GW01221014

Tragedy, Modernity and Mourning

Tragedy, Modernity and Mourning

Olga Taxidou

Edinburgh University Press

© Olga Taxidou, 2004

Edinburgh University Press Ltd
22 George Square, Edinburgh

Typeset in Ehrhardt Monotype
by Servis Filmsetting Ltd, Manchester, and
printed and bound in Great Britain by
The Cromwell Press, Trowbridge, Wilts

A CIP record for this book is available from the British Library

ISBN 0 7486 1987 9 (hardback)

The right of Olga Taxidou
to be identified as author of this work
has been asserted in accordance with
the Copyright, Designs and Patents Act 1988.

Contents

Acknowledgements		vi
	Introduction	1
1.	The Allure of *Antigone* or Antigone and the Philosophers	18
2.	Oedipus/Anti-Oedipus: The Philosopher, the Actor and the Patient	41
3.	*Trauerspiel*, Tragedy and Epic	72
4.	Euripides and Aristotle: Friends in Mourning	106
5.	The Heroism of Hercules and the Beauty of Helen	133
6.	Mourning and Tragic Form	159
7.	Brecht – Beckett – Müller: Modern Tragedy and Engagement	193
Index		210

Acknowledgements

This book has benefited immensely from the wisdom and generosity of Eduardo Cadava, John Frow, Jane Goldman and Liana Theodoratou. I am deeply grateful to them. My thanks also to Oliver Taplin, who supported this project at the early stages. Athena Athanassiou, Lauren Martin and Vassiliki Kolocotroni, through many a heated conversation over the years, have helped me shape its basic premises. My colleagues at Edinburgh University helped provide an environment that, despite the odds, is still congenial to intellectual activity. Anne Mason and Rachel Evans with their technical expertise and grace helped complete the final version of the typescript. Without Jackie Jones at Edinburgh University Press – her humour, patience and insight – this project would never have reached fruition.

I am thankful to the Arts and Humanities Research Board of Great Britain, whose award allowed me to complete this book.

Introduction

'It's a tragedy,' solemnly announced a spokeswoman from the US Defence Department on 25 March 2003. She was commenting on the loss of military and civilian lives in the course of what euphemistically has been called 'friendly fire' during the US attack on Iraq. Indeed, this use of the term 'tragedy' to mean something inevitable, transcendental, beyond our reach or control expresses the received view of the term as one that negates history and political responsibility. At the same time, it adds an aestheticising tone to an event that has specific political causes and effects. While doing so, it also harks back to an imaginary shared European tradition of high art that helps to conceptualise and embody historical and personal trauma. The fact that this act of aggression can be read as a 'tragedy' allows for it to be de-historicised, emptied of meaning and responsibility, and finally read across a trajectory of human suffering that is part and parcel of the human condition. In effect it is a classic use of humanism to justify barbarism. Personal and historical responsibility and accountability are subsumed under the all-encompassing notion of the tragic.

This transcendental use of the term tragedy has a long and distinguished history. From Plato onwards, the reading of tragedy that has dominated western metaphysics is one that sees it as part of an idealist legacy that is both aestheticising (Plato's double fantasy) and depoliticising. This legacy has enormous implications not only for theories of aesthetics but also for ethics, and for theories of subjectivity. Indeed, as the love affair between Athenian tragedy and German Idealism clearly exhibits, the 'tragic' is one way of reconciling the aesthetic, the ethical and the political. Freud's fascination with tragic form occupies a similar trajectory, as subjectivity itself is said to be shaped by forms and structures that follow the tragic ruse. And it is this overarching use of the term tragic that can at once negate historical and political reality and offer some consolation for personal trauma. If the missile bombings of market places in Baghdad are tragedies, then we who are watching them on television can at once be relieved of responsibility and offered, with some comfort, a *pharmakon* of sorts (in the sense of both poison and cure) that can ease the pain we feel from identifying with the victims. It is tragic because it is part of being human. This use of the term tragic does not rely on empathy and identification but rather on distance and objectification. What we are asked to feel while watching the victims on television is not simply a kind of humanism that empathises with their pain within a tragic understanding of the world, but rather a kind of inhumanity that is relieved that this is happening to them rather than to us. The sense of 'it could never happen here' is what is really reinforced by this use of the term tragedy. The actual pain and suffering is negated together with our responsibility for it.

This book sets out to challenge this received notion of tragedy. Its basic claim is that tragedy as a specific mode of performance, far from celebrating the transcendental and metaphysical, acts as a critique of these categories. The study of tragedy proposed here sees it as key to the development of the democratic *polis* and the notion of the citizen. Rather than reading tragedy as a general term that can encompass all genres, media and feelings, it attempts to re-examine the origin of tragic form at the moment of its genesis within the domain of Athenian democracy. As a specific mode of artistic production that is civic and collective, mythological and historical, private and public, written and performed, it is an essential constituent of the collective 'dream of democracy' that the Athenian *polis* supposedly embodied. The reading of tragedy suggested here views it as formative of this utopian democracy but also critical of its exclusions and barbarities. Rather than offering an antidote to suffering and pain through an all-encompassing reconciliation, tragic form emerges as a radical form of critique that interrogates the basic assumptions and foundations of western democracy.

I am aware that this version of tragedy might be seen as a rather eccentric one, especially in relation to the more common view outlined above. Tragedy's fondness of heroes, myths, Dionysiac frenzy, sacrifice and transformation are all notions that make contemporary literary critics very nervous indeed, particularly since they all bear the mark of universalism. Tragedy has been so implicated in the European project of the Enlightenment and the violence that it has generated (indeed it often has been used to justify that violence) that any attempt to reclaim the term for the purposes of a radical critique seems either a waste of time or doomed to lapse into the same theoretical pitfalls as those it sets out to scrutinise. This is so much the case that Terry Eagleton's recent book on tragedy sets as its main goal the appropriation of tragedy for the purposes of a left, radical critique. He illuminatingly outlines the awkwardness felt both by

Marxist cultural critics and by the so-called postmodernists (as always undifferentiatedly subsumed into one category) when it comes to tackling the idea of the tragic:

> As an aristocrat among art forms, its tone is too solemn and portentous for a streetwise, sceptical culture. Indeed, the term hardly scrapes into the post-modern lexicon. For some feminists, tragic art is far too enamoured of sacrifice, false heroics and a very male nobility of spirit, a kind of highbrow version of ripping yarns for boys. For leftists in general, it has an unsavoury aura of gods, myths and blood cults, metaphysical guilt and inexorable destiny.[1]

In truth, it is difficult to disagree with such a statement. However, it is also interesting to note that quite predictably the first category of identity politics that gets criticised is that of the 'feminists', admittedly qualified by the use of 'some'. The ethical and political bankruptcy of postmodernism, the general poverty of a theory, is read through the workings of feminism. There are very good reasons for feminists to be weary of tragedy as well as for cultural leftists. And the study of gender cannot be separated from the general study of tragic form. Eagleton's ambitious project continues to reclaim the tragic through a revalidation of the metaphysical, transcendental and paradoxically the theological (in its Christian guise)[2] for the purposes of a left, cultural critique. In many ways it is an admirable thesis both in its scope and its depth. The subtitle of his book, *The Idea of the Tragic*, suggests the use of the term made throughout the analysis: that is, without consideration to form, period, genre or reception. The emphasis is entirely on the 'idea' of the tragic, with almost total disregard for the genre's formal or material aspects. I suspect it is challenging tragedy as a 'genre' in the first place. I cannot help but wonder whether this adamant use of the tragic in an attempt to reclaim the metaphysical might not slip into the same idealism that has haunted the term, or the idea of the term, since its first Platonic manifestation.

Not so much in opposition to studies like the above (and it is true that there aren't that many) but possibly as part of the same project, this book tries to re-conceptualise the term tragedy through a double movement. On the one hand, it tries to map out an alternative genealogy of the term. In this sense it revisits, through the lens of recent neo-historical approaches and through performance theory, the 'golden moment' of Athenian democracy that gave birth to a very specific mode of theatre with its own set of performance conventions. This approach tries to bridge the gap between purely discursive readings of tragedy – ones that usually conflate tragedy and philosophy – and more historical and materialist readings, which tend to focus on the production of performance and on the civic dimension of the institution of theatre. On the other hand, and taking on board the more recent scholarship on Athenian tragedy, it also revisits that crucial encounter between tragedy and modernity that helped to shape modern notions of ethics, the relationships between the aesthetic and the political, and modern notions of subjectivity. This encounter is nowhere more clearly and dramatically staged than through the interactions between Athenian tragedy and German Idealism and Romanticism. I would also claim that this dialogue between the 'ancients and the moderns' also resurfaces in the ways Freudian psychoanalysis rewrites tragic form for the purposes of delineating its own epistemology, particularly in relation to the concept of the modern subject.

This analysis tries to reclaim the secular rather than the theological/metaphysical aspect of tragic form, or rather puts forward the suggestion that the tension, sometimes creative sometimes destructive, between the secular and the theological forms a structural element of tragic form itself. It is really a matter of historical interpretation, proposed mainly by schools of western philosophy, as to where the stress falls. It is also true that most, if not all, theories of tragedy stress the theological, metaphysical and idealist strands in this tradition. This is especially dominant in post-Christian readings of tragic form, which see the sacrifice of Christ as the last embodiment of Dionysus, as Nietzsche would have it, making tragedy impossible in a monotheistic world. This is the line of thinking that constantly announces the 'death of tragedy', with George Steiner as its more vocal spokesperson. Eschatological and nihilist in its tone, this school of thought sees tragedy as obsolete in a world that can no longer recuperate pain, loss and suffering as part of a metaphysical project. However, if we rethink the whole relationship between the metaphysical and the secular as forming a constituent element of tragic form itself, and if we see tragedy as the forum for such a debate, then we might be able to map out ways of talking about loss and suffering that are not necessarily metaphysical and theological, or at least contest the hegemony of those terms.

I believe that the idea of tragedy as solely transcendental and metaphysical results from the intricate and sometimes fraught encounters between tragedy and philosophy. This net is a particularly complex one to disentangle, as it haunts almost every study of tragedy since Aristotle's famous definition in the *Poetics*. According to this line of argument, tragedy comes first, followed by philosophy, in a developmental model that sees tragedy, that is, the aesthetic, as rehearsing debates and thought processes that are then taken over by philosophy. This reinstates the discursive hegemony of philosophy while relegating tragedy to the realm of the sublime or the transcendental. It also relies on the deeply embedded concept of a 'fall', a fall from the organic unity between tragedy and the *polis*, the cosmological and the secular, the aesthetic and the political, and the individual and the collective. And after this 'fall', after the death of tragedy, we enter the world of reason, critical thinking and philosophy.[3] In turn tragedy itself and its negotiation of notions of death and suffering are redistributed into the realm of the metaphysical, once the organic, ideal unity has been forever severed.

We are told that in the age of Sophocles tragedy was about the fall of great men who acted as scapegoats for the well-being of the state. Somehow there is a seamless process of representation at work here. The kings, the gods, the sacrifice, the ritualistic dismemberment are acceptable as part of a pre-philosophical sensitivity, a 'golden era' that is disrupted with the arrival of Socrates and critical thinking. This is more or less the legacy compounded by Nietzsche in his *Birth of Tragedy* (1872) and has more recently been appropriated in an attempt to reinvigorate the subversive aspects of tragedy.[4] This postmodern reading of tragedy through Nietzsche may have resulted in some very interesting contemporary performances, but I would claim it occupies the same idealist trajectory. As Walter Benjamin's criticism of Nietzsche insightfully claims, it opens up 'the abyss of aestheticism'. Rather than talk of shifts and ruptures, from the mythological to the historical, from the collective to the individual, from the ritualistic to the critical and so on (all embodied in the concept of the fall, but also, ironically, in the concept of progress), it might be more useful to assume that such a golden, organic moment never existed. The perfect identification between discourse and praxis that was the Athenian miracle might have been fractured at its very source.

In this sense tragedy is not something that we are always trying to resuscitate by reclaiming the transcendental and theological. It is not the almost-dead body of the aesthetic into which critics desperately try to breathe life, sometimes with embarrassment, sometimes with pride. And it certainly is not a form that once worked, in its wonderfully organic splendour, but since the advent of modernity has lost its power to impact on our psychic and material lives. This analysis puts forward the suggestion that such an organic moment never existed, that the shift from the so-called pre-modern period to modernity is at least problematic and that tragedy is not lost in the process of such a shift. Rather, it wants to underline the somewhat old-fashioned suggestion that tragic form comprises a site of struggle. It is a conflictual *topos* where the King does not simply and unproblematically stand for the state and its people but acts as a ruse through which the whole concept of power is questioned. It is not so much that tragedy conjures up bygone heroics and 'primitive' rituals that make it seem old-fashioned and inadequate to deal with contemporary pain and suffering (because the advent into modernity has certainly not diminished these). It is more the reading of tragedy as something forever lost, always in the process of being regained, together with the ultimate resort to the transcendental, that makes it appear insufficient to deal with our pain and suffering. This is why the use of the term by the US Defence Department seems clichéd and insulting. However, if tragedy is and has always been about barbarism, rather than simply charting the movement towards more democracy, more individuality, more civilisation, then a very different interpretive arena transpires, one that sees tragic form as a conflictual site, one that helps construct the collective dream of the democratic *polis*, but also and crucially undermines it by bringing centre stage the exclusions and the violence on which the project of democracy is/was based.

It is fascinating to note that we have inherited this transcendental 'idea of the tragic' from Plato. This does not come as a surprise from the great philosopher of idealism. However, what is equally important is that Plato also was the great anti-theatrical philosopher. His famous repudiation of mimesis relegates theatre to creating a 'double fantasy', one that can only further remove and aestheticise the ideal world. The concept that mimesis can interact with the world or offer a critical judgement that may possibly reveal a truth is alien to Platonic thinking. Furthermore, the whole notion of enactment through mimesis, for Plato, can only initiate a process of decadence and degeneration, spreading through the audience like a disease. Indeed, the contaminating quality of mimesis is what Plato fears most. He believes that this process of contamination, instigated by enactment, can trigger a social epidemic. This is why Plato bans tragedy and the aesthetic in general from his ideal republic. We revive this Platonic legacy every time we read tragedy as part of a transcendental project. It is a legacy that negates the power of mimesis and is deeply anti-theatrical. For Plato, tragedy as mimesis relies on the basest emotions of pity and fear, it distorts reality (or the ideal world), and in the end is simply a form of bad philosophy.

What takes place in this reading is the agonistic relationship between tragedy and philosophy. Interestingly enough, Plato's analysis engages the fact that mimesis and tragedy are theatrical. His fear and loathing of tragedy derive from the fact that he reads it as performance, as a discourse that relies on the physical, the collective and the civic – something which Aristotle refuses to do.[5] Equally fascinating is the fact that, although Aristotle furnishes western philosophy with a definition of tragedy, it is Plato, the great anti-theatricalist, who provides us with the transcendental, the 'mystical' idea of tragedy, as Stephen Halliwell calls it.[6] It is this idea that seems to have caught on, one that derives from an attempt to dismantle the impact of tragedy as a theatrical experience. This spectacular, physical, collective, physiognomic (as Benjamin would call it) dimension of tragedy is one that ironically has been of the least concern in theories of tragedy. Even Aristotle, trying to recuperate the social/therapeutic function of tragedy, contra Plato, has little to say about issues of performance. Hence the contemporary criticism voiced against him by many classicists and performance theorists that he 'writes about tragedy like a philosopher'. In a sense most writing about tragedy that ignores its material modes of production is writing that treats tragedy as if it were philosophy. Ironically the great anti-theatrical philosopher Plato is a rare example of a philosopher who views tragedy as a theatrical event. It is almost a case of 'know your enemy', as Plato's abhorrence of the performance event points towards ways in which tragedy could undermine both philosophy and the totalising powers of his republic. The reasons why he bans tragedy from his ideal state are understandable in Platonic terms. Tragedy distorts the ideal world, through the process of mimesis, which feeds into people's basest emotions, and which also incidentally feminises them (enactment being the resort of the feminine). It has the power to trigger collective emotions and incite collective action against the state. In the same gesture, Platonic thinking either sublimates this idea of tragedy or relegates it to the transcendental (possibly because of the power it has outlined previously). It is this anti-theatrical legacy that helps create and consolidate the metaphysical and idealist reading of tragic form.

In opposition to the deeply embedded anti-theatrical tradition initiated by philosophy, this analysis wants to reintroduce the theatrical dimension of tragedy into the debate. The long tradition of reading tragedy as an 'idea' that can cut across modes of production, genres and historical periods results more or less from the idealist legacy which sees tragedy as one of the finest examples of the 'Greek miracle', in a gesture that actually negates history and the materiality of the theatrical experience. However, tragedy, like the democratic project itself, appears to be fractured at its centre. In this way the emphasis on performance, rather than resorting to a schematic, or poststructuralist formalism, hopes to reinstate a reading of tragedy that sees the aesthetic inextricably linked with the political. I am aware that this approach also goes against the grain of reading tragedy as the quintessential aristocratic art form, one that is all about kings and heroes and never about the 'common man.' Nonetheless, I want to suggest that tragedy has always been about democracy. This notion of democracy, however, one that we still inhabit today, is not simply about progress, visibility and civilisation, but also about violence, exclusion and barbarism. In many ways, tragic form has always explored the barbarism at the core of the democratic *polis*.

This emphasis on the historical and performative dimension of tragedy also introduces the concept of mourning as central to tragic form. In its neo-historical context, the appearance of tragedy as a specific set of artistic conventions and as a civic institution has been read in the context of a renegotiation between practices of lamentation, mourning and the law within the workings of the democratic *polis*. The significance of mourning for tragedy is another category that has been underexplored, possibly because death, like many a 'high' tragic concept, has always been the domain of the transcendental. However, the insistence on mourning as a material practice that opens up a creative dialogue between tragedy and the city-state, mainly through the law, could also point towards ways of historicising the form. It is less, as Nietzsche would have it, that the Greeks invented tragedy in order to come to terms with death, than a case of reading tragedy, through mourning, as a way of reiterating death into the praxis of life. Since death is a contested field, whoever controls death is crucial for the functioning of the city-state. Mourning transpires as another agonistic *topos* within the democratic *polis*. Recent studies by classicists, anthropologists and archaeologists stress the importance of mourning both for the creation of the laws of democracy and for the creation of tragic form. Indeed, as most scholars agree, after the outlawing of public, female and oral mourning by Solon in the sixth century BCE, we have the advent of two discursive modes into which mourning is channelled. These are the tragedy and the official, state funeral oration, the *epitaphios logos*. These two discourses of mourning might be read against each other: one appears as mourning reconfigured through the aesthetic and the other through the political.

This battle over death helps create tragic forms and performance conventions. An oral tradition, predominantly female, is rewritten as a set of performance conventions where we have no female performers or members of the audience. At the same time, the official state logos, with its first cenotaph (after the first year of the Peloponnesian War), also claims the absent bodies of the dead for the purposes of constructing the identity of the new Athenian and democratic citizen. The interface between these two discourses is very fruitful indeed; it helps us read the preoccupation with death that tragedy constantly enacts not solely in transcendental terms but also in material terms as another site of struggle between the secular/civic and the metaphysical. The state funeral oration first delivered by Pericles validates the transcendental notion of death through the concept of the *pro patria* sacrifice. It is spoken over the absent bodies of dead soldiers and reclaims those dead bodies through the body of the state. On the other hand, mourning, as part of tragic form, excessively laments, theatricalises and feminises (or re-feminises) death in such intricate ways as to turn it into performance convention. This version of dealing with death, where the dead body is constantly present, is blatantly opposed to the sanitised death of the cenotaph, a vacuum that disguises the barbarism of war.

Reading tragedy as a discourse of mourning might help us overcome the embarrassment that materialist criticism sometimes encounters when dealing with notions of death. Equally, dealings with death bring us to that other great taboo: immortality.[7] How is immortality constructed? Is it through the workings of the official state logos with its heroes or martyrs or is it through the historical memory of the aesthetic? Either way, tragedy's claim over the dead and immortality has to be read in tandem with the state's jurisdiction over the same categories. To paraphrase Gillian Rose's insightful notion of mourning becoming the law,[8] how does mourning become the aesthetic? I would venture to propose that tragedy presents us with a discourse and a practice that claims death for the purposes of the aesthetic while also scrutinising the state's jurisdiction over the same field.

The stress on mourning will also lead us inevitably to the centrality of gender for tragic form. As an oral, female tradition – one that is also associated with barbarism and otherness – mourning is reinscribed into tragic form in a process of appropriation that negates the female. In a neat package this transition has also been read as one that charts the movement from ritual to art, from myth to history, from matriarchy to patriarchy and so on. I would like to challenge this slightly schematic view by examining the idea that these transitions are never fully achieved and are always unsuccessful. Furthermore, tragic form might itself examine the ways in which this reading of progress is always haunted by what it excludes or attempts to overcome. The function of gender is crucial in this context. Athenian tragedy is a homosocial art form, one that is based on the negation of the female. On the other hand, the female always returns with a vengeance on to the Athenian stage. As always represented, for there were no female performers, and as always physically absent, for there were no women in the audience, the fascination with the female transpires as one of the great obsessions of tragic form. I would go so far as to claim that this classic love/hate relationship with the female defines one of the structuring forces of tragedy. This may account for the convention of men playing women on the Athenian stage. It is in this sense that performance convention needs to be read into our understanding of tragedy. If we read tragedy as a discourse of mourning, one that tries to deal with death in aesthetic terms, while also taking over this domain from what would have been traditionally feminine, then a very intricate and complex set of relationships surface. These examine the connections between mourning, tragedy and the always represented, but never present female. One could go so far as to claim that for all these reasons tragedy is a gendered form.

Far from expressing an all-encompassing humanism, tragic form is based on the specific repudiation of the female, which in Athenian sensibility would be the same as the slave and the barbarian. In turn this reading poses general questions as to whether we can then proceed to understand tragedy in other periods and in other genres without taking on board this fundamental issue. For it is not simply a case of a feminist distaste for posturing heroics or fallen kings, but rather that this negation of the female is structural and formative of tragedy itself. More specifically, this analysis examines the ways in which tragedy, as a form of mourning, initiates a very difficult relationship with the female body and in particular its reproductive function. What it proposes instead is the notion of the male homosexual sublime, where male-to-male *philia* is the ultimate relationship. The centrality of *philia* is scrutinised in this book. It is presented as formative of tragedy in ways similar to those that negate the female. The emphasis on *philia*, male-to-male friendship, as Derrida's recent insightful analysis of the concept demonstrates,[9] is also a way of reconciling the personal and the political, and of dealing with the ethical, another basic concern of tragedy.

Psychoanalysis figures on the scene at this point of the analysis. From a psychoanalytical perspective mourning appears crucial for both subject formation and gender differentiation. Coupled with the fascination that psychoanalysis has for tragedy, particularly when it comes to notions of subjectivity, this opens another fruitful encounter – one that sees the origins of the modern subject as somehow rehearsed on the Athenian tragic stage. The emphasis on mourning as providing both themes and forms of tragedy brings together the historicity of recent classicist approaches with the somewhat ahistorical interpretations proposed by psychoanalysis, at least in the Freudian legacy. At the same time, more recent readings of mourning and its relevance for the formation of gender, as seen in the work of Judith Butler and Joan Copjec, are brought into the analysis in an attempt to re-evaluate tragedy as a discourse of mourning, while also critically assessing the schools of psychoanalysis that view the psyche as a tragic stage.

Interestingly enough, Plato's anti-theatricality is matched by his abhorrence of mourning.[10] For Plato, excessive mourning is barbarian and feminising. It contains the danger of triggering an epidemic of uncontrollable grief and in the end, like tragedy, it stops the philosopher from thinking clearly. It theatricalises reality and can only give rise to self-pity, never critical thinking. I would like to suggest that tragedy as mourning helps create an interpretive arena that places the feminine, the barbarian and the performative centre stage and thereby includes the elements that the Platonic, idealist view would negate.

This Platonic view of tragedy, the one that we more or less inhabit today, has been compounded by the interaction between tragedy and German Idealism and Romanticism. The reintroduction of mourning, and the emphasis on the performance dimension of tragedy, informs the excursions that this study takes into the dominant field of philosophy. Two figures stand out majestically from this encounter. They are, of course, Antigone and Oedipus. Antigone has been associated more with the nineteenth century and Oedipus with the twentieth (because of the impact of psychoanalysis). Most consequent readings of Antigone, from Derrida's through to Judith Butler's and Joan Copjec's, are in some sense in dialogue with Hegel's famous interpretation. In discussions about the limits of the law or the mapping of democracy itself, Antigone looms largely as the one 'character' from Greek tragedy who somehow embodies all the debates about the legitimacy of critique, while also gendering them. From the perspective of psychoanalysis, Antigone offers us ways of reading the relationships between the symbolic and the imaginary, between desire and the death drive, and, more recently, a model for different lines of kinship. The reading of Antigone in this book reviews these existing ones while also introducing her performance and performative dimension within a web of relationships that underlines her function as the state's designated mourner within a male homosocial and homosexual sublime. It further investigates the appropriateness of Antigone as a symbol of resistance and critique, especially for feminism.

The obsession with Antigone is only matched by the fascination that both philosophy and psychoanalysis reserve for Oedipus. Since the twentieth century has been termed the 'Oedipal Century', this study problematises the notion that the Oedipal story is pivotal both for the creation of the subject and for the formation of civilisation in general. Through more recent anti-Oedipal approaches and again through an emphasis on performance, it suggests that the myth and the tragedy might be fractured at their source and that they already encompass an anti-Oedipal critique. Instead of Oedipus presenting us with a paradigm of the reasoned, philosophical subject, it/he may present us with ways of reading a type of hysteria that is also embedded within the same notion of the subject. This reading of a hysterical Oedipus goes against two fundamental premises of Freudian psychoanalysis, that of hysteria as quintessentially feminine and that of Oedipus as the reasoning subject, the first philosopher, as it were. Although the twentieth century is littered with adaptations and rewritings of Oedipus, almost none of them feminise him. This analysis allots Oedipus his proper gender, that of male, and examines the fantastic possibility of a feminine Oedipus.

Antigone and Oedipus also function as examples of how the philosophies of modernity read tragedy mainly through the notion of character. Difficult as that may be to sustain, even in Aristotle's definition where tragedy is said to be mimesis of a praxis, it nevertheless provides a very significant analytical trope. This approach claims that such an obsession with the trials and tribulations of tragic character derives mainly from the fact that most theories of tragedy base their analysis on Sophocles. Of all the tragedians, Sophocles is the one who is said to herald the new humanism. He was very popular in the dramatic contests and he wrote during the height of the so-called 'golden era'. His friendship with Pericles and his success with the Athenian audience have helped create one of those great mythic couplings that have haunted the study of tragedy to this day. Sophocles the poet and Pericles the politician inhabit an organic space where the aesthetic and the political appear seamlessly integrated. The tragedies of Sophocles derive from the Greek miracle and in turn celebrate this. One of the ways that this is achieved on the stage is through an examination of the concept of the individual and of his relationship with the state. This reading sees the genesis of the subject on the Greek stage through the workings of an all-encompassing, and now classical, humanism. Sophocles is viewed as the poet-laureate of Athenian democracy and his versions of Oedipus and Antigone stand as emblems of both subjectivity and citizenship.

In addition to questioning the validity of such a claim, this book takes a fresh look at the work of Euripides in an attempt to create a poetics of tragedy that is based on the Euripidean rather than the Sophoclean model. Writing during the Peloponnesian War, Euripides charts a crisis within the project of Athenian democracy. His work underlines its contradictions and sets up a critical, combative relationship with the city-state, rather than an organic one. Euripides is the poet who quite consciously severs the supposed organic link between tragedy and the city-state. In self-imposed exile, a fate worse than death in the Greek sensibility, he leaves Athens and writes his last tragedies while a guest at the court of the King of Macedon. These tragedies are not written to be performed at official state events. They are written without state sanction and funding. They are works of exile. Like the tragedies that Euripides wrote while still at Athens (mostly unsuccessful ones), they too are about the shortcomings of democracy. They give the stage over to women slaves and barbarians, while relegating the function of the gods to machines. Turning the divine into a meta-theatrical convention, Euripides shows us why he is the great experimentalist of the tragic stage. We might even say that Euripides is the first modern playwright. His work sets up a critical relationship with the city-state and proposes the function of tragedy as a way of intervening, subverting and not necessarily celebrating the workings of power.

The Athenian tragedians were known as poets in a scheme of things that really relegated the literary and textual function of their theatre to a very small component within a greater performative and civic event. Interestingly enough, Euripides, the stage philosopher, as he was known, and the great stage experimenter, highlights the textual function of tragedy, particularly when he writes in exile without the whole edifice of the Athenian state to provide that supposedly seamless shift from text to stage to performance event. It is in this sense that I believe his stage experiments are almost endemic to his overall project. Without the solace and funding of the city-state, Euripides proceeds to reinvent tragic form. At the same time, he redefines notions of authorship in relation to the performative aspects of tragedy and to the state institution that was theatre. In this way, he ceases to be a tragic poet and becomes a playwright in the modern sense. In a fascinating twist of fate he may be said to have become a playwright as a result of the effects of exile, male-to-male *philia* and *philoxenia*, hospitality. However, as Derrida's reading of hospitality points out, in its Latin etymology the term conflates the idea of the host with that of hostility.[11] In an enactment of this double bind of hospitality, Euripides, as legend has it, is attacked by dogs and dismembered by them, at the orders of Archelaos, the King of Macedon, his host turned enemy.

While Aristotelianism tends to stress the significance of Oedipus, Aristotle's other favourite tragedy remains quite neglected. This is *Iphigeneia in Tauris* and it provides the springboard for an approach that is based on the politics and aesthetics of Euripides rather than Sophocles. The centrality of *philia*, *philoxenia* and mourning for tragic form are re-examined with this Euripidean model as the driving force.

The conflation of Aristotle and Aristotelianism also creates one of the great caveats within modern performance theory. This is parallel to the readings that see tragedy as being solely about kings, heroes and dead rituals. It is also the reading that stresses the function of tragic character within the workings of humanism. It sets up a direct lineage between Aeschylus and Ibsen, identifying schools of performance that couldn't be more different. It constructs tragedy as the precursor of bourgeois individualism. As such, it can never provide a fruitful encounter, let alone model, for a type of theatre that would aspire to be anti-naturalist, anti-humanist, interventionist and critical. As long as tragic form was seen as identical with the shortcomings of the project of the European Enlightenment, it could never be useful for the workings of a political theatre within modernity.

This is the critique that Brecht voices against Aristotle and Athenian tragedy. Brecht, the great anti-Aristotelian theorist of the twentieth century, bases his definition of epic theatre on a repudiation of tragedy. Through his characteristic 'crude thinking' and in the manifesto style of the European avant-garde, Brecht declares the death of tragedy in order to announce the birth of epic theatre. His epic theatre will in turn reclaim the secular and the revolutionary, categories that were denied efficacy according to Brecht's reading of tragedy. Ironically, Brecht's reading of tragedy is distressingly similar to that of German Idealism, and his reaction against this tradition might also account for his full-blown attack on tragedy. Following the double movement in this book, this analysis tries to reconcile Brecht and tragedy. Unless such a reconciliation is achieved, it would be very difficult, almost impossible, to reclaim tragedy for the workings of a secular, radical aesthetic. It is primarily this rift that has relegated tragedy to the function of high art, embodying a metaphysical politics that can never account for historical suffering or help bring about historical change.

The abyss opened up by Brecht between epic and tragic theatre might be bridged by Walter Benjamin and, in particular, his work, *The Origin of German Tragic Drama*.[12] This study, with its emphasis on allegory, mourning and catastrophe, bears startling similarities to Athenian tragedy. It also seems to be haunted by the spectre of Hölderlin and his studies on tragedy. Hölderlin's notion that tragedy occupies a 'speculative imagination' is formative of Benjamin's writings on both the *Trauerspiel* and on epic theatre, and provides a useful link in the reconciliation of tragic and epic forms. In turn, a more Benjaminian reading of epic, through mourning and speculation, might act as a corrective to the somewhat naively formulated optimism of the Brechtian project, injecting it with the necessary 'pessimism of the intellect'.

Either way, though, Brecht remains a central figure in this debate. Any attempt to create a theory of tragedy as a political and radical critique will always have to confront the edifice of epic theatre. In truth, it is a formidable construct to unravel. In its manifesto fervour it has created a legacy that continues to this day, as we see in the work of Augusto Boal, for example, who also builds his notions of a political theatre in opposition to the model created by Aristotle and Athenian tragedy. Sometimes this legacy has been read as embodying a Marxist critique of tragedy. I would suggest that this is a reductive reading of both Brecht and Marxist criticism in general. Through a rehabilitation primarily of the function of mourning, tragedy and epic are seen as mirroring each other in their attempts to claim the secular and the radical. Furthermore, this proposal of a melancholy version of epic theatre also helps to link Brecht to other contemporary projects that have rewritten the concept of tragedy.

Traditionally, the great modernist debates about engagement and autonomy have also been reconfigured as attitudes towards the tragic. At one extreme of the spectrum, Brecht defines epic theatre against the dead body of tragedy and, on the other, Beckett, read as the great paradigm of autonomous art, supposedly mourns the impossibility of tragedy. Either way, these two theatrical projects have always been read against each other. This has been compounded by the fact that they have been respectively adopted by the two opposing trends within the Frankfurt School. Benjamin stands as the great champion of engagement, with Brecht's epic theatre, while Adorno, with his study of Beckett, is seen as the spokesperson for autonomy. This debate has also been reconfigured as an agon between high art and popular art. The redefinition of tragedy proposed in this book may help close the rift created within modernist schools of performance regarding the efficacy of political theatre.

The death of tragedy has been more or less propagated since the end of the so-called Greek miracle. In turn the inability of a godless world to sustain the metaphysical and transcendental has led to readings of tragic form within modernity that attempt to reclaim the above categories for the function of the aesthetic. This project tries to disassociate tragedy from its transcendental interpretations and puts forward the notion that tragic form has always been secular and critical, underlining the contradictions and exclusions within the democratic project itself.

History has always occupied an ambiguous position in studies of tragedy as it has been read as dealing primarily with myth. However, as the work of Euripides clearly shows, far from absent, it forms one of the main structuring forces of tragic form. And the first extant tragedy that we have is Aeschylus' *The Persians*. This is a play that charts through the function of mourning the barbarities inflicted by the Greeks on to the Persians, while supposedly trying to 'liberate' them from a tyrannical regime. Through the force of mourning, the play asks the Athenians to identify with the Persians and with their loss. It stands as a visceral and insightful critique of war and empire, and sets up some of the great oppositions within the form, between civilisation and barbarism, between Greek and non-Greek other. The play, of course, proceeds to undermine these oppositions and show them as interchangeable, in the same way as the Athenians can be the Persians. This is where the tragedy lies: in the form, function and meaning of a historical drama in which loss and suffering are recuperated through mourning. This use of the term tragedy does not abdicate empathy and responsibility, but, on the contrary, it voices a historical critique that places both ourselves and the victims within a historico-political trajectory that can be accounted for and that, more importantly, is changeable.

The centrality of Antigone and Oedipus has plagued the reception of tragic form for at least the past two centuries. This book would like to help shift the emphasis towards the Euripidean model and the more historical tragedies like *The Persians*, which, far from appearing dated and steeped in a mythological reality, could have been written today, and could indeed help explain the workings of the US Defence Department, rather than dismissing them and our responsibility through the mainstream use of the term tragedy. As a way of reintegrating death within the workings of life, mourning might help create new ways of talking about tragic form that create historical accountability, radical critique and introduce the possibility of change. Like Benjamin's Angel of History, this notion of change will not solely rely on the concept of progress but will have a mournful eye fixed on the past, on its catastrophes and ruins. It is in this rubble that tragic form can be found and not in the great monuments of history.

Notes

1. Terry Eagleton, *Sweet Violence: The Idea of the Tragic* (Oxford: Blackwell, 2003), p. ix.
2. For an elaboration of significance of the redemptive power of Christianity in Eagleton's work, see a review of *Sweet Violence*, David Simpson, 'It's not about Cheering up', in *London Review of Books*, 3 April 2003, pp. 17–19.
3. This notion of the 'fall' is also evident in Eagleton's critique of postmodernism's inability to deal with tragedy. See David Simpson, 'It's not about Cheering up', p. 19.
4. For the impact of this subversive reading of Nietzsche on classical studies see M. S. Silk (ed.), *Tragedy and the Tragic: Greek Theatre and Beyond* (Oxford: Clarendon Press, 1996), see 'Everything to do with Dionysus', pp. 257–83.
5. See Edith Hall, 'Is there a *Polis* in Aristotle's *Poetics*?', in M. S. Silk (ed.), *Tragedy and the Tragic*, pp. 295–309.
6. See Stephen Halliwell, 'Plato's Repudiation of the Tragic', in *Tragedy and the Tragic*, pp. 332–49.

7. See Joan Copjec, *Imagine There's No Woman: Ethics and Sublimation* (Massachusetts: MIT Press, 2002), pp. 18–25, for a reading of immortality through a psychoanalytical study of Antigone.
8. Gillian Rose, *Mourning Becomes the Law: Philosophy and Representation* (Cambridge: Cambridge University Press, 1996).
9. Jacques Derrida, *The Politics of Friendship*, trans. George Collins (London and New York: Verso, 1997).
10. See Henry Staten, *Eros in Mourning* (London and Baltimore: The Johns Hopkins University Press, 1995), for an analysis of Plato's repudiation of mourning.
11. Jacques Derrida, *Of Hospitality: Anne Dufourmantelle Invites Jacques Derrida to Respond*, trans. George Collins (Stanford: Stanford University Press, 2000).
12. Walter Benjamin, *The Origin of German Tragic Drama* (1963), trans. John Osbourne (London: Verso, 1998).

CHAPTER ONE

The Allure of *Antigone* or Antigone and the Philosophers

In 1978 the film *Germany in Autumn* was made in response to the Stammheim suicides of the Baader–Meinhof group. This was a collaboration between Heinrich Böll and a number of prominent directors (Rainer Werner Fassbinder, Edgar Reitz and Vokler Schlondorff among others). The Böll–Schlondorff sequence, a reworking of Sophocles' *Antigone*, presented a panel of TV executives who refused to show a production of the play that explicitly included Antigone's suicide after Creon's refusal of burial rites for her brother, who is seen as a rebel against the state. The film itself is framed by two funerals, one official (the funeral of a victim of the Red Army Faction) and the other the unofficial mourning of the dead prisoners.[1] It is fascinating that this moment in post-war German history should be refracted through the retelling of a tale as old as *Antigone*. This seems less astonishing, however, if we contemplate the longstanding relationship that *Antigone* has had with German philosophy, particularly within the context of Romanticism and Idealism. In discussions about the relationships between kinship and the law, kinship and the state, and in examinations of the limits of the democratic state in particular, from Hegel and Hölderlin onwards, the figure of Antigone occupies a privileged position. In testing the limits of liberalism and the possibilities of Utopia within the same gesture, Antigone acts as an appropriate precursor/model for Ulrike Meinhof. However, this chapter sets out to explore a number of contradictions and ambiguities that the 'character' of Antigone embodies. Either as a redemption of philosophy or as a heroine of the eternal revolt against the state (or as an almost mythical combination of both), Antigone has captured the imagination of the philosophers of modernity. Indeed, in many cases she has been read as the emblematic bridge that helps cross the great 'dividing line' between the aesthetic and the political.

There have been numerous discussions about the allure of Antigone within German Idealism and Romanticism.[2] It forms part of the fascination that late eighteenth-century German thought has with Greek tragedy. This 'return' to antiquity remains part of the constant negotiation between 'ancients' and 'moderns' and re-energises the longstanding but difficult relationship between tragedy and philosophy. The turn to tragedy is part of a critical enterprise that strives to incorporate the aesthetic. As Miguel de Beistegui and Simon Sparks state in their introduction to *Philosophy and Tragedy*:

> If such a passage to tragedy was able to take place, then it was only because tragedy itself was envisaged as a passage, as a bridge thrown over the abyss opened by the critical philosophy; it is because, in other words, tragedy was envisaged as a 'solution' to the problem inherited from Kant, and in the wake of a path opened by him: that of the (re)construction of the critical edifice by way of the mediating role of 'those judgments which one calls aesthetic'.[3]

Much of the philosophical thinking about *Antigone*, in its attempt to realign the text within a broader project, tends to treat the textual and discursive construction of a piece of theatre (and indeed a piece of theatre that has an 'organic' relationship to the *polis*) as if it were already philosophy – as if the text explicates philosophical debate that is 'animated' through the use of actors and an audience. This philosophisation of tragedy, and in particular the work of Sophocles, creates one of the great stumbling blocks in the relationship between tragedy and philosophy. It implies an almost total disregard of formal issues (other than the ones pertaining to translation from classical Greek), and it tends to appropriate theatre discursively within philosophy in ways which contemporary performance theory strives to avoid. *Antigone*, mainly because of the attention the text has attracted, seems to suffer from this *philosophisation* more than most classical texts of Athenian tragedy. Most readings of the play assume a humanist reading of Antigone as a character, indeed most readings assume she is a woman (ignoring the crucial convention of the Athenian state of male-only actors and audience). This homosocial aspect of the play, for example, also needs to be theorised. Indeed, there is a whole dimension of the play as a work, as a form of production, rather than simply as a text, that needs to be considered in any discussion that seeks to problematise the central position that *Antigone* occupies within philosophies of modernity.

It is the same, more or less, ontological attitude that sees Antigone not only as a humanist character but as a transhistorical or ahistorical one at that. This touches upon a broader problem in the interface between German Idealism and classical Greek thought in general. In its most extreme rendition this can be seen in Heidegger's reading of Hölderlin's translations of Sophocles, which leads him to proclaim that 'to be Greek is to be German'.[4] This quasi-ontological reading of Antigone has plagued (in the Artaudian sense) her reception to this very day. Most readings suffer from the same attitude that takes it for granted that Antigone is indeed a female character. The potential of a performative reading of the figure of Antigone, one that could take on board the intricate connections between actual performance and performativity, remains largely unexamined. As this chapter hopes to examine, the way Antigone is made and the formal aspects of her representation on the stage bear huge relevance to matters of interpretation and philosophical validation.

What Antigone actually *does* is also crucial to the way she has been read. The centrality of the act of mourning can be and has been read thematically or allegorically as the mediating factor in the relationship between the individual and the state. In fact, recent interpretations for the stage in the midst of the AIDS crisis have repoliticised the act of mourning that is the kernel around which all the debates in this play are structured. The more general relationship between tragic form and death ritual is reworked in almost unique ways in this play-text. Antigone questions the structural connection between death and tragedy and the ways in which this relationship is reconfigured into notions of mourning and melancholia. However, the act of mourning that Antigone claims and represents might also be one that helps to construct her as a dramatic figure. Mourning is something that Antigone does; it may also be pertinent to her representation on stage.

'I do admit it. I do not deny it,' responds Antigone to Creon's challenge. Indeed, through this double performative Antigone both owns her deed and makes it public. These two very simple and direct sentences, coupled with the act of covering a dead body with earth (an act that is also performed twice, but never in front of the audience), have had a significant impact on philosophical thinking about ethics and the law. Furthermore, the figure of Antigone herself, possibly comparable only with that of Oedipus, has captured the imagination of philosophers of modernity. From Hegel, Hölderlin and Nietzsche to Brecht and Benjamin, at the tail end of this tradition, the attraction to tragic form is part of a conscious attempt to theorise, to philosophise (and I do not believe the terms to be interchangeable, as I hope to demonstrate later on) the aesthetic. With Brecht and Benjamin the reworking of tragic form also becomes a way of politicising the aesthetic. In his book on the literary and dramatic versions of Antigone, George Steiner counts over one hundred thousand translations and imitations of Antigone in German alone in the last two centuries. This fascination, what Stathis Gourgouris calls our affliction with

Antigone, gains a new momentum in the post-war period, where once again tragedy is called upon to provide 'a therapeutic gesture in a world defined by Culture having become the agent of annihilation of culture', echoing Adorno's famous aphorism on the impossibility of poetry after Auschwitz.

From the work of Hegel to more recent reformulations by Gillian Rose and Judith Butler, Antigone is central to thinking that both examines the borders of the state, the *polis*, but, nevertheless, continues to believe in the possibility of critique. In this chapter I will be looking more closely at two recent readings of Antigone; one is her appearance in Gillian Rose's *Mourning Becomes the Law* (1996) and the other Judith Butler's recent reinterpretation in *Antigone's Claim* (2000). I have chosen these texts because I believe they typify in many ways two of the main approaches taken in the appropriations of Antigone by philosophy. Butler's reading tries to incorporate Antigone within a feminist/queer project. She writes, 'I began to think about Antigone a few years ago as I wondered what happened to those feminist efforts to confront and defy the state.'[5] For Gillian Rose, Antigone is significant as part of her attempt to resuscitate a philosophy that has lost its power of critique. For both these readings the act of mourning itself, as an aesthetic rite and as a political right, is problematised in the midst of the AIDS crisis and forms a backdrop to their interpretations. Of course, this struggle to claim the dead and to politicise the act of mourning is central to the play as well.

Out of all the roles proposed by Athenian tragedy – and there are many to choose from (Klytemnestra, Cassandra, Medea, Agaue and so on) – why has Antigone been the one to become the emblem of the relationship between the individual and the state, the outside and the inside of the limits of the law, the boundary between the living and the dead? For Lacan, Antigone enacts the transition between the imaginary and the symbolic (never quite inhabiting either). She has come to enact a set of binary oppositions (also refracted through gender) that are constitutive to the way philosophy rewrites the aesthetic and hence to the way the aesthetic is reformulated as the political. From Hegel's configuration of Antigone as the 'irony of society' to Butler's recent reclaiming of her as a queer heroine, she delineates both the limitations of the state and the possibility of a critique of those limitations.

Antigone's transgression consists of her burying her brother, Polyneices, even though her uncle, King Creon, specifically prohibits such a burial. Polyneices leads an army against his brother, Eteocles, claiming the kingdom of Thebes for himself. Both brothers die in the battle and Creon, their maternal uncle, seizes power, whereupon he pronounces one of the brothers, Polyneices, to be a traitor and denies him proper funeral rites, leaving the body bare and exposed. This particular drama chronologically takes place after Oedipus has committed the Oedipal complex and has been banished to Colonus, outside Athens. It is the last of the Theban trilogy, even though it was performed first. The dates for the performance of *Antigone* are 442–441 BCE; for *King Oedipus*, 429–420; *Oedipus at Colonus*, 401, after the death of Sophocles. It is probably significant that *Antigone* was performed first, especially in view of the kinds of models of kinship she proposes.

Hegel's famous interpretation of Antigone in *The Phenemology of the Spirit* sees her as the 'eternal irony of the community'. For him, she represents the law of the household gods and Creon represents the law of the state. His interpretations insist that the laws of kinship give way to the laws of the state; they also presuppose the separability of kinship and the state. And it is on this issue that Butler's revision of Hegel is crucial to her own attempt at constructing a version of Antigone that represents alternative models of kinship. She writes:

> For two questions that the play poses are whether there can be kinship – and by kinship I do not mean the 'family' in any specific form – without the support and mediation of the state, and whether there can be the state without the family as its support and mediation. And further, when kinship comes to pose a threat to state authority and the state sets itself in a violent struggle against kinship, can these very terms sustain their independence from one another? This becomes a textual problem of some importance as Antigone emerges in her criminality to speak in the name of politics and the law: she absorbs the very language of the state against which she rebels, and hers becomes a politics not of oppositional purity but of the scandalously impure.[6]

And this, in many ways, becomes the crux of the problem for Butler, who at once states that Antigone has a 'passionate attachment' to Creon (to use the term she coins in *The Psychic Life of Power*) but at the same time examines the possibility of her acting as heroine for different types of kinship. In particular, she is interested in questioning anti-Oedipal models of subjectivity. However, I do not believe that Antigone is the most appropriate champion of such a cause.

Rather than placing Creon in opposition to Antigone, Butler's view sees how the two actually mirror each other. This is not lost on Hegel either, as he states that 'there is immanent in both Antigone and Creon something that in their own way they attack, so that they are gripped and shattered by something intrinsic to their own being'.[7] What Butler reads as a revision of Hegel, in many ways exhibits her own 'passionate attachment' to Hegelian thought. Either way, in terms of the conventions of tragedy itself, this is not particularly original or unique to Antigone. Throughout the play, Antigone and Creon constantly change places, echoing each other. She is called a man, she is described in manly terms and the language of rhetoric that she employs could only have been used by a man at the time. There is an interesting exchange between Creon and Haemon, his son, who is about to marry Antigone:

> Creon: Would you call it right to admire an act of disobedience?
> Haemon: Not if the act were also dishonourable?
> Creon: And was this woman's action dishonourable?
> Haemon: The people of Thebes think not.
> Creon: The people of Thebes!
>   Since when do I take orders from the people of Thebes?
> Haemon: Isn't that rather a childish thing to say?
> Creon: No. I am King, and responsible only to myself.
> Haemon: A one-man state? What sort of state is that?
> Creon: Why, does not every state belong to its ruler?
> Haemon: You'd be an excellent king – on a desert island.
> Creon: Of course, if you're on the woman's side –
> Haemon: No, no – Unless you're the woman. It's you I'm fighting for.[8]

In this telling exchange where the possibility of power outside the state and without subjects – a desert island – is examined together with the reversal of gender roles, we have a kind of trope which refers to a reworking of the tragic convention. In most tragedies where women perform some form of transgression – and this is what most tragedies are about – the women figures – like Klytemnestra or Medea – are described as behaving like men, as moving like men and talking like men. Indeed, they were men, men in women's clothing in a performing tradition that had no women performers. Futhermore, the whole civic event of going to the theatre in classical Athens was a homosocial event in so far as women were absent not only from the stage but also from the audience. This convention of male actors playing both men and women is, I believe, constitutive of tragic form and one to which I shall return later.

Another way in which Antigone has been claimed as a quasi-feminist or even queer heroine is by underlining her refusal to marry Haemon and her decision to choose death instead. Butler writes:

> In this light then, it is perhaps interesting to note that Antigone, who concludes the Oedipal drama, fails to produce heterosexual closure for that drama, and that may intimate the direction for a psychoanalytic theory that takes Antigone at its point of departure.[9]

The quest for a psychoanalytic theory that originates with Antigone and not Oedipus is an interesting one. Butler picks it up from George Steiner in his book on the literary configurations of Antigone.[10] However, such a quest is doomed at its outset because Antigone, the daughter/sister of Oedipus, is so absolutely implicated in the Oedipal drama that it would be almost impossible to read her outside those terms. Even as she enacts the perversion of that drama in its originating moment she is so structurally bound to it that an existence outside it is almost inconceivable for her. Just as she enacts the perversion of the law, its irony, without which the *polis* could not exist, she at once enacts the perversion of the Oedipal family, whose existence is also linked with the *polis*. In mourning the death of her brother Polyneices, she is in a sense also mourning the banishment/civic death of her father Oedipus as these two positions have been perverted throughout the play. As in the case of Electra the banishment death of the father creates an attachment to the brother-cum-father. In both cases, the act of mourning validates this. And like Electra, I would maintain that Antigone supports the house of the father rather than proposing something radically different.[11] Out of all the positions she occupies – that of the man, brother, father even – the one she refuses to occupy is the position of the mother.

> O but I would not have done the forbidden thing
> For my husband or for any son.
> For why? I could have had another husband
> And by him other sons, if one were lost;
> But, father and mother lost, where would I get
> Another brother, Creon condemns me and hales me away,
> Never a bride, never a mother, unfriended,
> Condemned alive to solitary death.
>
> (900–10)

It is a strange kind of kinship that is proposed here; one that is drastically different, for example, from that which Klytemnestra supports in *The Oresteia*, where the blood connection between mother and child is what is propagated. This is a notorious passage, one where neither the law of the city (linking her to her supposed husband) nor the laws of nature (linking her to her supposed children) provide the acceptable pattern of kinship. It is this quest for alternative lines of kinship that seems to have sparked Butler's exciting approach. However, Antigone seems to substitute both patterns with her obsessive *philia* for her brother Polyneices. This is in many ways reminiscent of the male-to-male relationships between warriors/heroes, where homosocial and homosexual friendship is constituted within the discursive domain of the *polis*. In this way Antigone's relationship with her brother mirrors the male-to-male relationship of *philia*. In the process Antigone herself occupies a male position. Again parallels can be drawn between this brother/sister relationship and the Electra/Orestes one. The male couple or pseudo-couple is reproduced through a traffic of women. According to one version of the myth, Electra marries Pylades, who is originally Orestes' companion. The *philia* of Orestes and Pylades is strengthened and reproduced through the bonding of Electra and Pylades. Of course, in the case of Antigone there is no such outlet and her strong attachment to her brother can only be reproduced through her 'marriage to death'.[12] Here I think the etymology of her name plays a significant role. Gourgouris writes:

> The preposition *anti* means both 'in opposition to' and 'in compensation of'; *gone* belongs in a line of derivatives of *genos* (kin, lineage, descent) and means simultaneously offspring, generation, womb, seed, birth. On the basis of this etymological polyphony (the battle for meaning at the nucleus of the name itself), we can argue that Antigone embodies both an opposition of kinship to the *polis*, (in compensation for its defeat by the *demos* reforms), as well as an opposition *to kinship*, expressed by her attachment to a sibling by means of a disruptive desire, *philia* beyond kinship. But her name also embodies opposition at a generative level, an otherness at the core, for it may be translated either as 'generated in the place of another' or also 'born to oppose', which is to say: bearing (generating) opposition/compensation. A freer rendition could easily be 'in the place of a mother', whereby the womb that generates opposition displaces the mother as premier figure of socialization, as the first pedagogue of sublimation.[13]

The etymological ambivalence of her name further serves to heighten the difficulty of placing her. She stands neither *for* nor *against* kinship. She cannot be read as a proponent of natural or cultural reproduction. Along an axis that covers both condensation and substitution she comes to represent anti-generation itself, according to Froma Zeitlin. Of course, it is crucial to point out that meaning does not reside in etymology alone and that it would be a strictly philological view that saw a direct correspondence between etymology and meaning. However, the particular polyphony with which the name Antigone presents us, compounded by the fact that she is a creature of the stage, further underlines her performative dimension.

In enacting the etymology of her name, in giving us its gestic dimension, Antigone occupies a number of positions which all problematise the concept of generation, production and reproduction. She identifies with the father, the brother and even the uncle. Interestingly enough, she does not identify with the sister, Ismene. The one position that is glaringly absent from the narrative of the play and the one her name does not allow her to occupy by definition is that of the mother. All the positions she stands in for are, of course, male, in a meta-theatrical gesture that nods towards the actual theatrical convention she embodies. Just as she stands in for a number of male positions, a male actor is standing in for her. In a seamless symbiosis of form and content the final gestic articulation of her name turns her into a man. Furthermore, in turning into a man who negates generation itself, Antigone enacts one of the main anxieties of Athenian tragedy, the anxiety of reproduction and its disassociation from the female body. From the court scene at the end of *The Oresteia*, where through the intervention of another manly female – that of Athena – the female body is deemed to be a mere vessel and the father is seen as the true and in fact sole parent of a child, to the works of Euripides, where this is read in an almost self-referential manner,[14] there is an anxiety about reproduction that permeates the whole of Athenian tragedy. This may be associated with the paradox of reconciling the existence of the reproducing female body with a world order where desire and power both originate from and are returned to the male. Within the predominantly homosocial and homosexual *polis*, the act of reproduction itself becomes a kind of *aporia*; one that is endlessly enacted on the Athenian stage.

Nevertheless, this homosocial world relies on heterosexuality for the purposes of lineage (kinship) and the *polis* (citizens, soldiers), the very two categories that Antigone's name negates. In this sense Butler's claim that Antigone fails to achieve heterosexual closure, although appropriate in constructing her as a queer heroine, could be further scrutinised. The anxiety is not over homosexuality (and here I think there is a problem in the way these terms are applied transhistorically) but over reproductive heterosexuality, or rather the harmonious coexistence of both systems (and by homosexuality in this context I mean male homosexuality).

It is true that Antigone fails to consummate her relationship with Haemon, but the text does proceed to heighten this and grant a kind of hypostasis that is very close to romantic love (as we understand the term today). Moreover, it is one of the few texts of Athenian drama where a relationship between a male and a female role approximates that of romantic and altruistic (on the part of Haemon at least) love. The famous ode to love by the chorus testifies to this:

> Chorus: Where is the equal of Love?
> Where is the battle he cannot win,
> The power he cannot outmatch?
> In the farthest corners of the earth, in the midst of the sea,
> He is there: he is here

> In the bloom of a fair face
> Lying in wait.
> [. . .]
> But here is a sight beyond all bearing,
> At which my eyes cannot but weep;
> Antigone forth faring
> To her bridal-bower of endless sleep.
>
> (780–800)

This is one of the few passages in Athenian drama where love, *eros*, is not associated with power, revenge, lineage, or frenzied madness. Indeed, it is a very humanist reading of *eros*, echoing a previous choral ode, the ode to *anthropos*, which charts his progression through conquering nature to the founding of language:

> Wonders are many on earth, and the greatest of these
> Is man, who rides the ocean and takes his way
> Through the deeps, through wind-swept valleys of perilous seas
> That urge and sway.
> He is master of ageless Earth, to his will bending
> The immortal mother of gods by the sweat of his brow,
> As year succeeds to year, with toil unending
> Of mule and plough.
> He is the lord of all living things; birds of the air,
> Beasts of the field, all creatures of sea and land . . .
> Hunting the savage beast
> [. . .]
> The use of language
>
> (400–28)

I believe these two passages can be read in conjunction, whereby the humanist sensibility proposed in one is mirrored and coupled with this 'new' notion of *eros* presented in the other. The anthropomorphism and the anthropocentrism of the first ode needs to be underpinned through the heterosexual love celebrated in the second. But who is the *anthropos* of the first ode? I think it is Antigone herself (in the context of Protagotra's 'man is the measure of all things'). This ode is immediately followed by Creon's question: 'Do you admit, or do you deny the deed?' To which, of course, Antigone gives her notorious reply: 'I do admit it. I do not deny it.'

But how does Antigone come to theorise the position of *anthropos* in Sophoclean terms? Through the process by which she is turned into a man. And it is important to remember that *anthropos* does not exactly mean 'man'. One of its etymologies has it mean 'the appearance of man'.

Antigone talks and walks like a man. In dramatic terms, that is, she appears to be a man. The convention of men-playing-women is significant here as well, as it would have been a male actor assuming the role of a woman, who then appears to behave like a man. Antigone is a man-cum-woman-cum-man who at once tests the limits of *anthropos* and the *polis*. In fact, Hegel's irony proves to be more ironic than he may have originally intended it to be. This structural link between the humanism and heterosexuality is one that I would like to explore a little further.

Antigone's relationship with Haemon is what turns her back into a woman. Nevertheless, this is a relationship that is not meant to be, as the only domain that can contain it is death. The manner in which this 'love' is eventually consummated is also very significant. Antigone is said to be married to death; her tomb is her bridal chamber ('Her bridal-bower of endless sleep'). Here, again, Sophocles' text cites an established dramatic convention (probably one derived from myth) whereby marriage, for female roles, is structurally linked to death. Iphigenia is told she is going to a wedding when she is led to the stake. Cassandra appears on a wedding chariot with Agamemnon on his return from the Trojan War, at the very moment she is prophesying her own death. And there are numerous examples where this paradigm is perverted, particularly in Euripides. Through an overdetermined, almost catachrestic, use of this convention, Antigone appears as married to death, as the ultimate bride of Hades. However, her forceful denial ('no wedding day; no marriage music'), far from failing to reproduce heterosexual closure, I would argue, only serves to validate heterosexuality in a quasi-romantic manner, while also accounting for the anxieties about reproduction mentioned earlier. What is denied presence in this world is validated and glorified through death. Again, the text portrays this through an emblematic use of existing convention. In *Tragic Ways of Killing a Woman*, Nicole Loraux examines the ways in which death is portrayed on the Athenian stage and underlines the determining function of gender.[15] She says that where suicide is concerned women kill themselves by hanging and men by the sword. It is the act of closing an orifice in the case of the women and obviously the act of penetration that is enacted in the case of the men. And here is how these two emblems, the noose and the sword, appear in the messenger's speech:

> Messenger: We went
> And looked, as bidden by our anxious master.
> There in the furthest corner of the cave
> We saw her hanging by her neck. The rope
> Was of the woven linen of her dress.
> And, with his arms about her, there stood he

> Lamenting his lost bride, his luckless love,
> His father's cruelty.
> When Creon saw them,
> Into the cave he went, moaning piteously.
> 'O my unhappy boy,' he cried again,
> 'What have you done? What madness brings you here
> To your destruction? Come away, my son,
> My son, I do beseech you, come away!'
> His son looked at him with one angry stare,
> Spat in his face, and then without a word
> Drew his sword and struck out. But his father fled
> Unscathed. Whereon the poor demented boy
> Leaned on his sword and thrust it deeply home
> In his own side, and while his life ebbed out
> Embraced the maid in loose-enfolding arms,
> His spurting blood staining her pale cheeks red.
> Two bodies lie together, wedded in death,
> Their bridal sleep a witness to the world.
> How great calamity can come to man
> Through man's perversity.
>
> (1217–43)

This double-suicide is highly staged in an almost meta-theatrical manner. By turning the cave – and the psychoanalytical resonance is obvious here – into a stage, the love that is denied presence in life is redeemed in death through the spectacular use of the two gendered emblems of suicide – the noose and the sword. The mention of 'man' – *anthropos* – towards the end of this sequence is also significant. Turning this scene into a parable, the pedagogic dimension of love/death becomes clear. Furthermore, the heterosexual relationship (all the more powerful for taking place in death) reinforces the overall humanism of the text. And this particular use of the cave-cum-stage, I would argue, is also a nod towards Plato's cave and his general anti-theatricalism, in an attempt to stress the humanist and pedagogical qualities of the institution of the theatre itself. This is a dominant feature of the work of Sophocles in general; a point that is not missed by Aristotle, as he chooses the Sophoclean canon to theorise his Poetics and reinstitute the civic, pedagogical dimension of theatre contra Plato. I also would argue that this validation of heterosexuality accounts for the popularity of the play. Steiner writes about the attraction that this play exerted on the Romantic sensibility:

> There is only *one* human relationship in which the ego can negate its solitude without departing from its authentic self. There is only *one* mode of encounter in which the self meets in another, in which ego and non-ego, the Kantian, the

> Fichtean, the Hegelian polarities are made one. It is a relation between man and woman, as it surely must be if primary rifts in being are to be knit. But it is a relation between man and woman which resolves the paradox of estrangement inherent in all sexuality (a paradox which incest would only enforce). It is the relation of brother and sister, of sister and brother. In the love, in the perfect understanding of brother and sister, there is *eros* and *agape*. Both are *aufgehoben*, 'sublated'. In *philia*, to the transcendent absoluteness of relation itself.[16]

It is fascinating that this heterosexuality of the play, which in the Romantic context can be read as the sublimation that is at the 'nub of the dialectic' itself, mirrors the convention of male-to-male *philia*. In the Greek sense, the only and first 'real thing' is the male-to-male relationship. The others, be it brother–sister or man–woman, are mere substitutes. The man–woman relationship especially is twice removed from the object of desire and thus a substitute of a substitute. In this context, linking it with the death drive, and sexualising death in the process, does not seem so extreme.

Far from failing to reproduce heterosexual closure, Antigone's non-reproducing and now dead body only serves to validate heterosexuality, which in turn helps construct the notion of *anthropos*, on which the idea of the Athenian citizen is based. What better way to reinforce the power of the democratic *polis* than by testing the limits of its law through those who are denied presence in it, that is, women. Antigone, a travestied woman, becomes the locus of the anxieties of the homosocial democratic Athenian citizen. Her final gesture of suicide, which turns her into a heroine, is redefined within the discursive domain of the *polis*. This is why I think it is difficult to sustain a feminist or queer reading of Antigone. I have, however, already started to 'queer' her myself in this analysis through reference to dramatic convention.

I would like to shift the perspective a little now and draw attention to what it is that Antigone actually does, what it is that her criminal act consists of. She wants to claim the right to mourn her brother. She buries him twice – and the repetition is significant here – defying the laws of the *polis*. Mourning is a contested site in Athenian tragedy, a site of struggle. We know from recent structuralist and/or anthropological approaches that 'excessive female mourning' was outlawed in the sixth century BCE. It was considered eastern (i.e. barbarian) and feminising. Furthermore, the dead bodies mourned were more often than not the bodies of young men who died at war. So the act of mourning itself, conducted by women, was seen as a threat to the expansion of the Athenian empire. Its subsequent outlawing is parallel to the rise of tragedy as a distinct set of artistic conventions and as a social institution. Gail Holst-Warhaft writes:

I have suggested that the state of Athens may, consciously or unconsciously, have channeled the passion of lament into its two great rhetorical inventions, the funeral speech and the tragedy.[17]

In turn these two great rhetorical traditions serve to unify and in many ways construct the city-state. Richard Seaford writes:

> Tragedy ... is a product of the developed city-state, of cult in which the growth of public participation in death ritual had contributed to the process of political unification.[18]

This thesis is parallel to the one put forward by Loraux in *The Invention of Athens*, where she suggests that the funeral oration, the *epitaphios logos*, and tragedy emerge as the two main discursive modes through which the Athenian city-state imagines, represents and finally reproduces itself.[19] And, of course, this process is also a gendered one. In this context, it is significant that Antigone chooses the act of mourning to express her defiance against the laws of the state. It is also significant that this happens during the so-called golden moment of the classical period. This is the moment when the institution of theatre establishes the supposed organic relationship to the city-state (a relationship that will haunt studies of theatre throughout the ages), when we have the ultimate identification of discourse and praxis: a golden moment that gives rise to the theory and practice of democracy itself. Within the heart of this gold-rimmed bubble we have a young, beautiful girl standing up against the laws of the state. It is almost perfect. We begin to see the attraction/affliction that this image exerts.

The *epitaphios logos*, the funeral oration, was first spoken as a public speech by Pericles during the Peloponnesian War. It is a type of speech-to-the-unknown soldier, an official state speech that at once claims the dead for its own and through them reinforces its own political power. According to popular belief, Pericles and Sophocles were best friends, reinforcing the supposed organic coupling between the politician and the poet. Sophocles was very popular in the dramatic contests. Antigone's claim to mourn can probably be read as the mirror image of the *epitaphios logos*, setting up a binary opposition between official and unofficial modes of mourning, which are also gendered. It is, however, a binary opposition that even in the act of opposing helps construct the identity of the Athenian city-state.

In this context, I would like to look at the way Antigone is referred to in the work of Gillian Rose. This approach sees in her the possibility of critique, a critique that at once opposes and furthers the democratic project. In *Mourning Becomes the Law* she draws parallels between a reading of a painting by Poussin, *Gathering the Ashes of Phocion*, and Antigone. She writes:

> What is the meaning of these acts? Do they represent the transgression of the law of the city – women as the irony of the political community, as its ruination? Do they bring to representation an immediate ethical experience, 'women's experience' silenced and suppressed by the law of the city, and hence expelled outside its walls? No. In these delegitimate acts of tending the dead, these acts of justice, against the current will of the city, women reinvent the political life of the community.
>
> By insisting on the rites of mourning, Antigone and the wife of Phocion carry out that intense work of the soul, that gradual rearrangement of its boundaries, which must occur when a loved one is lost – so as to allow the other fully to depart, and hence fully to be regained beyond sorrow. To acknowledge and to re-experience the justice and the injustice of the partner's life and death is to accept the law, is not to transgress it – mourning becomes the law.[20]

Throughout her book, Gillian Rose deliberately uses the term 'work' instead of 'text', 'the former implying the labour of the concept inseparable from its formal characteristics as opposed to the latter with its connotations of signifiers, the symbolic and semiotics.'[21] While this emphasis on materiality is very attractive, it nevertheless relies on an opposition between materiality and discursivity that sees them as mutually exclusive. Indeed, particularly in the analysis of theatrical events the work and the text are interconnected. How Antigone is made and what she comes to represent are so bound up together, and so constitutive of each other, that to read them separately would only really give us a partial – usually anthropomorphic – interpretation of her.

Nevertheless, this is a very appealing analysis, hopeful in all its melancholy. It is part of her overall project in the last books to reinstate the power and the impact of critique to philosophy. She writes, opening her introduction, 'It is strange to live in a time when philosophy has found so many ways to damage if not to destroy itself.'[22] In many ways this is reminiscent of the initial bridge that tragedy was called upon to cross in the context of German philosophy in the late eighteenth century. According to this approach, Antigone and the wife of Phocion stand in for what Gillian Rose calls the 'third city', neither Athens nor Jerusalem, somehow going beyond the *either/or* and presenting a *third* possibility.

I really want to believe this about Antigone. I want to believe that she represents the possibility of political action beyond the all-determining binary opposition, a hopeful third way. And as far as *The Wife of Phocion* is concerned I think that Gillian Rose's reading is truly inspired. But I do not think that it amounts to a model that can then be applied indiscriminately to Antigone. There are many reasons for this. First, where does this city that Antigone represents reside? What is its *topos*? Is it the realm of the soul? Or is it a non-*topos*, a Utopia? And this 'new' law that mourning turns into, that mourning becomes, is it necessarily a better law, in an almost evolutionary sense? And who will mourn for Antigone once she has committed her deed? The answer to this is in the play itself. It is the *polis* itself that redefines Antigone's action, at once turning her into a hero and appropriating her transgression. Haemon says in the debate with his father, Creon:

> Your face is terrible [*deinon*] to a simple citizen
> It frightens him from words you dislike to hear.
> But what I can hear, in the dark, are things like these:
> The city mourns this girl; they think she is dying most wrongly and most
> Undeservedly . . .
> Surely what she merits is golden honour, is it not?
> That's the dark rumour that spreads in secret.
>
> (685–95)

After transgressing the limits of the *polis*, the play has Antigone returning triumphantly. After all, as Rose herself states, 'all meaning and all mourning belong to the city, the *polis*.'[23] Whether or not the law itself has benefited from the process is the question that begs an answer. Does this wandering on the outskirts of the *polis* represent in and of itself a new *polis* – a third city – or is it a momentary aberration of the original *polis* that serves only to highlight, theatricalise and in the end reinforce its power? According to this reading, Antigone's transgression is a gesture towards the possibility of the third city; Antigone herself becomes the emblem that redeems philosophy. But who occupies the place of Antigone? Who is the *anthropos* of this city, its citizen?

In this respect I think that both of the interpretations presented in this analysis exhibit a classical blind spot. Like most readings of Antigone, Butler's and Rose's commit a basic humanist fallacy in assuming she is a dramatic character with will and intention, conscious and subconscious and so on, and a woman at that. This touches upon one of the most problematic aspects of the relationship between tragedy and philosophy. In approaching tragedy philosophical thinking treats it in the best scenario like a realist novel and in the worst like a philosophical treatise that uses human examples. Concepts, ideas and debates are enacted on the stage by characters who supposedly have will and intention, conscious and subconscious. If we are to read Antigone, following the lead proposed by Gillian

Rose, as a text *and* as a work, then the way she has been created and the kinds of conventions that constitute her presence on the stage become crucial in any analysis we may want to undertake. I think that these conventions do not simply embody tragedy, help it to become visible, but are fundamental to tragic form itself. The traditional humanist readings of Antigone separate the writing of her from the doing of her, as it were. They take the discursive construct of the human/female Antigone as a finished product that then stands in for their interpreted Antigone. This process is based on a series of assumptions, or acts of faith:

- the separability of writing and doing
- the separability of watching/reading and doing
- on an empathic reading of the character
- on a kind of philosophical reflection that can separate itself from the drama – that resides in the audience, as it were, and not on the stage
- on the separation of tragedy and philosophy
- and on the fundamental premise that there is a reconstructed line of hermeneutics from the Greeks straight to the twentieth century (the Greeks as the childhood of mankind, as Marx would have it).

What I want to question here, in order to open this analysis up to some of the other trajectories of this project, is not so much whether tragedy and philosophy can or should be separated, but the kind of philosophy that tragedy proposes. If tragedy challenges the discursive hegemony of philosophy, it does it in a very interesting way. Tragedy is theatre and theatre is etymologically linked to *theoria* (*theorein*, to contemplate, to reflect). The philological history of the term *theoria* itself might help clarify the underprivileged status it has had, particularly in relation to philosophy. *Theoria* was translated from Greek into Latin as *speculatio* (from *specto*, to look at, to scrutinise) by Boethius. In Christian theology, however, this aspect of its meaning (that is, to speculate) was put aside (primarily by Thomas Aquinas) in favour of a more negative interpretation of the term. In the Christian context *speculatio* derives from *speculum*, mirror, and bears the traces of the distorted and confused image. Françoise Dastur writes in 'Tragedy and Speculation':

> But in Christian theology this meaning was forgotten, especially by Thomas Aquinas, who derives *speculatio* from *speculum*, mirror, and related the word to what Paul says in the first Epistle to the Corinthians (13. 12) concerning the vision of God whom we see now confusedly as 'in a mirror' but whom later, that is to say, after death, we will see 'face to face'.[24]

This shift in meaning from *theoria* as a type of *speculative* thinking to *theoria* as representing a distorted image, indeed one that can only be restored by the intervention of the divine, bears the indelible traces of anti-theatrical philosophy. So much so that Thomas Aquinas' derivation from *speculum* can be read as echoing the master of anti-theatrical philosophy himself, Plato. In turn the identification of things *spectacular* with distortion and corruption of the truth accounts for the difficult relationship between Christianity and theatre in general.

If, on the other hand, we try to restore to *theoria* its initial meaning of *speculative* thinking, then we have *theoria* as philosophy by other means. Interestingly enough, Kant keeps to the pejorative meaning of the term, while Hegel restores to it its original sense. For him, *theoria*, as speculation, has mystical dimensions. It is connected with insight and illumination that parallel the *visio Dei*. Hölderlin, echoing Kant, calls tragedy 'the metaphor of an intellectual intuition'. Nevertheless, as crucial as it is to *theoria*'s speculative, intellectual and intuitive dimension, it is equally important to maintain its spectacular and distorting qualities, that is, its particular 'theatrical' and 'theatricalising' aspects.

The possible combination of 'intuitive thinking' and 'spectacular distortion' creates a kind of practice that is at once reflective, distancing and aestheticising. *Theoria* and its derivative *theatron* (i.e. the place, the locus of *theoria*) could propose a type of philosophy that embodies the idea of distortion, reproduction, citation even. The coexistence of 'intuitive thinking' (speculative thinking), with spectacular, corrupting images that supposedly distort the real might help construct a reading of performance that is quite close to contemporary readings of the function of the performative. In this instance, however, what was traditionally read as 'corrupting' reality has to be read as 'citationally' commenting on it. In this sense, *theoria* might be read as a type of philosophy that encapsulates the concept of enactment, or, in other words, a type of philosophical practice that embodies enactment. It is this reading of *theoria* that needs to be incorporated into actual theatrical practice, as is the case with tragedy and tragic form more generally.

The intertwining of the *spectacular* with the *speculative* gives us a reading of *theoria* that is at once physical and metaphysical, visual and auditory, linguistic – in the strict sense – and extra-linguistic, material and discursive. Where the locus of philosophy is the mind, the locus of *theoria* is the body with all its senses. Possibly the difference between philosophy and *theoria* is that *theoria* needs to be experienced through the body – the senses, that is, the aesthetic. In this sense tragedy might already be philosophical and the type of philosophy it enacts (a *theoria*) is one that preexists the separation of the aesthetic and the philosophical; one in fact where such a separation is not only meaningless but inconceivable; where the doing and the writing cannot exist without each other; where meaning resides in the inseparability of these categories. This is very close to the contemporary reading of the performative. This is why dramatic convention needs to be included in any study of tragic form. Not simply as a kind of reading-in-context or as historical pragmatics, but as formative and constitutive of tragic form itself. If tragedy is a type of performative philosophy, then the conventions/formal aspects of this performance are crucial.

The figure of Antigone, not a woman and not a man but alternating between both, as the text requires, and inscribing both into the text, becomes a kind of Brechtian *gestus*. A figure that at once represents and demonstrates, who writes and does, who acts and enacts. And what is enacted through a series of travesties – indeed through a travesty of the law itself – is the ability of the law to inscribe its own resistance. The fact that this process is enacted through mourning is also significant. Mourning is central to Athenian tragedy in general, and I mentioned it as a site of struggle. This constant claiming of the right to mourn coupled with the transvestive/cross-dressing convention of the tragedy could lead us towards a reading of tragedy as melancholy philosophy.

The term melancholia is not used in a symptomatological sense, but possibly in a philosophical/performative sense. There is a long tradition in the philosophical definition of melancholia. In the Hippocratic writings melancholia is recorded as an illness and has parallels with the four humours (and hence a series of metaphorical manifestations in the seasons, the elements, etc.). With Aristotle, however, there is a crucial shift in the understanding of the term. In the *Problemata* (30, 1), which is attributed to Aristotle, a different definition of melancholia is proposed. It reads melancholia as a basic attribute of the philosopher rather than as a disease. He sees melancholia as a trait of an 'exceptional personality' as 'a well-balanced diversity' (*eukratos anomalia*), something that does not constitute a philosopher's disease but helps form his *ethos*. This recalls Montaigne's view that 'to philosophise is to learn how to die'.

I want to propose a way of reading the cross-dressing element of Athenian tragedy that combines philosophical/historical readings of melancholia (inspired by Benjamin's *The Origins of Tragic German Drama*) with psychoanalytical ones (as seen in the work of Kristeva and Butler's *The Psychic Life of Power*). According to both Kristeva and Butler, melancholia is constitutive of the formation of identity, particularly where gender differentiation and identification are concerned. According to Butler, 'drag allegorizes heterosexual melancholy', by refusing grief and at the same time creating 'passionate attachments'. So much so that she coins a distinctive aphorism which has now become notorious:

> In this sense the 'truest' melancholic is the strictly straight woman [something which is also mentioned by Kristeva], and the 'truest' gay male melancholic is the strictly straight man.
> [. . .]
> Can we finally ever resolve the question of whether sexual difference is the accomplishment of a melancholic heterosexuality, sacrilized as theory, or whether it is the given condition of loss and attachment in any set of human relations?[25]

The approach taken by this analysis does not claim that this model can unproblematically be applied to Athenian tragedy. However, I do think that this cross-dressing convention has been ignored and almost completely untheorised and that one way of accounting for it would be to say that it enacts a type of melancholia that has to do with anxieties about gender differentiation and identification.

If we return to Antigone and reread her as a man dressed as a woman who is claiming the right to mourn, and in doing so is testing the limits of the democratic *polis*, it is very tempting to read her as a melancholy character. Her melancholia, however, does not simply derive from her refusal to grieve according to the law, but also from the way this refusal is enacted, the kinds of forms it enacts and creates in the process of this refusal. I would say that the two are so bound up together (form and content) as to create a kind of predicament, one that is occupied by most female roles in Athenian tragedy. Indeed, I think that this cross-dressing aspect of Athenian drama is endemic to the form (i.e. in the *demos*, the public sphere, the civic dimension of the tragedy and also in the sense of an infusion) without which it cannot exist.[26] If in turn Antigone's act is read in the context of many acts that claim the rite/right to mourn, her deed is not unique – an aberration – nor is it necessarily transgressive. Butler writes:

> The insistence on public grieving is what moves her away from feminine gender into hubris, into that distinctively manly excess that makes the guards, the chorus, and Creon wonder: Who is the man here? There seem to be some spectral men here, ones that Antigone herself inhabits, the brothers whose place she has taken and whose place she transforms in the taking.[27]

If we include a reading of the forms she embodies, then her hubris is not as obvious, as she is already the man in whose place she stands. In this sense she occupies both the real and the spectral space on the stage. This reading of the convention of men-playing-women confuses the opposition between the two genders, between transgression and submission, in fact between the whole *either/or* paradigm that the play traditionally has been read as enacting. Butler inscribes melancholia into Antigone only in respect to what she represents, as a humanist subject, not in respect to how she is made as performance/performative convention.

Both through what she stands in for – woman as irony, as Hegel claims – and through how she is made, Antigone enacts, in gestural fashion, the momentary suspension of disbelief, the momentary outside of the *polis*, the Utopia, without which the *polis* could not exist. Through a travesty of the law, through feminising and theatricalising it, she looks at us; she winks at us, almost behind the mask. And it is an enchanting glance, one that has mesmerised philosophers and theatre practitioners for centuries.

Notes

1. For a discussion of the cultural impact of the Stammheim suicides, see Peter Wollen's review of Robert Storr (ed.), *Gerhard Richter: 'October 18, 1977'*, in *London Review of Books*, 5 April 2001, pp. 10–12. Wollen calls the film 'a *Trauerarbeit*, both a demonstration and an enactment of grief'.
2. For an insightful discussion of Antigone's pivotal role in the traditions of German philosophy and aesthetic theory, see the chapter 'Philosophy's Need for Antigone', in Stathis Gourgouris, *Does Literature Think? Literature as Theory for an Antimythical Era* (Stanford: Stanford University Press, 2003). Gourgouris asseses the significance of Antigone for Hölderlin, Hegel and Heidegger: 'The enchantment this drama exercises on philosophy may be termed an affliction.'
3. See Miguel de Beistegui and Simon Sparks (eds), *Philosophy and Tragedy* (London and New York: Routledge, 2000). This impressive book belongs to a long tradition of the 'philosophisation' of tragedy.
4. See Gourgouris, *Does Literature Think?* for a discussion of Heidegger's particular brand of Hellenism. 'We learn of the Greek language so that the concealed essence of our own historical commencement can find its way into the clarity of our word.' Gourgouris comments, 'surely, a remark that would have made Fichte and Humboldt proud', p. 137.
5. Butler, *Antigone's Claim* (New York: Columbia University Press, 2000), p. 1.
6. Ibid. p. 5.
7. G. W. F. Hegel, *Aesthetics: Lectures on Fine Art*, trans. T. M. Knox (Oxford: Oxford University Press, 1975), pp. 1217–18.
8. Sophocles, *Antigone*, trans. E. F. Watling (London: Penguin, 1974), lines 730–43. All subsequent references to the play-text are from this translation.
9. Butler, *Antigone's Claim*, p. 76.
10. George Steiner, *Antigones* (Oxford: Clarendon Press, 1984).

11. Steiner draws a similar parallel and extends it to include the sister: 'In Sophocles' extant dramas, the Antigone-Ismene pairing has its counterpart in Electra-Chrysothemis. Sophocles resorts twice to the same asymmetry of sisterhood and conflict', ibid., pp. 144–5.
12. At this stage I would like to refrain from reading this bond as an incestuous one. See Martha C. Nussbaum, *The Fragility of Goodness: Luck and Ethics in Greek Tragedy and Philosophy* (Cambridge: Cambridge University Press, 1986), where she claims that Antigone appears not to have a great attachment to Polyneices. Her claim is rather used more as a springboard for her attack on the law.
13. See Gourgouris, *Does Literature Think?* for a detailed analysis of the etymology, p. 26. He cites John D. B. Hamilton, 'Antigone: Kinship, Justice and the Polis', in Dora C. Pozzi and John M. Wickersham (eds), *Myth and the Polis* (Ithaca: Cornell University Press, 1991), p. 95; Froma Zeitlin, 'Thebes: Theatre of Self and Society in Athenian Drama', p. 126, and Warren J. Lane and Ann M. Lane, 'The Politics of *Antigone*, p. 177, both in Peter Euben (ed.), *Greek Tragedy and Political Theory* (Berkeley: University of California Press, 1986); Robert Graves, *The Greek Myths*, vol. II (London: Penguin, 1960), p. 380.
14. See Euripides, *Medea, Ion* and *Hippolytus*.
15. Nicole Loraux, *Tragic Ways of Killing a Woman*, trans. Anthony Forster (London: Routledge, 1992).
16. See Steiner, *Antigones*, p. 17.
17. Gail Holst-Warhaft, *Dangerous Voices: Women's Lament and Greek Literature* (London and New York: Routledge, 1992), p. 10.
18. Richard Seaford, *Reciprocity and Ritual: Homer and Tragedy in the Developing City-State* (Oxford: Clarendon Press, 1994), p. 328.
19. Nicole Loraux, *The Invention of Athens: The Funeral Oration in the Classical City*, trans. Alan Sheridan (Cambridge, MA, and London: Harvard University Press, 1986).
20. Gillian Rose, *Mourning Becomes the Law: Philosophy and Representation* (Cambridge: Cambridge University Press, 1996), pp. 35–6. She says of this painting, in an inspiring interpretation, 'The gathering of the ashes is a protest against arbitrary power; it is not a protest against power and the law as such. To oppose anarchic, individual love or good to civil or public ill is to deny the third which gives meaning to both – this is the other meaning of *the third city* – the just city and the just act, the just man and the just woman. In Poussin's painting, this transcendent but mournable justice is configured, its absence given presence, in the architectural perspective which frames and focuses the enacted justice of the two women. To see the built forms themselves as ciphers of the unjust city has political consequences: it perpetuates endless dying and endless tyranny, and it ruins the possibility of political action,' p. 26.
21. Ibid. pp. 7–8.
22. Ibid. p. 1.
23. Ibid. p. 103.
24. See Françoise Dastur, 'Tragedy and Speculation', in de Beistegui and Sparks (eds) *Philosophy and Tragedy*, pp. 78–9.
25. Judith Butler, *The Psychic Life of Power: Theories in Subjection* (Stanford: Stanford University Press, 1997), pp. 146–7, p. 166. In particular see Chapter 5, 'Melancholy Gender/Refused Identification', pp. 132–50.

26. Judith Butler writes in *Antigone's Claim*, 'Her melancholia, if we can call it that, seems to consist in this refusal to grieve that is accomplished through the very public terms by which she insists on her right to grieve. Her claim to entitlement may well be the sign of a melancholia at work in her speech,' p. 80. However, she does not read this melancholia into the very conventions that Antigone embodies, she only reads it into what she represents.
27. Ibid. p. 80.

CHAPTER TWO

Oedipus/Anti-Oedipus: The Philosopher, the Actor and the Patient

> One summer afternoon Mrs Oedipa Maas came home from a Tupperware party whose hostess had put perhaps too much kirsch in the fondue to find that she, Oedipa, had been named executor, or she supposed executrix, of the estate of one Pierce Inverarity, a California real estate mogul who had once lost two million dollars in his spare time but still had assets numerous and tangled enough to make the job of sorting it all out more than honorary.[1]

In Thomas Pynchon's *The Crying of Lot 49* there is a character called Oedipa Maas who never really enters into any sexual encounters, does not reproduce and is visited by a messenger-like pigeon, in an ironic allusion to hierogamy (holy rape), or the Christian version of it, the Annunciation. Indeed, this is one of the rare instances in literature where Oedipus is feminised. Like her male counterpart, who responds to the will of Apollo, Oedipa sets out to discover the true meaning of this will which arrives to her like an omen. She sets out on a hermeneutic journey, again not unlike Oedipus himself, charting the hallucinatory landscape of southern California of the 1960s, while trying to establish her position in the universe. The manner in which Oedipus is feminised is important as well. Oedipa Maas occupies a position reserved for young *parthenoi* (unwed girls) who are visited by a god in disguise, usually as a bird or animal. The holy rape that proceeds uses the body of the young girl as a bridge between the earthly and the divine, as a mediation for the word of the God, which then turns into flesh through this young female body. In mythic structure this is a quintessentially female position. Leda and Pasiphae are prime examples. Oedipus is the one character who more than any other in classical Greek thought is associated with the shift from the mythological understanding of the world to a more epistemological one. Furthermore, many readings of him see him as the first philosopher. In an act of inversion Pynchon's Oedipa Maas feminises and theatricalises the philosopher Oedipus and turns him into a debased version of the most 'unconscious', even unwilling mythic character: that of the young sacrificial virgin whose sense of self resides only in her body and only in as far as that body reproduces a god or demi-god. To compound the effect, in this instance the reproductive, quasi-motherly dimension of Oedipa Maas is never fulfilled. So she is even denied the mythological status of bridging, through her reproductive body, the two worlds, the divine and the earthly. Oedipus himself is called upon to fulfil a similar function. He, however, gets to do it through the use of reason and not through his violated body.

This use of Oedipus raises the more general question of whether the position of the character could ever by occupied by a woman. This is not a case of a feminist rewriting or reclaiming, as Oedipus and the history of his name are not areas that many feminist projects are eager to reclaim. However, if the story of Oedipus signifies the birth of a certain type of philosophy, not to mention psychoanalysis, then a whole tradition of thought and *episteme* could be indirectly or very straightforwardly gendered. Even to begin to unravel the various strands of this question – or possibly *aporia* – we need to investigate (to use a term that Oedipus is fond of) the ways in which the story and the play of Oedipus have been appropriated and interpreted by various intellectual projects ranging from Aristotelian philosophy to psychoanalysis. This seems like an almost impossible feat, particularly in view of the fact that the same intellectual trajectory is itself probably structured *Oedipally*. If the twentieth century or indeed the Enlightenment are seen to be the Oedipal phases of the history of thought, then how does one begin a critique of the Oedipal narrative without simply reproducing it. Is there a system of thought or a construct of subjectivity that is outwith and beyond an Oedipal understanding of the psyche and the world?

The interpretation of Oedipus by philosophy and by Freudian psychoanalysis goes hand in hand. The classical school of philosophy, taking its cue from Aristotle, and re-echoed in Hegel, sees Oedipus as the first philosopher. The story in this context enacts the transition from a mytho-cosmological view of the world to one where the world can be understood and ordered by reason. Oedipus' quest for self-knowledge in defiance of the will of the gods signifies a historico-anthropological phase in human development where we have the seeds of what we today understand as empiricism and progress. Similarly in Freudian psychoanalysis, according to the Oedipal complex – seen as the cornerstone of the creation of 'normality' – the child, through the intervention of a hostile or friendly father (depending on the school propagated), enters into self-consciousness, reason, progress, the world as we know it. In both these ramifications Oedipus himself successfully stands in for the very concept of civilisation. And it is a neat symmetry – one no doubt picked up by Freud – that once again sees in the 'Greek' world a mythic version, a subconscious mirroring of modernity. This symmetry itself, of course, with its emphasis on linearity, on 'befores/afters', on shifts and phases, on conscious and subconscious, on identification and mimesis (through the act of mirroring), can be said to manifest a classic Oedipal reading.

The analysis that follows proposes to look at Oedipus both in *Oedipus Rex* and *Oedipus at Colonus* through the lenses of more recent anti-Oedipal philosophy and psychoanalysis. The main question addressed is whether Oedipus the play is in itself Oedipal. Can we sustain a reading of the plays that ignores Freud? Is there any way in which the plays themselves, both as textual explications and as pieces of embodied theatrical experience, already encompass an anti-Oedipal critique, which has been ignored both by philosophy and by traditional psychoanalysis? Most readings of the play stress the significance of the development of the character of Oedipus in relation to his father and/or to the gods, with psychoanalysis substituting the Father for the gods. The reading suggested here sets out to look at Oedipus as one of many roles in these plays. In particular his so-called development will be analysed in relation not only to his biological father and the gods but also in relation to both his mothers, Iocasta, the biological mother, and Merope, the absent cultural mother. It is fascinating that, like psychoanalysis, and possibly taking their lead from it, most readings of Oedipus tend to ignore his relationships with his mothers. The other great feminine absence, whose spectre haunts Oedipus as both character and play-text, is the Sphinx. The significance of the Sphinx as mythological character and dramatic trope will be addressed in detail. Her suicide, crucial for the development of the subjectivity of Oedipus, is also mirrored in Iocasta's suicide. Oedipus is also a king; he is called a tyrant at one stage. The political and civic dimension of his existence also will be looked at in an attempt to politicise and contextualise his otherwise purely psychic life, rendered to him by psychoanalysis. Like *Antigone*, *Oedipus Rex* and *Oedipus at Colonus* are pieces of theatre, not philosophical documents. The discursive processes involved in the interaction between theatre and philosophy will again be approached in an attempt to re-theatricalise Oedipus and read him as a performing creation that is embodied, physical and requires the physical presence of others in order to exist.

Oedipus, the Philosopher

> Let me make the point here and now, before returning to it in greater detail: what Western thought has had to acknowledge, since the Enlightenment, as another scene, foreign to the reflective subject, is precisely what the Oedipean posture –

founding the subject as consciousness of self – excluded and denied. The gesture by which Oedipus situated himself so as to respond to the 'riddling bitch', guardian of the initiatory threshold, and the belief that he could abolish her with the word 'man' in a presumption of auto-initiation, are what will later be called consciousness and unconsciousness. Hegel glimpsed this but, for good reason, was unable to see its implications.[2]

Jean-Joseph Goux makes the case in *Oedipus, Philosopher* for a reading of the Oedipus story that does not see it as the canon but as the rare exception, the deviation from the canon of initiation myths. In a rigorous anthropological analysis Oedipus' journey to self-discovery and self-reflection – the very attributes that make him the first philosopher – is seen as itself initiating a new process of thinking, which is nothing less than a new developmental stage in the history of western thought. Whereas most philosophical readings of the myth, from Aristotle to Hegel and Heidegger, see it as metaphorically enacting the birth of reason and subjectivity, the one proposed by Jean-Joseph Goux, while remaining faithful to this trajectory, introduces a very interesting element: that of the myth as a failed initiation. Whereas the monomyth is 'resolved in the sequence matricide – engagement', Goux claims that 'the Oedipal myth is organized around the causal sequence patricide – incest'.[3] As examples of the monomyth he cites Jason's trials in acquiring the Golden Fleece and the feats of Hercules. In both these instances the hero's passage into adulthood and masculinity is preceded by the encounter and battle with a feminine monstrosity. In killing this feminine monster the hero 'frees' the real feminine living inside the monster and in the end marries her. So this monster/bride dyad is crucial in this form of initiation. The hero kills a monstrous, deadly, motherly female in order then to proceed to 'marriage' and an overall 'engagement' with the world. In this way, the hero becomes a subject, one that differentiates himself from the world and orders it accordingly, internalising the subject/object separation. Indeed the separability of those two categories relies, according to this model, on the murderous act that preceded it.

The Oedipus myth, however, introduces a deviation to this model. As Goux succinctly puts it, the shift from matricide-marriage to parricide-incest is a crucial one and signals Oedipus as a representative of a 'failed' initiation. Reading the myth as a deviation and not as the canon also touches upon many of the 'unthought' elements in Freudian psychoanalysis. These, according to this reading, are 'monstricide', and 'matricide', where the two categories very smoothly stand in for each other. Indeed, it is not a particularly radical or new reading that proposes that both the myth and its Freudian interpretations ignore the feminine unless as monster, mother or bride, with these very categories posing their own problems.

However, this initiation, despite its failure, continues to produce visibility, power and representation. It helps construct anthropocentrism and anthropomorphism. It posits 'man' at the centre of the universe, a position from which he can begin to understand, order and define. This radical act of separation is in the final analysis what makes man human. Indeed, it is a movement that has fascinated philosophers and psychoanalysts alike. The subject/object divide creates one of those fundamental binaries that then seems to be mirrored in most aspects of the psychic and material life of power. In his 'Notes to Oedipus' Hölderlin attributes 'the ideal beginning of the actual separation' to 'the necessary *arbitrariness of Zeus*'.[4] The separation itself is reverberated in the split between the earthly and the divine, reason and the sacred, ritual and art, and, of course, man and woman. The structural position of Zeus is in turn filled by 'the father', the divine, the law, language and so on, depending on the particular school of thought that is represented. All of these 'schools', nevertheless, seem to have the so-called 'Greek miracle' as their origin:

> Oedipus is emblematic of the movement by which the human subject, recognizing itself as the source and agent, withdraws what it had projected onto the external world, with the result that in a single two-sided operation of deprojection, the subject discovers the world as an object (rather than a sign) and situates himself as a subject. It would not be impossible to show that all the original features characteristic of the 'Greek miracle', whether we are concerned with philosophy, politics, or aesthetic representation, refer in one way or another to that operation.[5]

Furthermore, the analysis that shows all this to be part and parcel of the 'Greek miracle' is not the obscure, hidden one, but the one that has fuelled most interpretations of the play. In this sense Oedipus himself is read as the quintessential 'son of the city of Athens' (where Thebes can be read as the 'other' of Athens). The philosopher himself is said to be born out of the democratic *polis*. Indeed, democracy and philosophy seem to have a similar genealogy. This reading of the play sees it as the source of all knowledge and civilisation. However, it is not without prisoners, captives and murdered monsters on the path to self-knowledge and not without victims to this notion of anthropocentrism and individuation. This path that the son follows in order to take the place of the father and to institute the reign of his reason is not without obstacles. As Goux himself states:

> The limits of the first operation can be anticipated in a few words: to suppress the Sphinx with the reflective and anthropocentered response is not to destroy her forever, it is to internalize her . . .

> The myth of Oedipus, in its aftereffects, thus also has the following meaning: with the Sphinx's suicide, with the precipitation into the abyss of that symbol of symbolism, the heroic age of fear comes to an end, and the rationalist era of anguish begins . . . Anguish is the *pathos* of a culture without *pathos*.[6]

Would it be too crude an analysis after all this posturing of initiation, individuation and anguish to ask whether a woman could follow the same path? Or is this yet another reconfiguration of the feminine as the other, an important other without which subjectivity could not come into being, but one, nevertheless, which can only exist as suppressed, 'internalised', sublimated, the dark mirroring of the male psyche? This is the monster/mother that the son needs to turn into a bride in order to tame her and the world. But, alas, no matter how far he runs or what feats of the mind and body he can accomplish, he can never escape her because once that magical tie has been severed – the one that ties him to the mother's body or to a mythical understanding of the world – the son enters the world of anguish, where he both loves and hates the internalised female. This source of anguish both situates him as a subject but also creates his unease in the world. According to this narrative, the moment of positioning as a subject, the moment man finds a home in the world is duplicated by an equal and simultaneous sense of what Heidegger, translating the Greek *deinon*, calls *Das Unheimliche*, 'the unhomely' or the uncanny.[7]

'Am I made man in the hour when I cease to be?',[8] says Oedipus to his daughter/sister Ismene in the more reflective and contemplative tone of *Oedipus at Colonus*. If we turn this aphorism round and state that his undoing starts at the very moment of his being made a man (a process traced in *King Oedipus*), if these two processes are constituent and reflective of each other, then his unease is as much a part of his being as any other position he may occupy. The myth itself may be said to signify a 'failed' initiation rather than a successful one. For Oedipus may have opened the road to self-knowledge and reason but with that comes the anguish that springs from the same source. Oedipus' suffering no longer has the consolation of a collective mythological body to be returned to and remembered by. The *pathos* of the hero or the god in the mythic world – a *pathos* which would usually entail dismemberment – would be recollected, put-together-again, by what Artaud called the communal sacred, the collective cosmological and mythological view of the world. Once the relationship with this has been severed, man is thrust into anguish, his *pathos* no longer redeemable or sacrificial has only one resort: knowledge.

This is a familiar story; one where the quest for some kind of sacred symbol or ritualistic repetition turns into a life-long quest for knowledge. The hero himself is humanised and he assumes an anthropocentric position in the world. However, the only way the feminine is conceptualised according to this model is as part of the failure of the initiation, as the demonised monster/mother, or the idealised bride who has to be revealed within her. By internalising the Sphinx, Oedipus is quite literally made 'unhomely', he is thrown out of the house of the father. The burden of the feminine that he carries inside him haunts him for the rest of his life. It is interesting that Tiresias, the breast-bearing prophet, plays such a crucial role in the revelation of the truth. Tiresias, who not only has internalised the feminine but also externalised her on to his body, is the true voice of wisdom, as opposed to reason, in the Oedipus story. Oedipus, however, is doomed to roam blind on the outskirts of Athens, at Colonus desperately trying to seek refuge in the sacred temples, which he had previously shunned. He becomes a stranger to humans and the Gods. He is a stranger to himself.

At the core of his anguish, his *pathos*, like the murder or sacrifice which always appears at the primal scene of cultural production, is a fundamental and multifaceted misogyny. And this is where the tale is a familiar one. Anthropologists, psychoanalysts and even philosophers have scrutinised the Oedipal narrative and revealed the glaring misogyny at its core. But they say that this is a *sine qua non* for both the creation of subjectivity and cultural production. It is somehow part of the burden of being human. How desirable is it, however, to read the feminine in terms of horror, lack and castration? If this love/hate relationship with the feminine is what creates man's essential unease in the world, his strangeness, imagine what it could do to women! Somehow women are supposed to be compensated by the fact that the feminine, like matricide, is a vital precondition of being.

'Who of us is Oedipus here? Who the Sphinx?'

Friedrich Nietzsche, *Beyond Good and Evil*

The Sphinx may already be dead when the play opens but her suicide haunts the narrative and the action. On the one hand, her structural role in initiation rites and, on the other, her function as *psychopompos*, a transmitter of souls, make her a crucial figure in the way the story unravels and in the trials of Oedipus. According to the myth, the initiatory rites of the Sphinx were brought to Thebes by Cadmus. Cadmus founded the city of

Thebes after having slain a fierce dragon and then sowed its teeth in the ground. From these grew civil war and strife but also the alphabet. So the King who with a single stroke brought the war and violence but also the language and civilisation that actually created that 'mother' of mythological cities – Thebes – is also attributed with introducing the rites of the Sphinx. This package includes the idea of language/representation, war/violence and the ever-present monstrous female as the foundational elements of a city, where the city itself, the *polis*, can be read as an extension of the male psyche. The rites of passage over which the Sphinx presides signal the transition into manhood but also the entry into citizenship. The character of Oedipus himself might even act a cursor for the shift from the 'raw', 'natural', or mythological constructions of masculinity to those discursively created by the power of the city-state.

But the genealogy of the Sphinx deserves attention in itself. In mythic thought, Oedipus' transgression – sleeping with his mother – is not uncommon. According to Robert Graves, the Sphinx derives from a similar tainted lineage. She is the result of an incestuous coupling:

> Echinde bore a dreadful brood to Typhon: namely, Cerberus, the three-headed Hound of Hell; the Hydra, a many-headed water-serpent living at Lerna; the Chimera, a fire-breathing goat with lion's head and serpent's body; and Orthrus, the two-headed hound of Geryon, who lay with his own mother and begot on her the Sphinx and the Nemean Lion.[9]

The Sphinx might owe her teratomorphic appearance to this strange lineage. Her connection with Cerberus might account for her 'bitch' quality, while the hound that guards hell might also account for her structural relationship with death. Cerberus is associated by Graves with the Egyptian dog-headed god Anubis, who led souls to Hades. Furthermore, Anubis seems originally to have been the death goddess Hecate. Her animal and human/feminine dimension links her back to its Egyptian source. Oedipus' repetition of the mythic pattern at once reinforces it and heralds a new era. The fact that his act in many ways mirrors the genealogy of the Sphinx places him firmly within the mythic world.

This aspect of his initiation is one that needs further attention and analysis. It is not so much that Oedipus breaks off from the old ritualistic world of cyclic repetition in order to initiate the new world of reason. The Oedipal story really needs to be read as encompassing both worlds. Like the Sphinx 'whose composite body represents the two parts of the Theban year – lion for the waxing part, serpent for the waning part'[10] – the body of Oedipus needs to be read as a hybrid, not as a singular anthropomorphic entity. Indeed, if we regress slightly from the heroic, humanist reading of Oedipus and read him for what he is, a mythological character, then his fate already fits a pattern; he is already within a mythic convention. That is not to say that the mythic world he inhabits is one devoid of reason. As Adorno tells us, 'myth is already enlightenment'. Rather, his mythic body, like the body of the Sphinx, is contaminated, plagued as much by his newly found consciousness as by the very convention he is doomed to repeat in accordance with myth's circular logic. Robert Graves offers an interesting interpretation of Oedipus, an interpretation that is, however, modified by his own schematic view of a matriarchal culture – the 'cult of the goddess' – that was overruled by the ascendance of patriarchy. Still, his view of Oedipus as belonging to a mythic structure is worthy of note:

> Was Oedipus a thirteenth-century invader of Thebes, who suppressed the old Minoan cult of the goddess and reformed the calendar? Under the old system, the new king, though a foreigner, had theoretically been a son of the old king whom he killed and whose widow he married; a custom that the patriarchal invaders misrepresented as parricide and incest. The Freudian theory that the 'Oedipus complex' is an instinct common to all men was suggested by this perverted anecdote; and while Plutarch records (*On Isis and Osiris* 32) that the hippopotamus 'murdered his sire and forced his dam', he would never have suggested that every man has a hippopotamus complex.[11]

The fascinating aspect of this analysis is that Graves exhibits a high sensitivity to the function of myth. His critique of Freud is insightful. Yes, why not a 'hippopotamus complex'? Obviously, because a hippopotamus is not human. However, within mythic thought the two categories are interchangeable, a fact that Graves' analysis acutely points out. This aspect of Oedipus – his monstrous, hybrid dimension – is one that usually gets written out of interpretations of the play. Furthermore, Oedipus is a mythic character that is staged for the purposes of tragedy. This adds yet another dimension. His so-called consciousness, or at least his quest for one, could also be read into the way dramatic form functions. The fact that myth is already citational once staged also opens up the possibility for distance, critique and *theoria*. The genealogy of the Sphinx is also interesting regarding the play as performance, especially given the structural, albeit mythic, link between the Sphinx and Dionysus. The connections between Dionysis and the Sphinx are stressed by Jane Ellen Harrison in her reading of the Vagnonville Crater:

> In any case the same conjunction appears on the Vagnonville Crater; a Sphinx is sitting on a choma ges [mound] which Satyrs are hammering at with picks, as though for the Anodos of Kore.[12]

This Anodos of Kore, a scene which is also depicted in a black, red-figured bowl painted by Myson, represents an interesting moment when birth and death merge.[13] For Kore can be seen as ascending from what looks like a tomb. She is greeted by dancing satyrs who have released her from death-into-life by hammering open the mound from which she springs, in egg-like fashion. On the top of the mound there is a seated Sphinx. The Sphinx and the Kore can be seen as mirroring each other: one is the monstrous female, the initiate has to overcome; the other is the 'virgin' he reveals, frees and reaps as his reward. In this context, the Sphinx is connected not only to funeral rites but also to fertility rites as the presence of Dionysus and his satyrs bears witness. However, when analysing these representations, we must keep in mind the fact that they are precisely that: representations. They are already artistic renditions of rites from an age where these rites may or may not have been practised. What is significant is that the presence of the Sphinx as an emblem both of funeral and resurrection is structurally linked to Dionysus, the god of theatre. Goux writes of this interconnectedness:

> The symbol of the Sphinx refers to a notion whose power and persistence are very familiar, the notion that death is rebirth, and thus the supreme rite of passage . . . To conceive of dying as the crossing of an initiatory threshold, that is, as a violent separation from the secular world followed by a rebirth on another ontological level, is to express confidence in the soul's survival. The theme is such a recurrent one that we seem to be touching here on a genuine anthropological invariant. Initiation is a symbolic death, and real death is an initiation, the most solemn of the rites of passage, the most important of thresholds.[14]

As insightful a comment as this may be, it tends to reinforce the separation between the secular world and the ontological world, the one that Oedipus is about to inhabit. Rather than underline the notion of thresholds and divisions, I believe that the simultaneous presence of the Sphinx and Dionysus tends to highlight the discursive interdependency of both. To conceive of the idea of rebirth as ontologically other than death somewhat misses the point that may be raised here. Furthermore, to read into this some notion of a permanent, almost transcendental, soul that exists before and after the initiation also misses the materiality and the theatricality of the event/depiction. The presence of Dionysus together with the Sphinx, rather than gesturing towards an eternal soul that survives death (a very Christian idea indeed) – that dies and is born again – might on the contrary connect Oedipus with the chthonic, bodily, material, performative elements of his existence, where the body/soul/mind separation is ultimately undermined. Oedipus' initiation is not meant to be overcome; it is part of a continuum; it is ritualistically repeated.

But, any depiction of death once more raises the issue of the relationship between tragedy and philosophy. And this is another way in which Oedipus has been read as the first philosopher. However, this claim is constantly undermined by the presence of both the Sphinx and Dionysus. In a sense they are there to disrupt his quest for pure knowledge and reason, and to render to death its non-reconciliatory, but also playful character. The relationship that has been established between the Sphinx and Dionysus, rather than initiating a process of philosophical thinking, enacts in a highly theatricalised form the structural interdependency between *telos* (end) and *telete* (ritual). As Jane Ellen Harrison writes in *Epilegomena to the Study of Greek Religion*:

> Moreover death itself is not a crisis so clearly marked as with us, a man dies socially when he ceases to be able to dance his tribal dances. The notion of death as an initiation has left manifest traces in Greek religion. That to die is to be initiated into the 'Higher Mysteries' was to the Greek a literal fact.[15]

The shift in readings from Harrison to Goux is a significant one. Harrison's version, heavily influenced by the so-called 'Cambridge ritualists' – admittedly a school of anthropology that has received much criticism lately – still underlines the significance of the performative (and aesthetic) dimension of death. Death as an end, as a *telos*, is what seems to be undermined by the presence of ritual, *telete*. The simultaneous presence of Dionysus and the Sphinx defuses the 'real' of death, its final *telos*, and the 'unreal' of Dionysus, his performative dimension, his power to mask and transform. In this way, death, with all its philosophical efficacy, is aestheticised through the theatricality that Dionysus represents, while Dionyus and his *thiasos* of satyrs present a kind of dancing philosophy. It is not so much that there is an ontological shift that proceeds to philosophise the aesthetic – a shift that Oedipus enacts – but rather a continual to-and-fro between the two categories. Both Dionysus and the Sphinx, *telete* and *telos*, philosophy and the aesthetic, preside over the same event and help materialise the presence of *kore*. To see the relationship between *telos* (end but also aim) and *telete* (ritual) as one that valorises philosophy rather than performance (dance, tragedy and so on) requires an act of faith if not simply interpretation. Indeed, as has been noted throughout this book, tragedy and death – in its ritual, civic and political dimension – are interdependent. This, however, does not necessarily result in a reading of tragedy as the necessary precursor of philosophy. If the initiatory, theatrical and performative aspects of tragedy are constitutive of philosophy and, by the same token, the reflective, ontological and teleological dimension of philosophy help make up the tragic gesture, then we are proposing a very different notion of one or both of these terms, in which the whole process of initiation and the idea of a fixed aim or end might be read as interchangeable:

> You too have seen our city's affliction, caught
> In a tide of death from which there is no escaping
> Death in the fruitful flowering of her soil;
> Death in the pastures; death in the womb of woman;
> And pestilence, a fiery demon gripping the city,
> Stripping the house of Cadmus, to fatten hell
> With profusion of lamentation.[16]

Despite having solved the riddle of the Sphinx, the city of Thebes is still suffering from pestilence and infertility, from the signs of death. Oedipus is again called to answer death with reason. However, his initiation, as mentioned earlier, might be read as a failed exercise. There are ample deviations from the typical structure to allow this reading. He does not kill the Sphinx, but instead forces her to kill herself. He does not commit matricide but parricide. He does not get the bride in the end, entering the world of the fathers as a reconciled, resurrected man, but ends up blind and in exile.

Instead of the traditional slaying of the monstrous female, Oedipus manages to eradicate the Sphinx through the use of his intellectual powers rather than through physical force. He makes the 'riddling-bitch' fall off a cliff by uttering a single word: 'man'. That is the answer to her famous riddle and subsequently becomes 'the measure of all things'. This monolectic answer has been hailed as the start of philosophical reflection. It signifies the end of ritual repetition and the entrance into the world of linearity, progress and knowledge. In uttering the word 'man', *anthropos*, Oedipus gives birth to himself as a reflective being, as a philosopher. However, the fact that the violence perpetrated is not physical does in no way mean that the violence has disappeared, or that the new era heralded by Oedipus/man is not one without violence. As the founding myth of Thebes indicates, the civilisation introduced by the alphabet goes hand-in-hand with the barbarism of war. Both seem to grow from the same seed. The fact that Oedipus does not slay the Sphinx, does not cut her up into pieces, is no signal for the end of violence. The force of the word 'man' is what drives her off the cliff. The concept of 'suicide' presupposes subjectivity and agency, two categories that are difficult to sustain in mythological characters. Indeed, they are the very categories to which Oedipus is about to gesture through his travails. To attribute them to the Sphinx seems slightly premature. The uttering of the word 'man' from the lips of Oedipus can be said to be like a curse, a word that has magical powers, whose effect can be physically felt on the recipient. It is the performative function of Oedipus' answer, 'man', that causes the death of the Sphinx. Oedipus himself, while articulating the word, in a sense straddles both worlds. The word 'man' appears both as the last instance of the magical and the sacred, and as the first example of reason. In using the performative function of the word, Oedipus still inhabits the mythological world. The Sphinx is driven off the cliff by the power of the word rather than killing herself. After her death, Oedipus himself can be read as becoming the man he earlier proclaimed. Rather than interpreting Oedipus as a failed initiation, the reading proposed here sees his version as a variation on the theme and not a radical departure from it. The entry into the world of philosophical reflection and reason chartered here is not one without violence and monstrosity.

The Oedipean *gestus*, as it is seen here, ceases to signify definite beginnings and ends, earth-shattering shifts from one world-view into another. By uttering the word 'man', Oedipus inhabits both worlds at once: the mythological and the epistemological. The word has the power to send the Sphinx to her death while constructing him as a subject. Rather than expressing the separability of two distinct worlds, the break between magic and reason, between myth and philosophy, the Oedipean posture enacts how the two categories are constitutive of each other, implicated in each other's lives, and how they are infected by each other. So Oedipus' aspiration, both physical and psychic, towards 'manhood' does not do away with monstrosity and horror. Indeed the Sphinx may have thrown herself off a cliff, but the world she represents continues to haunt Oedipus. The first philosopher is also a monstrosity. He is called a tyrant, his mother is his wife and his children are his siblings. Having internalised the Sphinx, Oedipus now carries her murder inside him like a miasma. He also takes over her function as a *psychopompos*, as a carrier or transmitter of souls. Rather than expressing the foundational 'break' from one world into another – from unconsciousness to consciousness, from the world of the mother to the world of the father, from barbarism to civilisation – the Oedipal *gestus* may be said to enact the very process of mediation itself, a process enriched and contaminated by both the preceding and the newly heralded systems.

The Sphinx did not so much as kill herself as was blown over the cliff by the force of Oedipus' utterance: *anthropos*. Any attempt to reinvestigate the feminine in the Oedipal model needs to start with the Sphinx:

that she is quite literally blown over does not necessarily result in her total and utter banishment. As Goux claims, she is internalised by Oedipus. Oedipus' gesture, which was supposed to rid the world of ritual and violence and herald the dawn of nothing less than modernity itself, sets forward its own mechanism of violence and repetition. For as we know his troubles are far from over. The feminine that he was supposed to expunge from the world returns with a vengeance. Rather than having its head chopped off and being contained, the feminine has spilled out everywhere, particularly on to the Athenian stage. So much so that it has even occupied Oedipus's own self.

Oedipus' quest for self-discovery is also a quest for self-creation. In trying to get rid of the feminine, he tries to give birth to himself. In sleeping with his mother, he in a sense becomes his own son. In the play he is called *homogenes*, born of the same, not of the other. He quite literally attempts to think himself into existence. According to Aristotle, god is a being that can 'think itself'. But, if god is indeed that being and that being alone then Oedipus inhabits a world where hubris and subversion are possible, and possibly desirable. Oedipus, however, is not the only one who inhabits the ever new/always same, strange world. The Sphinx also revisits all the female roles of the play: Iocasta, Merope, Antigone and Ismene. All these women – played by men – are as categorically damned as Oedipus himself. Iocasta, who bears the most direct relationship with, hence experiences the most vicious attack from, the Sphinx, mirrors her act – or rather its reception – and kills herself, employing the dramatic convention of the noose. Antigone has a passion for death that never quite resolves the either/or that her act sets up. Interestingly enough, the only woman who dies a 'natural death' is the cultural mother, Merope, the one whose love and labour created the philosopher that is Oedipus.

This reading of the relationship between Oedipus and the Sphinx sees them as almost interchangeable. Rather than the Sphinx representing everything that Oedipus needs to overcome in order to be a reflective man – ritual, death and so on – she comes to inhabit him. In this way, Oedipus himself might be said to be feminised, presiding over ritual initiation into reason and philosophical thinking; it is a philosophical mode, however, that has already been theatricalised and feminised by internalising the Sphinx. On the other hand, the Sphinx herself may be said to have acquired consciousness at the very moment of her death.

> Jocasta: At least your father's death is a relief.
> Oedipus: Agreed; but while *she* lives, I am not safe.[16]

The '*she*' to which Oedipus is referring here is not his biological mother but his cultural mother, who in the play is called Merope, the wife of King Polybus of Corinth. Oedipus' attempt to give birth to himself presupposes a radical reworking of his relationships with his various mothers. These 'mothers', be they monstrous (Sphinx), life giving (Jocasta), or nurturing (Merope), all have to be overcome in order for Oedipus to achieve manhood. All these mother figures, in the strict Freudian sense, are pre-Oedipal. They have all fulfilled their roles before the play starts. Oedipus now has to undo them so as to become a subject and enter the world of the fathers.

Oedipus' difficulty is mirrored in the Freudian 'difficulty' of conceptualising the pre-Oedipal and the post-Oedipal mother. It is true that this area has been addressed by a variety of schools of psychoanalysis, ranging from Kleinian object relations theory to more recent Deleuzean anti-Oedipal theory and theories of hysteria.[18] All these approaches, as will be discussed further on in this analysis, offer very useful, sometimes conflicting, ways of reintegrating anti-Oedipal models of subjectivity into the project of psychoanalysis. What I would like to examine is how these 'mother figures' appear in the myth and in the play, and I shall propose an interconnectedness among them. The Sphinx, Merope and Jocasta, broken down as they are into three different entities, help form the web of meanings, concepts, symbols that prompt Oedipus to reconfigure the feminine and more specifically the maternal. If Oedipus is to become *homogenes*, born of the same (himself, the fathers) and not of the other, then the ways these 'mother figures' are presented is crucial for any reading of the play and for any model of subjectivity that, rightly or wrongly, takes its cue from the play.

The received etymology of Oedipus is 'swollen foot', based on the fact that his feet were deformed by the nail-wound by which the shepherd carried him when taking him to Corinth. However, Robert Graves cites a possible source of a different etymology. He writes:

> According to another version of the story, Laius did not expose Oedipus on the mountain, but locked him in a chest, which was lowered into the sea from a ship. This chest drifted ashore at Sicyon, where Periboea, Polybus's queen, happened to be on the beach, supervising her royal laundry-women. She picked up Oedipus, retired to a thicket and pretended to have been overcome by the pangs of labour. Since laundry-women were too busy to notice what she was about, she deceived them all into thinking that he had only just been born. But Periboea told the truth to Polybus, who also being childless, was pleased to rear Oedipus as his own son.[19]

Following this version of Oedipus' rebirth, his name means 'son of the swelling sea'. Rather than being born again through the act of having his feet pricked and hung upside-down, this version of the story gives him a more feminine birth. Instead of the mountain of Cithaeron we have the swelling sea and enclosure in a chest. It is also significant that Periboea, his adopted mother, mimics the act of giving birth in a gesture that 'copies' nature, the swelling of the sea. This identification of the womb-bearing woman with nature has its own lineage and no doubt it is one aspect of the story that Graves – the Graves of the white-goddess theory and of matriarchy – finds attractive. Nevertheless, without necessarily having to expand it into a grand theory of matriarchy, Bachofen style,[20] this version of Oedipus' rebirth from nature into culture, as it were, from one mother into another, offers interesting interpretative possibilities. In this version of the story, Oedipus is not mediated from the King of Thebes to the King of Corinth; rather he is transmitted from one motherly body to another. The birth scene is particularly attractive to any analysis that sees the very process of enactment as already self-referential, as performative. In copying nature, Periboea performs the ultimate 'unnatural' act. She does something which can be construed as mimetic and interpretive, that is, aesthetic.

In the play Periboea is referred to by Oedipus as Merope (eloquent or bee-eater). The connection with bees, queen bees in particular, is another emblem of the feminine. It also connects Merope to the Sphinx. In Aeschylus' *Seven Against Thebes*, the Sphinx is called 'the man-snatching Cer'. *Cer* belongs to the same family of words as *cerion* (honey-wax), *cerinos* (waxen) but also comes to mean 'fate', 'doom' or destiny'. In the plural *ceres* it denotes 'spites, plagues, or unseen ills'.[21] Hence the use of the epithet for the Sphinx. This connection between Merope and the Sphinx, as part of the female-dominated bee-world again is useful in trying to establish some sort of genealogy for the mothers of the play. Furthermore, *cer* and *cerinos* may also refer to the material of wax itself and its ability to change shape and be moulded. This shape-shifting, masking quality – another gesture towards the aesthetic – again is interestingly identified with the feminine.

'Woman is so artistic' writes Nietzsche in a famous aphorism.[22] This *cerinos-e-on* quality that the Sphinx shares with Merope might also point towards a reading of motherhood as pure materiality, as the substance that sustains life. This would be in line with Aristotle's theories of reproduction, where he identifies matter with the female parent (and sees this mainly in terms of menstrual blood) and form with the male parent.[23] This theory is echoed in Freudian psychoanalysis, where the relationship with the mother, the material 'thing', is seen as something that needs to be overcome. In the case of Oedipus, this 'overcoming' leads straight on to the quest for intellectual existence. However, the *cer* (both the wax and the pestilence) that characterises Oedipus' lineage substantially qualifies the 'matter' under consideration. For *cerinos* also implies easily moulded, shape-shifting, transforming and masking. Rather than signifying the 'real' of matter, it points towards artificiality and falseness. It is this 'artistic' quality that Oedipus inherits from his mother figures (wax figures?). And as with any wax figures that have ritualistic, performative qualities, he has to exorcise himself of them. Whether he does so successfully or not determines whether or not he enters the 'real' world of the fathers, abandoning the false, 'artistic' world of the mothers. If, however, these two worlds are not so absolutely and utterly separated, particularly on the Athenian stage, then the impact of *cerinos*, as shape-shifter and shape-giver, as feminine, theatrical and overtly aesthetic, may have been so far underestimated.

It is not merely a case of Oedipus having internalised the Sphinx and his mothers. Having, in a sense, given birth to himself, turning himself into his own mother, he also embodies those very qualities he so yearns to be rid of: falseness, femininity, artificiality. His world of reason will be marred forever by the artificiality and self-referentiality that he inherits from his *cerinoi* ancestors. The philosophy that he is supposed to initiate is undermined, plagued by the tragedy that helps create him. In this sense the pestilence that dwells in his body – and in the body of the city-state – is both the poison and the cure to his predicament, his *pharmakon*. This is compounded by the fact that the Oedipus story is a piece of theatre, a drama and a *dromenon*, both an artwork and a ritual. It is not coincidental in this context that sites of ancient Greek theatres were usually built next to or on the ruins of temples to Asklypios, the God of medicine.

> Such suffering needs to be born twice;
> once in the body and once in the soul.[24]

Oedipus' quest for rebirth becomes, in a sense, a quest for the 'Oedipal complex' itself. For what is being established in the process is a narrative that acts as the foundational 'story' of subjectivity, human desire, civilisation and 'normality'. This narrative is very neatly enacted through a family drama, which is in turn reiterated, with variations, by philosophy and psychoanalysis. There have been various critiques of the Oedipal complex that attack the familial dimension at the expense of the socio-political. The work of Wilhelm Reich and more recently Deleuze and Guattari challenge the notion that desire originates from a familial drama and that it is something purely psychic and always repressed.[25] Instead of prioritising the familial dimension, which is always heterosexual, Deleuze and Guattari, following Reich, see desire as rooted in social context. The material nature of the unconscious is stressed, as opposed to its purely psychic life in Freudian terms. Furthermore, the reproduction of the unconscious is seen as a social and historical passage as well as a familial one. This is a tradition in psychoanalysis that privileges the material and the bodily over the psychic, the linguistic (as in the work of Lacan) and the discursive. It could also present ways of reading the myth and the play that go against the dominant reading that sees it as the primary site of the Oedipus complex. This analysis, so far, already has been anti-Oedipal in stressing the aspects of the play that directly or indirectly undermine its status as the *Ur-myth* of human subjectivity.

Another possible way of reading the Oedipus story is by introducing the discourse on hysteria. Hysteria has a long and somewhat thorny relationship both with traditional medicine (from the ancient Greeks onwards) and psychoanalysis. Without providing a historical survey of the term and its quasi-clinical interpretations, for the purposes of the approach taken here, I would like to focus on Juliet Mitchell's recent comprehensive study of the term 'hysteria' in *Mad Men and Medusas*.[26] Mitchell's analysis draws attention to the possibility that the Oedipal complex might be founded on the vanishing/repression/transference of hysteria, particularly since hysteria traditionally has been feminised. She writes in her introduction:

> I shall argue that, in particular, the relationship between hysteria and psychoanalysis has been haunted since its inception by a crucial omission: that of sibling relationships. Secondly (and linked to this) is the problem of male hysteria. It is ironic, but necessary, then, to point out that the repressed sibling and the repressed male hysteric came together in the person of Sigmund Freud at the very outset of psychoanalysis . . . However, I believe that the repression of the male hysteric has partly led to a misdirection of psychoanalytic efforts from looking at the symptoms of hysteria to trying to replace them with an understanding of femininity in general.[27]

This identification of femininity and hysteria (present in the etymology of the word) is one of the aspects of the term that her study attempts to dispel. The idea that hysteria cannot only be masculine but also foundational to the way masculinity is constructed could usefully enable an alternative reading of Oedipus. Like Mitchell's reading of Freud, who channels his personal *petite hystérie* into his weaving together of the Oedipus complex, Oedipus, the first philosopher, the first intellectual, the first psychic subject, might be tainted by hysteria at his very inception. These hysterical traits reintroduce the material, the bodily and the maternal back into a reading of Oedipus and the kinds of subjectivity he proposes.

Defeminising hysteria is not an easy task. Throughout its history it has been associated not only with femininity but also with histrionics, falseness and theatricality. Again, we note a structural link between the feminine and the theatrical and performative. Mitchell writes:

> Quite simply it became femininity. It was generally considered that at one end of the spectrum hysteria became a parody of ultrafemininity; at the other end was motherhood. As Michel Foucault put it, woman was hystericized all the way 'from nervous woman to mother'. However, Foucault's observation totally misses the point: motherhood can be hysterical. Hysteria was made woman, not vice versa.[28]

Another aspect of hysteria that is significant is its highly mimetic quality. It mirrors, identifies with and reproduces. This mimetic quality is what sometimes accounts for its disappearance. It learns to disguise itself as something else. The mimetic, artistic quality, however, also has been used to make hysteria feminine. As far as traditional psychoanalysis is concerned, it lacks the tools to identify hysteria, as hysteria can easily disguise itself within the framework offered by psychoanalysis:

> After the discoveries of psychoanalysis, language and the story (narrativity) instead of the body have been deployed by the hysteric as a major means of enacting mental conflict. In such a situation, hysteria is not cured by psychoanalysis (although it can be), but rather it becomes camouflaged within linguistic mimesis and the Oedipal or pre-Oedipal constellation of the treatment that psychoanalysis imposes upon it.[29]

According to this reading, the Oedipal complex already entails hysteria, albeit in a disguised fashion. This propensity of hysteria towards mimesis might also account for its 'healthy' appearance in what Mitchell calls 'certain artistic practices', especially in the performing arts. Without necessarily identifying artistic creativity with hysteria, which again would fall back on the Freudian theory of artistic creation, there might be some validity in this notion, particularly in relation to its relevance to performance in artistic terms and the performative in terms of theory. In this sense Oedipus himself enacts a type of hysteria in his frantic search for self-identity, where phantasmic pregnancy has always been a classic symptom of hysteria.

The banishing of hysteria is also linked with the emphasis placed on vertical relations (that is, father/son) in the construction of subjectivity at the expense of horizontal, sibling relations. The vertical cathexis tends to stress the familial drama, whereas the horizontal one has the potential to expand the nexus of relationships into a socio-political framework. The relationships with siblings might offer a model for the way desire circulates rather than the relationships with parents alone. I would argue that the Oedipal story in its hysteric dimension offers models for sibling relationships as well. In giving birth to himself by sleeping with his own mother Oedipus also becomes the brother of his children. He is their brother and their father. If we take the Oedipus story as encompassing *Antigone*, *Oedipus at Colonus* and possibly *Seven Against Thebes*, then there is much material for a non-Oedipal, vertical, model of subjectivity, while equally there is plentiful scope for examining horizontal models (Antigone–Ismene, Antigone–Polyneices, Eteocles–Polyneices, and so on).

Such an all-encompassing theory of hysteria is in danger of almost completely negating the Oedipal complex. As Mikkel Borch-Jacobsen writes in a review of Mitchell's book, 'shouldn't we conclude according to good psychoanalytical logic, that the Oedipus was a symptom of his [Freud's] unresolved hysteria?'[30] If indeed we follow this logic through then Oedipus is a symptom/victim of the Sphinx rather than the other way around. The highly mimetic quality of hysteria makes it particularly versatile and in some respects overwhelming. It can hide underneath anything and anyone. It is not necessarily replaced or substituted by other 'objects', but remains unchanged behind the disguise. Borch-Jacobsen's critique of this aspect of hysteria as a general theory of psychoanalysis is telling:

> In other words, hysteria is not itself an artefact but the truth of all artefacts, enabling one to criticise all those who take the artefact for the thing itself.[31]

Borch-Jacobsen's insightful critique of this reading of hysteria states that Mitchell simply substitutes the Mummy/Daddy (citing Deleuze) of Freudian theory with the little brother/little sister model, whereby hysteria reaches all the parts that the Oedipal complex does not. It becomes a kind of 'other' of Oedipus and in this way remains quintessentially Oedipal itself. As he says, 'one could easily repeat the same hermeneutic feat with cousins, the uncle, the maid or the postman'.[32]

Borch-Jacobsen's own contribution to psychoanalytical theory might also prove useful in trying to approach Oedipus in a way that is neither absolutely hysterical nor constrictingly Oedipal. If hysteria is the 'other' of the Oedipal theory, Borch-Jacobsen flatly denies the presence of 'otherness' in the creation of subjectivity. Identification and mimesis play the central role in his approach. Denying both Lacanian linguistic notions about the subconscious and more traditional Freudian ones, his view of desire does not see it as that which needs to be repressed by an external force. Indeed the notion of power and possession seem alien to him. He states of the subject that, 'Its basic verb is "to be" (to be like), not "to have" (to enjoy).'[33] By extension the opposition between ego and object, self and other, inside and outside ceases to exist. Rather, he believes that there is a strong emotional tie that unreservedly binds the ego and the object; so much so that the subject is constituted by that tie between ego and object, between self and other. It is the mimetic identification of ego with object that creates the subject. Desire itself is seen as primarily mimetic, where the urge to be like, as in enacting or playing, does not mean that the mimicked object needs to be overtaken or mastered. It has no aim or goal. Its function is simply to enact and it is always an in-betweenness, a negotiating, a to-and-fro, and not a victory and a loss.

If we proceed to bring this anti-Oedipal view of subjectivity into the Oedipal myth then some of its fundamental premises seem to dissolve. The ego–object distinction, for example, so vital for the interpretation of the myth that sees it as the start of anthropocentrism and philosophy, vanishes. Oedipus' spelling out of the word 'man', rather than initiating the split between the two worlds, the world of myth and the world of reason, projects one on to the other, and proceeds to mimic. In this sense Oedipus does not simply internalise the Sphinx, but through a process of identification and mimesis becomes her. This is perhaps why he does not need to kill her physically. Borch-Jacobsen writes:

> The matrix of desire and, by the same token, the matrix of rivalry, hatred, and (in the social order) violence: 'I want what my brother, my model, my idol wants – and I want it in his place.'[34]

This view of desire as mimesis and identification displaces the centrality of 'murder' as the prime act of cultural production and proposes rather the act of representation itself. It also has the interesting effect of de-sexualising desire, which might also be a way of de-gendering it, with all the possibilities and dangers that such an act may entail. Either way, the Oedipal narrative is upstaged it is no longer the originating and generative moment of human subjectivity. According to this model, Oedipus is already a desiring subject before he encounters the 'Oedipal complex', before he kills his father and sleeps with his mother. The Oedipal moment is not seen as the prime moment of sublimation between the individual and culture. The psyche, according to this reading, and it is a reading that has generated a significant body of interpretations from the work of Judith Butler to that of Cornelius Castoriades, is always and already social.[35] The real itself does not exist before representation. As Castoriadis says, 'society and the psyche are inseparable and irreducible to one another'.[36] There is no distinction between representational and affectual desire. The psyche is primarily artistic and this is not simply a metaphor. It performs, identifies and mimics, and presents and represents.

This approach that reconfigures the relationship between the narcissistic ego and the object denotes desire not as a murderous act but as a mimetic and representational one. It undermines the centrality of the Oedipal complex and it allows for the possibility of a socio-historical reading of the psyche. It also highlights the significance of the aesthetic and the performative, not in opposition to the historical and the political but in a way that sees these categories as constitutive of each other. By removing the emphasis from the category of 'otherness' as the *sine qua non* of subjectivity, it also reconceptualises the function of gender. This aspect of the approach, together with the emphasis on mourning as a psychic and social activity, will be explored in the next chapter.

The intriguing aspect of the Oedipal story before and beyond the Oedipal complex is that it can sustain a multiplicity of readings. The anti-Oedipal interpretations proposed here serve as a pointer to the ways both the myth and the play-text can generate a versatile and sophisticated critique of the received Freudian version of the narrative. Could it be that the Oedipal narrative already is and always has been anti-Oedipal? And if this is the case then we have to reconsider seriously the ways we have been reading Oedipus. Rather than enacting breaks and shifts (from myth to history, from the aesthetic to the philosophical, from woman to man, from ontology to epistemology, etc.), the story might be structured in terms of identification and mimesis, through the acts of mourning and loss. Rather than reason, triumph and knowledge being initiated by Oedipus' curse of 'man', the story might enact yet another journey into ambivalence and loss, an almost permanent state of mourning that transfigures and masks itself within tragic form. It also re-energises and prioritises the function of the aesthetic in the creation both of subjectivity and of philosophical discourse. The emphasis on the aesthetic and the performative, together with the all-pervasive mourning that the play-text is both structured by and enacts, points towards a reading of the Oedipal story as a form of melancholy philosophy that deals with loss and ambivalence rather than will, reason and triumph. And this is the tone in which King Oedipus ends:

> Then learn that mortal man must always look to his ending.
> And none can be called happy until that day when he carries
> His happiness down to the grave in peace.[37]

The closing lines of *King Oedipus* do not signal the end of the drama. His troubles are not over yet. He has become *apolis*, without a city, and in *Oedipus at Colonus* he appears roaming on the outskirts of a new city in an attempt to find an appropriate resting place, somewhere to take his new-found 'happiness' or knowledge.[38] Note that this 'happiness' does not end with death nor is it buried in the grave. Rather, he carries it with him, like a *psychopombos*. The closing lines of this play prepare us for the next one. *Oedipus at Colonus* is mainly concerned with Oedipus' quest for a burial place. Accompanied by his daughter/sister Antigone, Oedipus is looking for a place to die. As he carries within him the miasma of his predicament, this proves a difficult task. However, through the workings of hospitality and male-to-male friendship, he manages to find this place on the outskirts of Athens. Oedipus, the first philosopher, having attempted to give birth to himself, now tries to orchestrate his own funeral. In doing so, he also predicates the types of mourning that will follow his death (something that Antigone inherits).

The way the myth is acted out in all parts of this trilogy is crucial for our interpretation of the Oedipal complex. The reading of Oedipus as a hysteric might be further supported through a reading of *Oedipus at Colonus*. The opening lines of the play point to some of its main concerns:

> Tell me, Antigone – where have you come to now
> With your blind old father? What is this place, my child?
> Country, or town? Whose turn is it to-day
> To offer a little hospitality to the wandering Oedipus?
>
> (1–4)

Through the workings of male-to-male friendship and hospitality, as will be examined in detail in the next chapter, Oedipus' predicament is redeemed. From a carrier of pestilence and disease he is turned into a gift for Athens, a *pharmakon*, that carries both the poison and the cure. The appearance of Thesues, the King of Athens, and the friendship he offers Oedipus is significant, as it is through his relationship with Theseus that he manages to find his last resting place. Equally significant, however, is the exact location of this grave. Not only is it on the outskirts of Athens – the shift from Thebes to Athens charting the shift from the subconscious to the conscious – but it is also next to another grave. This is the grave of the Furies. One of the 'natives', as the play calls them, *autochthones*, has to advise Oedipus, the stranger, about this other sacred place:

> Countryman: it may not be touched, and none may live upon it.
> Dread goddesses own it, daughters of Earth and Darkness.
> Oedipus: What may I call these holy ones in my prayers?
> Countryman: As you will; to each the custom of his country;
> We call them here the All-seeing Kindly Ones.
>
> (40–5)

These are, of course, the Furies turned into the Kindly Ones, at the end of *The Oresteia*. It seems like Colonus is the burial ground for everything that Athens wants to expunge from the *polis*. Athens keeps the Furies on its borders as both a reminder of the horrific threat they pose and as a trophy of their supposed victory over them. Oedipus will occupy a similar position. His burial place will be a predominantly feminine domain. Having internalised the Sphinx, Oedipus now brings her to rest in good company. The resting place he is searching for needs to accommodate her as much as it needs to accommodate him. We also need to note the inversion that has taken place. Oedipus, having internalised the 'sun of knowledge', as Hegel would have it, is now blind. However, the Furies, having been appropriated as the 'Kindly Ones', are characterised as 'All-seeing'. Surely, this trope questions not only the agent of knowledge in this schema but the schema itself. It is more than irony that sets up the Furies – the chthonic, murderous and monstrous females – as the ones that can 'see' and Oedipus – the thinking, rational man – as the blind one. Oedipus' blindness is more than compensated for by the 'gift' that he brings to Athens:

> Oedipus: Theseus, your noble kindness in these short words
> Permits as brief an answer. Who I am,
> Whence born, from what land come, you know and have said.
> It remains to tell my errand, and all is told.
> Theseus: Then tell me that.
> Oedipus: I come to offer you
> A gift – my tortured body – a sorry sight;
> But there is value in it more than beauty.
> Theseus: What value?
> Oedipus: Later you shall know, not now.
> Theseus: When will this gift be known for what it is?
> Oedipus: When I am dead, and you have buried me.
>
> (545–60)

The gift that Oedipus leaves Athens could perhaps be read as significant as the journey into knowledge and self-discovery that he has undertaken in the previous play. Appropriately this gift needs to be buried before its impact can be felt on the city of Athens. Like the Furies, who also require burial before they can be turned into the Kindly Ones, the gift that Oedipus carries in his tortured body must find a resting place before it too can be buried (appropriated, sublimated, repressed etc.). Interestingly enough, it resides in his body and not in his mind. Its value is greater than beauty and knowledge. But what is this gift that is at once poisonous and therapeutic? And why is it so important for the city of Athens to be on the receiving end of this process, as its host?

I would claim that the gift that Oepidus bestows upon Athens is perhaps the gift of hysteria itself. Having imbibed the Sphinx, Oedipus now carries her firmly within himself. The resting place he chooses is fittingly also a burial place for the other monstrous females that Athens has distanced from its centre, but not expelled completely. Rather than turning the Sphinx into philosophical angst and reflective contemplation, Oedipus' body has traversed her, has copied her, has theatricalised her. In his attempt to give birth to himself, his failed initiation has in some ways turned into an initiation of another sort. Mimicking pregnancy, his body carries within it hysteria rather than his own subjectivity. What was to free him from the horrific world of the mother returns to torture his body. This phantasmic pregnancy – a mark of hysteria – is also inverted. Birth is not its outcome but death. This inversion of the feminine and the masculine, or even the conflation of the two is mirrored throughout the play. The brothers' decision to abandon Oedipus is seen as feminising. Evoking the Sphinx's Egyptian lineage, Oedipus says:

> What then? They ape Egyptian manners, do they,
> Where men keep house and do embroidery
> While wives go out to earn the daily bread?
> Instead of troubling themselves about my business,
> They sit at home like girls and let you two
> Bear all the burden of my calamities.
>
> (338–45)

In a direct reflection of the above, Oedipus is about to perform a similar inversion. The strongest marker of 'Egyptian manners' in the play is the Sphinx herself. Having internalised her as a form of hysteria perhaps, he needs to find a way of first burying her and then turning her into a gift for Athens. A similar path is followed in *The Oresteia* with the Furies, who, in many ways, will be the hostesses for the Egyptian 'riddling bitch'. In this notional scheme of the phantasmic pregnancy that we have been setting up, Oedipus needs modes of kinship that will provide him with a framework for the birth/burial of his gift. His biological, Oedipal family can no longer do that as it is in crisis. Having occupied all possible positions within the Oedipal triangle (father, mother, child), and, in some ways, also having conflated them into one (his hysterical, Sphinx-carrying body), he now needs a bond that will attempt to relieve him from his predicament. And it is a predicament that is integral to the Oedipal legacy. It is this bond that will turn his 'tortured body' into a gift for Athens. The Oedipal bond is replaced with the homosocial *philia*. It is through the workings of male-to-male friendship and hospitality that this gift can find a final resting place. Theseus welcomes Oedipus and, in effect, becomes his last primary attachment, substituting his relationships with his 'family'. He says:

> The kindly intention of such a man must be respected.
> Not only on the ground of hospitality
> To a friend and ally, but also for the goddesses' sake
> Whose suppliant he is, and the boon he will bring to us
> Such claims compel me to accept his overture
> And house him within our city.
>
> (660–6)

The goddesses protecting Oedipus are the Furies. It is out of respect to them and to the functions of hospitality and friendship that Theseus agrees to 'house' Oedipus. This 'house', as Theseus fully knows, will be Oedipus' grave. There is one condition, however, that Theseus has to fulfil in order to receive Oedipus' gift: he has to keep the location of his grave a secret.

The bonding impact of such a shared secret proves more effective than any tie the Oedipal family can provide. Having gone through the necessary shifts that have transformed Oedipus from a miasma into a *pharmakon*, it is crucial that that gift/cure remain within the domains of the *polis* and not the family. This is achieved, I would claim, mainly through the governing of the function of mourning. The direct impact of Theseus' secret is to prohibit Oedipus' daughters from mourning him. Indeed, this emphasis on the inability to mourn might be the motor that propels Antigone into her own tragedy. Towards the end of the play, Antigone and Theseus have the following exchange:

> Theseus: Now, daughters, dry your tears. Kind death
> Has gently dealt with him; and we
> Share in his blessing. We must not weep;
> Our grief would provoke the gods to anger.
> Antigone: Yet hear a petition, son of Aegeus.

> Theseus: What is it you ask?
> Antigone: Only to see
> Our father's grave.
> Theseus: That cannot be.
>
> (1749–58)

Once again, the battle over the right to mourn is crucial for the outcome of the tragedy. Oedipus' entry into the homosocial relationship of friendship also marks his entry into Athens. However, as his acceptance by Athens can only be completed after his death, the ways in which he is mourned have also to be controlled by the *polis*. And this sets the scene for the final play of the trilogy, the *Antigone*.

Reading the Oedipal drama as a trilogy, rather than concentrating on the single play, might help reveal some of the complications of the narrative itself. Rather than charting the path into self-knowledge, subjectivity and ultimately civilisation itself, the Oedipal story might be more incongruous and disjointed than the traditional Freudian or philosophical readings allow for. The emphasis on the whole trilogy rather than solely on Oedipus' journey of self-discovery unravels a story that entails parricide but also, and importantly, matricide. Following Goux's primarily philosophical account helps foreground the function of the feminine, on the one hand, but relegates that to the sublime-repressed-subconscious, on the other. This we are told is turned into philosophical angst and ambivalence. However, hysteria might present us with another way of reintroducing gender into the Oedipal narrative. If the story is read as a whole, then Oedipus' journey from Thebes to Athens, via Corinth, might already be a narrative of hysteria. Together with the narrative that sees this as a journey into self-knowledge, differentiation and identity formation, there exists the story that reads hysteria as its double. It is not so much the case, as Freud is accused, of basing the Oedipal complex on the negation of hysteria, as the possibility of hysteria being written into the story all along and forming its constitutive shadow. The difficulty we have today in approaching hysteria is compounded by the fact that we rely heavily on the notion of differentiation as the main trope of any classification, a process that may have its origin in the classical Oedipal story. If, however, hysteria's main mode is mimesis and identification (rather than murder and replacement) then it possibly has been there all along, dove-tailing Oedipus' journey. Mitchell writes:

> But again, this definition is dependent on our medical culture that 'murders to dissect', a culture built on differentiation as a basis for classification. Once again, it is not that hysteria is necessarily organic or non-organic, but that our definition

always demands a distinction between the two. This creates problems, for such distinctions may not have mattered to the ancient Greeks.[39]

The emphasis on differentiation as classification also produces the reading of the Oedipal story that sees it in terms of thresholds, great shifts that signal the passing over of myth into history and tragedy into philosophy. It is also the primary distinction that feminises hysteria. In this way Oedipus' journey awards him the trophy of knowledge and leaves behind it a trail of hysteria that is conveniently identified with the feminine. If, however, the feminine – the Sphinx in this case – is not something that needs to be overcome but integrated, mirrored and copied, then this fundamentally changes the nature of the journey in the first place. And this may be primarily why Oedipus does not have to kill the Sphinx. He takes over her through the process of naming himself ('man'). Rather than killing her, through identification and mimesis he copies her, and, in a sense, becomes her too. Instead of charting the triumph over hysteria, the Oedipal narrative might help expose the mechanisms by which hysteria is sublimated and subsequently feminised. Not only a rational and reasoning being, but also, and crucially, a hysterical one, Oedipus' plight might help to decode the ways in which hysteria became feminised in the first place. Rather than reading hysteria as the great forgotten aspect of Freudian psychoanalysis, this interpretation of the Oedipal story sees hysteria as being there all along. There are probably at least two ways of reintroducing hysteria into the Oedipal story: the classically Freudian one, which relegates hysteria to the feminine and the sublime, and the other, which views hysteria and its mimetic function as a vital aspect of subjectivity formation and not simply as its repressed, as its feminine other.

If we read *Oedipus at Colonus* as a vital component of the Oedipal story, then we perhaps could even propose a reading of Oedipus as a hysteric. The gift that he brings to Athens – a poison turned gift – bears all the signs of hysteria and, since those signs are decoded as feminine he seeks shelter at the shrine of the Furies. As mimesis seems to be the main function of hysteria, his journey, from one into knowledge and reason, could now be read as mimicking the original journey of hysteria itself. In Greek thought this is visualised as the image of the wandering womb (and blindness). So the mind and the eye, the parts of the body that we traditionally associate with Oedipus, are accompanied by the womb. Oedipus' journey from Thebes (the subconscious) to Athens (the ego) via Corinth (culture-nurture) becomes a metaphor – the metaphor – for the original journey that the womb undertakes. As such it delineates the mechanisms that first create hysteria and then proceed to feminise it.

This effect is compounded by the theatrical nature of Oedipus' predicament. If, indeed, the psyche is artistic, with representation and mimesis as its primary functions, then the fact that the Oedipus story is a performance must surely bear relevance to the issues we are considering. Oedipus' journey with the internalised Sphinx, which he is attempting to copy and carry to Athens as a gift, is mirrored in the homosocial dimension of the drama; that is a drama where men copy women and perform for the benefit of other men. The dramatic conventions themselves fold over into the themes, the anxieties and the aspirations of the narrative. To a contemporary audience the protagonist of this drama, Oedipus, appears less of a philosopher and is primarily an actor. His primary function is not that of reflection, but mimesis and enactment. These aesthetic functions, however, are not sublimated but entail their own critical and reflective force. Read as a performance and not as a piece of animated philosophy, the Oedipal story also becomes the story of the birth of hysteria; it is a hysteria which in due course is feminised but throughout the story remains fundamental both to the protagonist's journey and to his final destination.

Notes

1. Thomas Pynchon, *The Crying of Lot 49* (New York: Bantam Books, 1967), p. 1.
2. See Jean-Joseph Goux, *Oedipus, Philosopher*, trans. Catherine Porter (Stanford: Stanford University Press, 1993), pp. 132–3.
3. Ibid. p. 27.
4. For an analysis of Hölderlin's reading of Oedipus, see David Farrell Krell, 'A small number of houses in a universe of tragedy: notes on Aristotle's περὶ ποιητικῆς and Hölderlin's "Anmerkungen"', in Miguel de Beistegui and Simon Sparks (eds), *Philosophy and Tragedy* (London: Routledge, 2000), pp. 88–116.
5. See Goux, *Oedipus, Philosopher*, p. 121.
6. Ibid. pp. 194–5.
7. For a discussion of Heidegger's use of the term *Unheimliche*, see Will McNeil, 'A "scarcely pondered word", The place of tragedy: Heidegger, Aristotle, Sophocles', in de Beistegui and Sparks (eds), *Philosophy and Tragedy*, p. 183, pp. 169–89. For a discussion of Heidegger's translation of *deinon*, see Stathis Gourgouris, *Does Literature Think? Literature as Theory for an Antimythical Era*, pp. 134–7.
8. *King Oedipus*, trans. E. F. Watling (London: Penguin, 1974) in Sophocles, *The Theban Plays*, line 421.
9. Robert Graves, *The Greek Myths*, Vol. I (London: Penguin, 1960), 34, p. 130.
10. Robert Graves, *The Greek Myths*, Vol. II (London: Penguin, 1990), 105.3, p. 13.
11. Ibid. 105.3, p. 13.
12. Jane Ellen Harrison, *Themis* (Cambridge: Cambridge University Press, 1912). Harrison cites further references for this image, see J. E. Harrison, *Delphica*, J.H.S. XIX (1899), p. 235, and *Prolegomena*, p. 211, fig.45; cf. also the krater in *Monumenti dell'Inst*. II. Pl.LV.

13. See Goux, *Oedipus, Philosopher*, p. 53.
14. Ibid. p. 56.
15. Jane Ellen Harrison, *Epilegomena to the Study of Greek Religion* (Cambridge: Cambridge University Press, 1921), p. 16.
16. *King Oedipus*, lines 20–6, p. 26.
17. Ibid. lines 1017–18, pp. 52–3.
18. See Juliet Mitchell, *Psychoanalysis and Feminism* (London: Allen Lane, 1974); Nancy Chodorow, *The Reproduction of Mothering: Psychoanalysis and the Sociology of Gender* (Berkeley: California University Press, 1978) Madelon Sprengnether, *The Spectral Mother: Freud, Feminism, and Psychoanalysis* (Ithaca: Cornell University Press, 1990); G. Deleuze and F. Guattari, *Anti-Oedipus: Capitalism and Schizophrenia*, trans. R. Hurley, M. Seem and H. Lane; preface by Michel Foucault (London: Athlone, 1984).
19. See Graves, *The Greek Myths* Vol. II, 105.c, p. 9.
20. J. J. Bachofen, *Myth, Religion and Mother-Right*, trans. Stanley A. Leavy, New Bollingen Series 84 (Princeton: Princeton University Press, 1967).
21. See Graves, *The Greek Myths*, Vol. I, 82.6, p. 280.
22. 'Finally, *women*: consider the whole history of women – *mustn't* they be actresses first and foremost? Listen to doctors who have hypnotised womenfolk; finally, love them – let yourself be "hypnotised" by them! What is always the result? That they try to be "taken for something" even when they are being taken . . . Woman is so artistic . . .' Friedrich Nietzsche, *The Gay Science* (1882), ed. Bernard Williams, trans. Josefine Nauckhoff (Cambridge: Cambridge University Press, 2001), p. 226.
23. See Kathleen C. Cook, 'Sexual Inequality in Aristotle's Theories of Reproduction and Inheritance', in Julie K. Ward (ed.), *Feminism and Ancient Philosophy* (London: Routledge, 1996), pp. 51–67.
24. *King Oedipus*, lines 1367–8, p. 62.
25. For an analysis of this debate, see Jan Campbell, *Arguing with the Phallus: Feminist, Queer and Postcolonial Theory* (London and New York: Zed Books, 2000).
26. Juliet Mitchell, *Mad Men and Medusas: Reclaiming Hysteria and the Effects of Sibling Relations on the Human Condition* (London: Penguin, 2000).
27. Ibid. p. 19.
28. Ibid. p. 161.
29. Ibid. p. 122.
30. Mikkel Borch-Jacobsen, review of *Mad Men and Medusas*, 'Little Brother, Little Sister', in *London Review of Books*, vol. 23, No.10, 24 May 2001, pp. 15–17.
31. Ibid. p. 17.
32. Ibid.
33. Mikkel Borch-Jacobsen, *The Freudian Subject*, trans. Catherine Porter (Stanford: Stanford University Press, 1988), p. 28.
34. Ibid. p. 27.
35. Judith Butler, *The Psychic Life of Power: Theories in Subjection* (Stanford: Stanford University Press, 1997); Cornelius Castoriadis, *The Imaginary Institution of Society: Creativity and Autonomy in the Social-Historical World* (Cambridge: Polity Press, 1987).
36. See Castoriadis, *The Imaginary Institution of Society*, p. 320.

37. *King Oedipus*, lines 1527–30.
38. Sophocles, *Oedipus at Colonus*, in *The Theban Plays*, trans. E. F. Watling (London: Penguin, 1974), pp. 69–124.
39. Mitchell, *Mad Men and Medusas*, pp. 119–20.

CHAPTER THREE

Trauerspiel, Tragedy and Epic

> In the ruins of great buildings the idea of the plan speaks more impressively than in lesser buildings, however well preserved they are; and for this reason the German *Trauerspiel* merits interpretation. In the spirit of allegory it is conceived from the outset as a ruin, a fragment. Others may shine resplendently as on the first day; this form preserves the image of beauty to the very last.[1]

These are the closing lines of Walter Benjamin's *The Origin of German Tragic Drama* (1928). With the emphasis on ruins, the view of history as catastrophe, the underlining of the significance of form (allegory), the mingling of spirits with buildings, the overall melancholy of the piece combined with its aphoristic flare, the book bears all the traces of Benjaminian thought and style: a mode of writing that would make a very marked contribution to theories of modernity. Within Benjamin's corpus, his book on the *Trauerspiel* occupies a crucial position and indeed has inspired a number of recent commentaries and interpretations, which mostly regard it within the framework of theories of modernity, particularly those pertaining to the relationships between aesthetics and politics.[2] This analysis initially wants to approach Benjamin's important book as a 'modern theory of tragedy'. Although it refers specifically to eighteenth-century Baroque German drama and more alarmingly constructs its theory of *Trauerspiel* against the so-called classical model of Greek tragedy, I would like to examine the possibility of approaching Benjamin's thesis as a way of reconciling the tragic and the modern. Almost against the grain of Benjamin's central thesis, this analysis presents a reading of the *Trauerspiel* as a way of bridging the overarching gulf between the ancients and the moderns.

Most approaches to *The Origin of German Tragic Drama* focus on the theories of allegory and melancholia, situating them in general within the modernist debates about form and content, aesthetics and politics, to which Benjamin makes several crucial contributions. However, the first two sections of the book – the 'Epistemo-Critical Prologue' and the chapter on '*Trauerspiel* and Tragedy' – have received very little attention.[3] In them Benjamin not only constructs a theory of subjectivity but also sketches out a theory of theatre for modernity. The fact that he uses the notion of the tragic to do so is fascinating both in terms of theories of subjectivity (something that he shares with Freud) and in terms of theories of aesthetics. These concerns, coupled with the historico-political dimension of the work, make it a precursor to the work of Bertolt Brecht. Indeed, Brecht and Benjamin became close if unlikely friends, a friendship that was to be frowned upon both by his Marxist colleagues (for example, Theodor Adorno) and by his German-Jewish companions.[4] Nevertheless, the relationship between the melancholy Benjamin and the hopeful Brecht helped to generate one of the most important bodies of work about the role of theatre and theory within modernity.

Both men, interestingly enough, defined their theories of theatre, whether *Trauerspiel* or epic, against the Aristotelian model of Greek tragedy. No matter how schematic or reductive their readings of Greek tragedy were, sometimes conflating Aristotle with Aristotelianism, the theories created from this encounter continue to shape the ways we understand performance today, its relation to the real, its reception by an audience, and its ability to create critique and change. The centrality of tragedy within this whole conceptual and methodological framework has barely been scrutinised. Usually constructed as representing unity, harmony and the organic (or pseudo-organic) coexistence of the political and the aesthetic, Greek tragedy becomes the emblem of everything antimodern, classical and humanist. For an aesthetic that was in search of formal expression for estrangement, fragmentation, alienation and antihumanism, Greek tragedy (in its appropriated and mainly Renaissance guise) became a polarised position against which Brecht and Benjamin could then proceed to define their own theories. However, this binary opposition was not without its own problems and inevitably there were areas of ambiguity and contradiction.

In the case of Benjamin one of these areas might be expressed through his relationship with Hölderlin. Hölderlin's notes to his translations of *Oedipus* and *Antigone* could be said to haunt Benjamin's study of the *Trauerspiel* and in many ways create links with Greek tragedy that the whole thesis of his book otherwise consciously resists. Indeed, this relationship with Hölderlin also connects Benjamin with the great tradition of German Idealism that has a very special relationship with Greek tragedy in its attempt to recuperate the aesthetic. Furthermore, Hölderlin's emphasis on theories of theatre as speculative philosophy bear their marks on Benjaminian thought in general and on modernist theories of theatricality. In a rare instance in *The Origin of German Tragic Drama*, where Benjamin abandons a crudely applied dialectical approach (which he admittedly borrows from Hegel), he sees tragedy as a precursor of the *Trauerspiel*:

> For in the theory of 'tragedy' the rules of ancient tragedy are taken separately, as lifeless components, and piled up around an allegorical figure representing the tragic muse ... In such a context of allegorical decay and destruction the image of Greek tragedy seemed to be the only possible, the natural sign of 'tragic poetry'. Its rules became significant anticipations of the *Trauerspiel*; its texts are read as *Trauerspiel*-texts. The extent to which this was, and continued to be, possible can be seen from Sophocles' translations of Hölderlin.[5]

Almost despite himself – since he castigates Hölderlin for turning to Greek tragedy – Benjamin acknowledges his debt to Hölderlin and inadvertently pays homage through him to Greek tragedy, which he has already constructed as a melancholy site complete with ruins and allegorical decay. This contradictory relationship with Greek tragedy also haunts the works of Brecht. Both men inherit this legacy from German Idealism, mainly through Hölderlin and Nietzsche, and want to differentiate themselves from it, while attempting to formulate a modern theory of theatricality, speculation and critique. However, these modernist theories of theatre, particularly as they became animated by dialectical materialism, as in Benjamin's later work and as in the works of Brecht, had to rid themselves of their idealist past. In the process they also had to abandon any connection to Greek tragedy.

This is the narrative that constructs Greek tragedy as the ultimate other of modernity. It posits Greek tragedy as the precursor of bourgeois individualism; in terms of theories of subjectivity and in terms of aesthetics its modern reincarnation is seen in the European naturalist movements. This is a somewhat eclectic and idiosyncratic reading of Greek tragedy that draws a direct line of progress and evolution from Aeschylus to Ibsen. As long as Greek tragedy was seen as constituting the spirit of Enlightenment thinking and as long as modernity was seen as a critique of the project of the Enlightenment, then Greek tragedy and modernity became sworn enemies. The attempt to construct a theory of theatre as critique and intervention almost always defines itself against Greek tragedy. It is seen as one of the foundations of classical European civilisation and as such any project which was about the celebration of modernity, as a movement of social emancipation and political critique, had to dismantle the edifice of Greek tragedy.

Interestingly enough, within the so-called historical avant-garde, there is quite a clear distinction in the attitudes towards Greek tragedy. At the one extreme there is the tradition that aspires towards metaphysical purity and aesthetic totality, and sees modernity as a threat to a nostalgic notion of a 'traditional past', and sees in Greek tragedy a model to be imitated. This legacy starts with Wagner's *Gestamkunstwork* and through the experiments of Edward Gordon Craig[6] and Yeats reaches the fascist aesthetics of the Italian futurists,[7] creating the only trajectory that has a place for Greek tragedy. As an emblem of a great tradition and as an expression of a great empire of the past, it is seen as offering the lost unity between audience and orchestra, between the collective and the individual, between aesthetics and politics – a unity that had once and for all been shattered by the advent of modernity. It is ironic that this is the only modernist performance tradition that reclaims Greek tragedy. It is a tradition that fears social and political change and is adamantly anti-feminist and anti-democratic. Greek tragedy, from the revivals of Oedipus in the circus tents directed by Reinhardt to the Italian futurist productions of tractor plays on hillsides, offers a way of combating modernity and somehow regaining a lost unity with the communal, the political and even the sacred.

At the other extreme of this spectrum is the legacy that embraces theatre as the quintessentially modern mode of art, probably only rivalled by the cinema (although there is a huge overlap in terms both of practitioners and theories). With theatre's reliance on an audience, it is seen as a way of resuscitating the collective dimension of art, and, with its synaesthetic approach, its use of many different kinds of artists, it is seen as a way of democratising the artistic process, and of offering an alternative vision of totality. Furthermore, the very making of theatre, the process from text to stage, is seen as a fruitful context for experiment and subsequently has generated very diverse and distinctly modernist languages of performance. This tradition, with its emphasis on materialism rather than metaphysics, on modes of production rather than on finished totalities, on the possibility, sometimes utopian, of radical change rather than on dwelling on any notion of tradition, sees Greek tragedy as epitomising everything that is evil, bourgeois and reactionary about European theatre. And, of course, this modernist tradition finds its most articulate and effective expression in the works of Benjamin and Brecht, and in their sometimes unlikely alliance. Rather than continuing this tradition, the analysis proposed here aspires to reconcile tragedy and modernity through the very work of Benjamin and Brecht.[8] This might seem like an odd undertaking as so much of their work relies on a superficial castigation of Greek tragedy. From Benjamin's aphorisms to Brecht's manifestos the so-called

Greek model is only referred to in negative terms; it is almost set up as a straw man, there to be torn apart and fragmented by the advent of modernity and the democratic projects it heralds.

Another tradition, as mentioned earlier, from which both theorists want to distance themselves is that of German Idealism and its fascination with Greek tragedy. Not only the work of Hölderlin, crucial for Benjamin's own intellectual trajectory, but also that of Nietzsche is vital in this context. His *The Birth of Tragedy* (1872) is impossible to avoid in any discussion about theatre and modernity.[9] Benjamin engages critically with it and highlights some of the problems that later commentaries and Nietzsche himself would raise. Its Apollonian/Dionysian binary is seen as schematic, but, more importantly, its lack of historicity and its exaltation of aesthetics is seen by Benjamin as highly problematic:

> The abyss of aestheticism opens up, and this brilliant intuition was finally to see all its concepts disappear into it, so that gods and heroes, defiance and suffering, the pillars of the tragic edifice, fall away into nothing . . . For what does it matter whether it is the will to life or the will to destroy life which is supposed to inspire every work of art, since the latter, as a product of the absolute will, devalues itself along with the world? The nihilism lodged in the depths of the artistic philosophy of Bayreuth nullified – it could do no other – the concept of the hard, historical actuality of Greek tragedy.[10]

Foreshadowing the aestheticisation thesis that he was to develop later on Benjamin,[11] this offers an insightful critique both of Nietzsche's interpretation of tragedy and the Wagnerian appropriations that were to follow and, in doing so, he tries to distance himself from this legacy. As an antidote to Nietzsche's statement that 'it is only as an *aesthetic phenomenon* that the existence and the world are eternally *justified*',[12] Benjamin emphasises 'the hard, historical actuality of Greek tragedy'. His book never proceeds to analyse this as it is concerned with German Baroque drama, but there are moments like the above, when he abandons the created opposition between *Trauerspiel* and tragedy and reads both as if they were part of the same trajectory or even genre. I would like to investigate these moments, when tragedy and modernist theories of drama are seen not in contrast but as possible mirrors of each other.

Benjamin's search for a theory of theatricality that is not simply an extension of philosophy also connects him with Hölderlin. There is a world of difference between Nietzsche's aesthetisation of tragedy and Hölderlin's theory of tragedy as speculation.[13] One reads tragedy firmly within a philosophical tradition while the other represents an attempt to theorise performance. It is in this sense that both Benjamin's and Brecht's projects of creating a kind of theatre that would be the aesthetic equivalent of dialectic materialism find an unlikely predecessor in Hölderlin.

While trying to grasp these sometimes contradictory elements within Benjamin's theory of the *Trauerspiel*, this analysis also follows the radical rereading of tragedy proposed by recent approaches. It is based on the premise that the schematic view of tragedy put forward by these leading modernist theorists is at best flawed, only able to function with the narrative of the aphorism or the manifesto. If, as recent approaches suggest, Greek tragedy is not the epitome of the European project of the Enlightenment, but a subtle and conflicting critique of that project, possibly conceived at the moment of its genesis, then very diverse hermeneutic possibilities emerge. Rather than viewing Greek tragedy as the site of the organic coexistence of the private and the public or of the aesthetic and the political, it appears to voice a critique of these categories while also helping to construct them. This reading of tragedy dispels the vision of it as the perfect immersion of discourse in praxis, the lost unity that can never be regained. Rather, if we see it as a site that already is and always has been fragmented, ambiguous and ambivalent, then it actually appears already to be part of modernity (destroying the opposition between tradition and modernity in the process).

Recent scholarship on Greek tragedy tends to focus on its discursive construction in relation to the development of the city-state, to funeral and other rites, to the dynamic of gender, to the function of Athenian law, to the development of empire, and so on.[14] All these approaches – anthropological, neo-historicist or psychoanalytical – have created a huge body of work that problematises the humanist, Renaissance interpretations of tragedy. Using theories of the *Trauerspiel* to approach Greek tragedy, this analysis intends to add to that body of work. However, it does not set out to create a 'new' theory of tragedy. What the *Trauerspiel* perhaps allows us to do is to examine the possibility of reconciling tragedy with modernity. Rather than seeing modernity as something which once and for all heralds the end of the tragic vision of the world and the artistic forms that that vision inspired (Steiner), reading notions of the *Trauerspiel* (back?) into Greek tragedy could help create a type of 'archeology' of the genre and its reception. With its emphasis on ruins and catastrophe, its use of the allegorical trope and its melancholy impact, the *Trauerspiel* might offer a way of reading tragedy that goes against the grain of most humanist readings that see it either as part-and-parcel of the 'Greek miracle', or as the prototype for the relationships among the aesthetic, the philosophical and the political within the project of the European Enlightenment.

However, I would like to resist reading Greek tragedy as if it actually were a form of *Trauerspiel*. Neither do I want to (re)construct the origins of Greek tragedy. Their relationships are seen neither in generative nor in causal, determinist terms. Rather, the analogy I would like to draw, one which Benjamin himself uses, is that of the constellation or the mosaic: 'In their supreme, western form the mosaic and the treatise are products of the Middle Ages; it is their very real affinity which makes comparison possible.'[15] If both the mosaic and the treatise are creations of Greek antiquity, then they might offer a way of approaching these otherwise disparate modes. Both modes, in their combination of the material and the textual, art and artistry, *techne* and *mechane*, offer analogies for tragedy as performance and as poetry, as theatre and as philosophy. The mosaic's reliance on the fragment, the chipped surface and its use both as decoration and as ritualistic ornament, also offers possibilities for approaching modes that seem very diverse and multifunctional. This analysis does not set out to view Greek tragedy as a precursor to the *Trauerspiel*. Rather it hopes to set up an intertextual dialogue between the two modes and their respective histories and receptions. Drawing the analogy of the mosaic and the constellation, it does not aim to create a finished, polished surface, but to create a way of reading tragedy and *Trauerspiel* that allows for the fragment, the ruin, and the incongruous existence of antiquity and modernity. In any case we as 'moderns' can only really experience Greek tragedy in terms of ruins and fragments, textual or otherwise. This project does not aim to smooth out the catastrophic and fragmentary nature of our reception of tragedy; instead, it proposes to see these aspects as an integral part of its aesthetic. In the dialogue with the *Trauerspiel* it is the essentially anti-humanist, non-organic, melancholy dimension of tragedy that will be explored and read within the overall context of modernity.

Theatricality and Speculation

The parallel between tragedy as an aspect of *theoria* and Hölderlin's view of tragedy as a form of speculative philosophy has already been drawn in this book. This nexus of concepts gains a new momentum in Benjamin's theory of *Trauerspiel*. Both terms seem to be re-energised and reapplied in a way that is typically Benjaminian and modern. Rainer Nägele writes:

> It is not by chance that Benjamin's most important epistemological text appears as a preface to a book on theatre and theatricality: theatre and theory are intimately linked not only through their common Greek root in *theorein* (to watch, see) but also in the two German terms *vorstellen* (put forward, present, imagine) and *dar-*

stellen (present, represent, depict) . . . *Vorstellen* and *darstellen* are both theatrical and epistemological concepts, and they structure the world and our knowledge of it in terms of position, that is, of relation rather than substance.[16]

Tragedy, *theoria*, *Darstellung* and *Vorstellung* create a mosaic of meanings and gestures that needs unravelling. What they all point towards is the inevitability of performance: the fact that there can be no reading of the tragic without the inclusion of performance and the performative. Benjamin's opening sentence of the 'Epistemo-Critical Prologue' points to this and to the fact that philosophical writing itself needs to be read within this constellation of concepts: 'It is characteristic of philosophical writing that it must continually confront the question of representation.'[17] This self-reflexive mode which needs underlining in philosophy is already and always present in tragedy through the presence of performance, through its *theoria*.

The connection of *theoria* to speculative philosophy is something that Benjamin inherits from Hölderlin's essays on tragedy and his notes to *Antigone* and *Oedipus*. This link also emphasises the aesthetic (in its original sense of pertaining to the senses) and the physical, the bodily. Indeed, *theoria* might be read as a form of philosophy where the separation between the philosophical and the poetological, between the word and the body, ceases to exist, or rather never existed in the first place. Hölderlin's famous definition of tragedy points towards this: 'The tragic, in appearance heroic, is idealistic in its signification. It is the metaphor of an intellectual intuition.'[18] In the opening of his 'Remarks on Oedipus', he writes:

> It will be good, in order to secure for today's poets, also at home, an existence in the city, to elevate poetry, also at home, given the difference of times and institutions, to the level of the *mechane* of the Ancients.
> When being compared with those of the Greeks, other works of art too lack reliability; at least, they have been judged until today according to the impression they produce rather than according to their lawful calculation and to the other methodical modes through which the beautiful is engendered . . .
> As men, we must first realize that it is something, that is, that it is something which can be known by means (*moyen*) of its manifestation, that the way in which it is conditioned may be determined and learned. Such is the reason why – to say nothing of higher reasons – poetry is in special need of secure and characteristic delimitations.[19]

Hölderlin's quest for a poetics of tragedy that is at once *techne* and *mechane* is attractive to Benjamin. This incorporation of the physical is also implicated in the ways tragedy acts as a form of *transport*, of mediation of the 'intellectual intuition'. This form of mediation, according to

Hölderlin, acts as a bridge to combat the eternal and 'limitless separation' between the earthly and divine, between the word and the body, between subject and object. It also is always self-reflexive:

> The tragic *transport* is actually empty and the least restrained. So, in the rhythmic sequence of the representations wherein *transport* presents itself, there becomes necessary *what in poetic meter is called caesura*, the pure word, the counterrhythmic rupture, namely in order to meet the onrushing change of representation at its highest point in such a way that very soon it is not change of representation which appears but representation itself.[20]

Hölderlin's notoriously dense term *caesura*, with its combination of physical and lexical qualities, its 'counterrhythmic rupture' (all present in the etymology of the word) and its ever-present fixation on representation prove very attractive for Benjamin. Indeed, the opening sentence of his book on the *Trauerspiel* could be read as an echo of Hölderlin. The term *caesura* also finds its way into Brechtian theory, particularly in his formulation of *gestus* – a crucial performative act, where the body and language both posit and 'alienate' the actor on stage and within a broader network of socio-historical interactions. *Gestus*, as a 'counterrhythmic rupture', can both impersonate and demonstrate, making the natural seem strange and wondrous, yet always historical. The lineage from *gestus* to Hölderlin's *caesura* is one which merits further investigation and offers yet another way of linking the 'tragic' with the 'epic' modes of theatre. There are ways, for example, of reading *gestus* and *caesura* within a genealogical context that includes the tragic conventions of *schemata* and *chironomia*. This reading, however, would have to elide the oppositions of tragic/*Trauerspiel* and tragic/epic, the very oppositions that help construct the 'modern' categories. Nägele writes:

> There is an analogy between the Hegel's and Hölderlin's differentiation of Greeks and Moderns and Benjamin's opposition between tragedy and *Trauerspiel*. Both of these scenarios portray the Greek situation as a scene of the formation of the yet unformed, of giving language to the yet unspoken. In contrast, the Moderns find themselves imprisoned in the fixed order of concepts; in Hölderlin's formulation, their bodies are already more spiritual. Benjamin's version of this scenario is that of individuals 'for whom the fully unfolded consciousness of the community allows no more latent meaning'. The communal language has no more taboos, no more mystery. The modern subject in the *Trauerspiel* is in search of the mystery, and the history of modern drama as *Trauerspiel* 'from Calderon to Strindberg' points at the 'future of this form as the form of the mystery'.[21]

This is a familiar scenario; one that sees the transition from 'Greeks' to 'moderns' as a series of great shifts, ruptures and breaks. The 'Greek' scene is viewed upon, with a mixture of nostalgia and horror, as the primary scene, 'the original sin', where the unspoken is given language and where flux is given form and where bodies are somehow more physical. It is a world that still accommodates taboo, mystery and presumably ritual. It is the absence of these within modernity that the *Trauerspiel* is called upon to replace. It is the same reading that claims the impossibility of tragedy in the modern world. The lack of mystery, taboo and ritual is usually pointed to as the reason for the 'death of tragedy'. If, however, such a scene never took place, and if tragedy enacts the always present and continual interdependence of these categories, then a very different scenario emerges. If tragedy is seen not solely as the organic mystery, the rite and ritual that keeps taboo at bay, or in place, if it is seen already as forming an art form with a language, indeed a performative language, then the shift proposed above ceases to function. Instead, what emerges is a view of tragedy as a performative, speculative philosophy, where form and content are of equal significance.

Hölderlin's observations on tragedy are conspicuously present throughout Benjamin's theory of *Trauerspiel*. As part of the tradition of German Idealism that sought to redefine tragic form and incorporate it within a broader aesthetic theory, they present a formidable body of work and a challenge both to the 'ancients' and the 'moderns'. With their emphasis on speculation, physicality, reception and mediation, and the notion of the *caesura*, they provide a useful springboard for ideas about the form and function of theatre within modernity. Indeed, this is a tradition that, however reluctantly, is followed by Benjamin and Brecht. Despite their attempts to shape a theory of theatre for the future, the legacy that they inherit from Hölderlin not only connects them with German Idealism but also draws more alarming parallels between their own work and the work of the 'Greeks', from whom they are desperately trying to be different, and against whom they define themselves.

Allegory and Ruins

> When, as is the case in the *Trauerspiel*, history becomes part of the setting, it does so as script. The word 'history' stands written on the countenance of nature in the characters of transience. The allegorical physiognomy of the nature-history, which is put on stage in the *Trauerspiel*, is present in reality in the form of the ruin. In the ruin history has physically merged into the setting. And in this guise history does not assume the form of the process of an eternal life so much as that of irresistible decay. Allegory thereby declares itself to be beyond beauty. Allegories are, in the realm of thoughts, what ruins are in the realm of things.[22]

This crucial quotation establishes the role of history and the significance of allegory for the *Trauerspiel*. At the same time, however, it can be read as both foreshadowing the function of history in Brecht's epic theatre and echoing the role of myth in Greek tragedy. This Janus-like quality of Benjamin's approach is what makes it a suitable interface between the 'ancients' and the 'moderns'.

The role of history, however, is one of the main differences between the Greek model and Benjamin's, where the *Trauerspiel* is seen as being steeped in historical subject matter and Greek tragedy to be based on myth. Eliding his own opposition, Benjamin seems to be reading history as a 'script', not only in empirical terms but in blatantly discursive ones. This is reminiscent of the placat-signalling of the Brechtian plays. It is very interesting that nature and history appear in the same compound term: 'nature-history'. Benjamin's physiognomy is at the same time material and materialist, physical and discursive.[23] This view of history manifests itself in the form of the allegory. Allegory, as opposed to symbol, is seen to encapsulate this version of history which does not see the physical/natural and the discursive/ideological as separate entities. This physiognomy materially appears in the form of the ruin. Things, like thoughts, are seen as fragmentary, unfinished, ambiguous and open to interpretation.

The function of myth within Greek tragedy can be seen to occupy a similar position. As many recent approaches show, the fact that Greek tragedy relies on myth (with a few notable exceptions) does not make it less historical. In fact the strict reliance on mythic structure, albeit one that is endlessly interpreted, allows for the use of allegory instead of symbol. Like the use of fables in bible stories, or in Brechtian plays, the centrality of myth and the communality it offers allow for the most 'classical' use of allegory as a tool of instruction and pedagogy. Against this strict intentionality, however, allegory also allows for ambiguity and interpretation. These two contra-punctual strands in allegory are what make it at once instructive and subversive. As the differences in the work of the tragedians shows, from Aeschylus to Euripides, this diverse application of the function of myth as allegory allows for celebratory tragedies (as mainly in the work of Sophocles) or for directly subversive ones (as in the plays of Euripides). Mostly, though, Greek tragedies do both. They tend to celebrate the Athenian state, while also exhibiting its limitations. And this double bind seems to be present right through from the first quasi-historical tragedy we have, *The Persians*, to the last clearly mythic one, *The Bacchae*. This paradoxical aspect of tragedy is something that Benjamin believes to have faded away from tragedy, only to be regained by modernity. He writes:

> The decisive confrontation with the demonic world-order which takes place in Greek literature also gives tragic poetry its signature in terms of the history of philosophy. In all the paradoxes of tragedy – in the sacrifice, which, in complying with ancient statutes, creates new ones, in death, which is an act of atonement but which sweeps away only the self, in the tragic ending, which grants the victory to man, but also to god – ambiguity, the stigma of the daimons, is in decline.[24]

On the contrary, I would claim that ambiguity is a structuring force of the tragic and it is one of those traits that make it both historical, as in, of its own time, and modern, of our time. And, of course, ambiguity is one of the direct effects of the function of allegory, so central to the reading of the *Trauerspiel*.

Nägele charts the genealogy of the opposition between allegory and symbol from Goethe, through Hegel, leading to Benjamin's formulations. This is an opposition that has generated a number of interpretations. Most rely on the manner in which the relationship between the particular and the general is formulated. This is not only a formal, aesthetic issue but also and primarily a political one. The relationship of the individual to the community and who mediates whom is of crucial significance. Brecht, for example, who views the individual as part of the historical process, uses allegory rather than symbol as the epitome of epic theatre. On the other hand, symbol, with its emphasis on closure, manages to hide the workings of history or to subsume them under the category of the particular. Goethe's phrasing of the effects of symbol as getting 'the general with it at the same time without being aware of it, or only late', also could read as a definition of the Marxist concept of 'false consciousness', or in more aesthetic terms as a function of the sublime. In general this is the reading that sees symbol as a function and expression of bourgeois individualism and allegory as a function of historical materialism, where the individual exists as part of the general and communal.

In epistemological terms the categories of 'idea' and 'concept' also require further analysis. Nägele states that these 'are invested with specific implications in the post-Kantian era: ideas emerge from synthetic reason (*Vernunft*), and concepts are produced by analytic reason (*Verstand*).'[25] He then continues to read *Verstand* in terms sketched out by Hegel in the *Phenomenology*:

> *Verstand* is linked in an associative chain to notions of dismemberment (*zergliedernd, Zergliederung*), dissolution (*zersetzend*), and sterility (coldness and dyness). Analytic reason is a threat to the wholeness of life, body, and beauty... It reaches from analysis to beauty, from thought to death as the power of negativity. And it is most of all in this moment of negativity and its threat to beauty that *Verstand* is most intimately connected with allegory.[26]

And it is this reading of allegory that for Benjamin is related to melancholy contemplation, ruins and the catastrophic view of history. This notion of the 'concept' as negativity and critique is also close to Hölderlin's view of tragedy as speculative philosophy.

Anxieties about dismemberment, dislocation, lack of wholeness can also be said to permeate Greek tragedy. From the dismemberment of Dionysus, a founding myth for the birth of tragedy, through its endless enactments to Pentheus' final one in *The Bacchae*, dismemberment seems to be a central theme and convention of tragedy. Furthermore, it is also refracted through the function of gender as will be examined further on. However, for the purposes of the function of allegory and all it implies, Greek tragedy can be read as steeped in negativity, where death and funeral ritual haunt the scene but also help create presence on the stage through specific conventions and enactments. The notion of allegorical personification might also prove useful in reading the function of 'characters' on the Greek stage. In the lectures on aesthetics Hegel writes:

> [Allegory's] next/first business is to personify general abstract conditions or qualities both from the human and from the natural world . . . and thus to conceive them as *subject*. This subjectivity, however, is neither in its content nor in its exterior form truly a subject in itself nor an individual but rather remains the abstraction of a general notion that receives only the *empty form* of subjectivity and can be called only, so to speak, a grammatical subject.[27]

This is an anti-humanist version of the notion of anthropomorphism or even anthropocentrism. Reading character, with intent and motivation, into any role on the Greek stage is problematic at best. These ideas of the 'empty form' and the 'grammatical subject' could provide a way of interpreting 'characters' on the Greek stage without resorting to anachronistic applications of psychology or subjectivity. Furthermore, they might also help to read the homosocial dimension of the Greek stage. The convention of men-playing-women, which usually gets omitted from interpretations of 'character', could find a useful counterpart in the idea of a grammatical subject that can in turn be enacted in a performative manner, drawing attention both to the subject it is 'being' and to the one that is being 'demonstrated'.

Reading the notion of character in this manner allows us to move away from psychological or psychoanalytical notions which inevitably will be anachronistic. To view character as a 'grammatical subject' and an 'empty form' also releases tragedy from any quasi-naturalist or humanist interpretations. Rather than seeing it as enacting the creation of subjectivity and anthropomorphism (and even philosophy), this allegorical reading of character allows for the constitutive relationship between being and appearance to be exposed. Symbol presents a seemingly seamless whole of being and appearance, where the essence is of vital importance. Indeed, appearance is only there to directly and unproblematically mediate the essence of a character. With allegory, however, a very different relationship emerges. Appearance is not the simple and undiluted expression of the essence of the character. On the contrary it is seen as helping to give shape and content to that character. Its being and its 'being demonstrated' are inextricably linked. Meaning can only really be derived from the interaction between the two. Neither has the ability, on its own, to generate the category of character. It is in this way that Hegel's negative formulation of character within the allegorical mode can prove useful in approaching Greek tragedy.

The convention of men-playing-women acquires added significance in this context. As anxieties about gender, its function and differentiation, play a pivotal role in Greek tragedy, how these issues are channelled through the notion of character is crucial. As the stylisation implied by the cross-dressing convention clearly demands, there can be no simple and direct identification of actor and character. Instead we are exposed to the complexity of relationships between being and appearance. As the men playing the women are 'naturally' not women, the whole 'nature-history', the *physiognomy*, of the category of gender is being interrogated, where biological sex and gendered sexuality are seen as two discrete units, which, nevertheless, can only materialise through their interaction. This historicising of the actor's body creates a set of acting conventions that fruitfully could be read within Hegel's notion of the character as 'grammatical form'. More obvious parallels could also be drawn with Meyerhold's[28] and Brecht's convention of the *dialectical actor*, who can at once be and show, who can impersonate and demonstrate. Again this analogy helps bridge the opposition of tragedy and *Trauerspiel*.

The use of allegory as an attempt to read 'character' in Greek tragedy also opens up another interesting hermeneutic dimension. In many ways the emphasis on gender, in terms of both conventions and themes, gives this category an added significance within the whole process of representation. This is something to which Benjamin's analysis is oblivious.[29] In many ways the underlining of gender as a constitutive element in the formation of the category of character is something of which modern theories of tragedy have been unaware, or have been uninterested in. The only way in which gender, and particularly the female, enters into this analysis is when it is identified with falseness, surface, appearance and pure theatricality. Again, Nietzsche's aphorism is vital in this context, 'woman is so artistic'.

Tragedy, on the other hand, cannot exist without theatricality. If theatricality itself is pure femininity, then what of Hölderlin's speculative philosophy? Tragedy, as a form of philosophy, can be read as a discourse which engages with the feminine, not only thematically but also in terms of its conventions. This 'engagement' with the feminine is not necessarily critical or 'feminist', which would be as anachronistic as reading psychology into the characters. It is, however, a mode of aesthetic production which scrutinises the formation and function of gender. Within the predominantly homosocial and homosexual world of Greek tragedy the role of women and gender is constantly under examination on the stage. One way of reading this obsession and the conventions it generates could be through the idea of the allegorical character. Hegel continues his adamant criticism of allegory:

> b. Second, the senses of the allegorical are at the same time determinate ones in their abstraction and recognizable only in this determination, so that now the expression of such specifications . . . has to step in as an explicatory predicate beside the subject. This separation of subject and predicate is the second side of allegory's coldness.
> Thus allegory is barren in two respects. Its general personification is empty, the determinate exteriority only a sign that, taken by itself, has no meaning.[30]

Against the vision of wholeness proposed by the rhetoric of the symbol, allegory appears as fragmented and disjointed; the separation of subject and predicate, of what the character 'is' and what it 'represents', is seen as something that generates 'coldness'. In terms of dramatic conventions this also could generate the kind of 'coldness' that is identified with abstraction and estrangement rather than empathy and identification. It implies a self-reflexivity that underlines the process of representation itself, where signs have no meaning in and of themselves; there is no essence in the world of allegory, only cold and fragmented appearance, according to Hegel. Nägele has an interesting contribution to make to this discussion:

> More and more clearly, the scene of allegorical anxiety reveals itself as the subject's anxiety of dismemberment, a phantasy of the dismembered body whose limbs and members take on an independent existence. Implied also is the anxiety of the cut of language through which the imaginary, substantial I is confronted with the grammatical I.[31]

I would add to this analysis that allegorical anxiety also reveals a particular anxiety about the feminine. In as much as the feminine is identified with histrionics and empty signifiers, with falseness and appearance, then this reading of allegory also appears to be a gendered one. It would not be incongruous for Hegel's thesis to proceed to read allegory as feminine and symbol, with its emphasis on wholeness and essence, as masculine. However, allegory is a specific kind of woman; it is a cold, barren woman. It is a woman deprived of her 'nature' as child bearer. Motherhood, woman's 'natural' role, is the only function that can restore the wholeness to her being. Deprived of it, she is cold and barren, lifeless. Since she can no longer fulfil her natural role, all she can do is reproduce falseness and empty signifiers, simply drawing attention to the absence of essence in her. She is pure exteriority, pure spectacle. Benjamin 'suggests connections between spectacle proper and allegory'.[32] Considering the parallels between femininity and spectacle and between allegory and the feminine, we might suggest that allegory and spectacle exhibit very specific anxieties about gender.

Nowhere are these more obvious than on the stage of Greek tragedy. More specifically, the notion of barrenness is also an anxiety that permeates many a Greek play. The delicate balance of reconciling a homosocial and homoerotic world with the fact that only women's bodies have the ability to reproduce generates one of the most creative anxieties in Greek tragedy. Fears about lineage, kinship and kingship are all refracted through the very specific love/hate relationship with the reproducing female body. 'If only men could have children without women', says Jason to Medea, and the phrase is echoed in many plays. In particular, this anxiety about reproduction can also be read into the men-playing-women convention, where the woman represented can only be 'barren and cold' as she is portrayed through a male body, a body already barren. However, in its dual drive towards celebration and subversion, this convention can also draw attention to the ways that gender itself is constructed. If gender is implicated in the ways that allegory functions, then the ways this is moulded for the purposes of the Greek stage could perhaps point towards ways of interpreting these specific dramatic conventions.

On the one hand, allegory is the site of anxieties about dismemberment and the function of gender. On the other, these anxieties are constitutive of the notion of the subject and character. Allegory allows for the expression of these anxieties and for the critique that follows. It is indeed a negative critique, but one that connects allegory with the analytical reason mentioned earlier. The coldness and distance that allegory exerts triggers critical thinking instead of emotional identification. The nod to Brecht is obvious here. Less obvious is the reading of Greek tragedy within this trajectory. In terms of reception, allegory leads towards an interpretation of mimesis as enactment and not identification. Allegory allows for a reading of mimesis that is primarily anti-Aristotelian. Rather than demanding identification, it generates distance. It allows for a reading of Greek tragedy that goes beyond psychological identification and opens the road to critical thinking and speculative philosophy. However, this reading of allegory is seen as a quintessentially modern trope and yet another point of opposition to Greek tragedy. Nägele writes:

> This is the essential topology that structures the rhetoric of the symbol-allegory opposition as well as that of bourgeois subjectivity and its interiority. Against it, a pathos of exteriority or of the surface emerges in Modernism: it revalorizes allegory in all its theatricality.[33]

The pathos of exteriority can also be read in all the dramatic conventions that Greek tragedy embodies, particularly in the cross-dressing aspect. To see allegory solely as a trope of modernity, with reflexivity and estrangement as its emblems, misses a potential genealogy of the term, which also could incorporate Greek tragedy. However, such a schema would have to go beyond the binaries on which most of the above readings rely. This is not to imply that Greek tragedy *is* modern, hence universal and eternal. Taking the analogy even further, our reception of Greek tragedy *as* moderns can only be through ruins and fragments. We can never occupy a place in that auditorium. We can, nevertheless, find a way of relating to the past as ruin and fragment. Allegory allows us to do this. Rather than identifying with the 'characters' in these plays, as if they were us in some form of collective delusion, allegory sets up a relationship of critical negativity which allows for a reading of the tragic as both theatricality and myth, and as speculative philosophy.

Lamentation and Mourning

> Mourning is the state of mind in which feeling revives the empty world in the form of a mask, and derives an enigmatic satisfaction in contemplating it. Every feeling is bound to an *a priori* object, and the representation of this object its phenomenology. Accordingly the theory of mourning, which emerged unmistakably as a *pendant* to the theory of tragedy, can only be developed in the description of that world which is revealed under the gaze of the melancholy man.[34]

The intricate relationships between tragic form and mourning and melancholia are ones that have been mentioned throughout this study. Using the model of the mosaic, I would like to sketch out a way of reading mourning and melancholy into Greek tragedy that involves recent anthropological and neo-historicist approaches, together with psychoanalytical views on the function of mourning in the formation of subjectivity.

The central role that lamentation and mourning play in helping to structure tragic form has been documented by anthropologists and classicists alike. The banning of female lament around the sixth century BCE is a crucial moment. The fact that it is outlawed, of course, does not mean that it vanishes. As Nicole Loraux states, it finds its way into tragic form.[35] Indeed, it is one of the most significant impulses behind the creation of tragic performance conventions. At the same time, it allows for death ritual itself to leave the domain of the female (the private and the domestic, the oral) and enter into the civic, political and discursive world of the male. This public participation in death ritual helps construct the identity of the Athenian citizen. In the *History of the Peloponnesian War*, Thucydides cites a moment where female lamentation is stopped to make way for the more political, male discourse of the official funeral oration:

> In the same winter the Athenians gave a funeral at the public cost to those who had first fallen in this war ... After the bodies had been laid in the earth, a man chosen by the state, of approved wisdom and eminent reputation, pronounces over them an appropriate panegyric; after which all retire. Such is the manner of the burying; and throughout the whole of the war, whenever the occasion arose, the established custom was observed. Meanwhile these were the first that had fallen, and Pericles, son of Xanthippus, was chosen to pronounce their eulogium. When the proper time arrived, he advanced from the sepulchre to an elevated platform in order to be heard by as many of the crowd as possible, and spoke as follows.[36]

Unlike the funeral oration, which can be read as a type of treatise,[37] tragedy filters lamentation ritual in more complex and fascinating ways. It is not a case of simple and direct appropriation, where the excessive femininity of lament and its flirtations with death are subsumed within the direct and overpowering discourse of the male oration. The very physiognomy of tragic form with its emphasis on the physical and the bodily, the presence of the audience and the use of theatrical convention all allow for a very diverse and contradictory relationship to death ritual. As has been mentioned before, death ritual is seen as constitutive of tragic form. The more traditional reading of this relationship from Nietzsche to Benjamin sees tragic form as somehow mediating death ritual in a manner that makes it either more palatable or transcribes it into the sublime. Tragic convention itself is seen as the filter, which somehow rids the stage of melancholy and instead reinscribes it with *pathos*. Benjamin writes of the chorus in this respect:

> Really the chorus of tragedy does not lament. It remains detached in the presence of profound suffering; this refutes the idea of surrender to lamentation ... Choric diction, rather, has the effect of restoring the ruins of the tragic dialogue to a

linguistic edifice firmly established – in ethical society and in religious community – both before and after the conflict. Far from dissolving the tragic action into lamentations, the constant presence of the members of the chorus, as Lessing already observed, actually sets a limit on the emotional outburst even in the dialogue.[38]

Against the suffering and the *peripeteia* of Greek tragedy, Benjamin posits stoic *apatheia*, the inability to suffer, feel *pathos* and learn from experience. The chorus is seen as mediating this process. As the representative of ethical and religious society, the communal spirit in general, the chorus can turn the excessive, oriental and feminising drive of lamentation into a pedagogical experience. It is there to turn the raw and unruly forces of lamentation into experience and knowledge. This very humanist reading of tragic form sees artistic form as something that shapes ritual and rite in a direct and uncomplicated manner. Regarding the chorus itself, its function as a simple interface between the individual and the collective, between form and content, has long been disputed. Rather, as choruses from *The Persians* to *The Bacchae* clearly exhibit, they can be unruly, lamenting, and highly subversive.

Melancholia is also constitutive of the creation of subjectivity, according to Freud, and more specifically, according to recent feminist psychoanalysts, it plays a significant role in gender differentiation. Within this broad framework melancholia can also be read into the cross-dressing convention of Greek tragedy. According to Judith Butler the notion of men-playing-woman always exerts melancholia. Melancholia, in Freudian terms, results from ungrieved loss, where the subject in the making has not been able or allowed to mourn a lost identification. If in this case the unmourned refers to the feminine, the great absent from the Greek stage, then the constant acting-out in performance 'may be related to the problem of unacknowledged loss', as Butler puts it.[39] If the construction of gender itself inevitably entails some form of 'acting-out', then the cross-dressing convention of Greek tragedy may be commenting on the process of gender differentiation itself. The performative aspect of this process is heightened in a self-referential manner, drawing attention to the modes of its representation. Furthermore, this acting-out always involves unresolved grief for a lost object of identification. In Butler's analysis this object almost always results from a homosexual identification and what is denied grief causes the melancholia. This analysis is valid when trying to account for 'compulsory heterosexuality' as Adrienne Rich terms it, where the subject-in-the-making has to renounce same-sex identification in order to comply with a heterosexual and heterosexist economy. However, in the context of Greek tragedy this approach needs further qualification. In the predominantly homosocial and homosexual (male) world of Athenian drama it is primarily the female who is denied identification and the grief that follows the subsequent loss. Indeed, in a world where desire derives from and is aimed exclusively at male subjects and objects, the female is relegated to the domain of absence and loss. We can almost say that it is a type of structural misogyny that is otherwise associated with homophobia. Rather than expressing the fear of homosexual identification, the drag element of Greek tragedy might point towards the more 'conventional' trope of misogyny.

It is also fascinating to point out, as Butler does, that the literary mode in and by which melancholia manifests itself is allegory. Allegory allows for the 'incorporation' of the grieved object of desire. In many ways the body of the mourner imbibes the body of the grieved object of desire. The men playing women on the Greek stage have already incorporated the bodies of the females they are acting out. In the same way that death ritual entails identification with the body of the dead person being mourned, the acting-out and the masking involved in cross-gender acting carry within its conventions the dead bodies of the women being portrayed on the stage. As a type of perversion of pregnancy and birth (an anxiety that runs throughout Greek tragedy), the male actors represent the female characters, quite literally creating them in the process. As this manner, however, can never be realistic, psychological nor naturalistic in its style and reception, they are also drawing attention to the ways in which the female is internalised and represented. Again the Brechtian concept of *gestus* proves useful.

This incorporation of the other in the very process of its representation implies a very particular mode of reception as well. As a trope of representation it sets up a very intriguing relationship with otherness. In many ways, since this other has been taken on, imbibed and internalised, it breaks down the opposition between self and other, between subject and object, creating a type of performative fluidity and flexibility when it comes to gender construction. This slightly poststructuralist reading has to be modified by the historical facts surrounding the production of Greek plays and the civic and political absence of women from Athenian life. It could be that this specific performance convention both reproduces this fact and subtly allows for its interrogation and subversion. Either way, the kind of reception it presupposes is not one of empathy and identification but one of immersion and cannibalism.

Aristotelian pity and fear do not necessarily presuppose psychological identification, as Brecht wrongly concluded. They might also harp back to drama's anthropological precedent in human sacrifice and cannibalism. The tropes of displacement, disposition (ecstasis), dismemberment and cannibalism are all endlessly refracted through Greek tragedy. Indeed, murder (or human sacrifice), which cannot be portrayed on the Greek stage (obscene), and which might be at the centre of cultural production, appears as a strong taboo of Greek tragedy. Its relationship with cannibalism, and the trope of birth-death-resurrection that cannibalism sometimes enacts, sets up a sophisticated mode of reception. Against the interior world of the subject, which psychological identification presupposes and reproduces, the trope of immersion and cannibalism is shamelessly exterior and physical. The identification, if any occurs at all, is on the level of the physical and the sensual, the aesthetic. In this way the pity and the fear (horror) derived from the tragic experience comes from the loss of subjectivity and individuality that immersion, dismemberment and cannibalism imply.

The idea of the tragic character emerges as a centrifugal force, dissolving, fragmenting and dismembering rather than creating any notion of subjectivity. How this notion of character 'puts everything together again' is also extremely significant because it does so in a highly theatricalised, performative way, which does not hide but, on the contrary, relies on the process of disintegration that preceded it. The conventions that embody these stylised 'characters' can be said to be full of the ruins of the whole characters that they have torn apart and cannibalised. These conventions, particularly the cross-dressing ones, allegorise anxieties about the formation of gender, subjectivity and character. The audience that in turn is asked to receive such a notion of character can only really do so in an equally cannibalistic manner. This combination of allegory, melancholia, physiognomy and *gestus* creates a form of reception that relies on physical immersion while also creating the kind of 'horrific' distance that generates speculative thinking. The fact that the relationship with the stage is primarily one of topology (of bodies, things and places) does not imply that it is anti-critical or anti-intellectual in general. The kind of 'thinking' it generates is at the level of concepts rather than ideas, mirroring the opposition of symbol to allegory. This embodied and performative mode of critical thinking creates a version of Hölderlin's speculative philosophy. Benjamin writes of this relationship:

> Rarely if ever have speculative aesthetics considered how close strict fun is to horror. Who has not seen children laugh when adults are horrified? How such childishness that laughs and adulthood that is horrified alternate in the sadist can be deciphered in the intriguer.[40]

Against the idea of the unified subject Benjamin posits the figures of the child, the sadist, the intriguer and the detective. In an odd constellation of types, rather than characters, Benjamin interrogates the proximity of horror and pleasure and the physicality on which they are based. It is fascinating that the type of the 'child' also appears in this context, as childhood is rarely theorised in philosophy other than as a preparatory stage for subjectivity, as is the case with psychoanalysis (or civilisation, echoing Marx's 'The Greeks as the childhood of Mankind'). These are all types that either fragment the notion of the unified subject or present it in a state of flux and change. And these are the types of roles, of course, that populate Brecht's epic theatre. The combination of childhood and philosophy also can be found in Brecht's concept of the naive theatre, where critical thinking has to be combined with a sense of the wondrous, as if the world is being discovered for the first time. This sense of wonder at the world is a fundamental axiom within modernism. It can be found right through the Russian formalist concept of estrangement to Brecht's alienation. The role of theatre and art in general is to make the ordinary extraordinary. 'To make the stone stoney' was Schklovsky's motto. The process of denaturalising the apparently seamless relationships between people and things also entails critical thinking. It is the oxymoronic combination of childhood wonder (and horror) with critique that creates for Benjamin speculative aesthetics. Theatre is seen as the perfect *topos* for such an aesthetic theory.

The proximity of fear, horror and wonder is something that merits further investigation. The etymology of *phobos* links it not only with fear but also with wonder. No doubt it is this fear/wonder, pleasure/pain combination that allows for the term *phobia* to function so well in psychoanalysis. If Aristotle's 'pity and fear' could also translate into immersion, horror and wonder, then tragedy presents us with a type of aesthetic theory that is already speculative. Rather than reading the *Trauerspiel* against tragedy, the model of reception that tragedy sets up and Aristotle theorises might be seen as exhibiting some of the aspects of the speculative philosophy that underlines Benjamin's thinking.

The analysis of tragic convention sketched out above also allows for the inclusion of gender into Benjamin's theoretical formulations. For all its sophistication and rigour Benjamin's approach seems oblivious to the workings of gender and its relevance to the construction of subjectivity. This is an aspect of his work that has started to receive critical attention.[41] What the work of contemporary critics like Rey Chow exposes is that, despite the fact that Benjamin has been hailed as the advocate of otherness and marginality, his work exhibits a blindness towards the category of gender. Furthermore, his notorious aesthetisation thesis and his attempt to explain fascist aesthetics all rely on a very problematic notion of gender, where aesthetic politics, which leads to fascism, is aligned with femininity. This feminisation is seen to undermine the proper masculine attributes of critical reflection and judgement. Here is a telling account of the role of femininity in the creative process:

> One [angle] deals with the creative conception and concerns the feminine in the work of the artist. This femininity exhausts itself with the completion. It gives birth to the work, but then it dies off. What dies in the master with the completed creation is that part in him in which he conceived the creation. Yet this completion of the work – and this leads us to the second aspect of the process – is nothing dead ... It takes place inside the work itself. And here, too, we are talking about a birth. The creation, in its state of completion, gives new birth to the creator. Not to his femininity, in which it was conceived, but rather to his male element. Newly inspired, he outdoes nature ... He is the male first born of the work that he had once conceived.[42]

Like another Oedipus, the artist gives birth to himself, mimicking the act of birth. Indeed, according to this formulation, the aim of artistic creation is the rebirth of masculinity, not from the body of the mother (nature), but through the work of art. The artistic process is seen as an initiation rite where the male artist (by definition) gives birth to himself, or rather is born again in the world of masculinity once he has killed the monstrous feminine. All the allusions to death and its association with femininity are striking both in this passage and in other early works by Benjamin.

What can we make of speculative aesthetics and philosophy once we have introduced the parameter of gender? Is it, too, gendered in the same ways as traditional models of philosophy? This analysis so far has attempted to include the category of gender in its approach. This is not done as a simple corrective to Benjamin. If we include Greek tragedy within the general trajectory of speculative philosophy rather than set it up as its eternal opposite, then the examination of gender is inevitable. We can even say that focusing on Greek tragedy while trying to create a genealogy for speculative aesthetics and *Trauerspiel* undoubtedly will lead us to introduce gender to the whole edifice of *theoria* and speculation.

This queering of Greek tragedy which states that it relies on a homo-hetero identification divide also helps to queer the philosophical thinking that is associated with tragedy. Gender differentiation, the anxieties it produces and the representation conventions it helps create have all featured in this approach. More specifically, the convention of men-playing-women can be seen to be constitutive and structural to a type of aesthetics that identifies artistic production with the construction of masculine identity. Introducing Greek tragedy to the study of *Trauerspiel* and speculation helps include gender in the analysis. This is not a simple corrective addition, restoring thematically something which has been absent. This analysis presumes that speculative philosophy allows for such a queering to take place. Indeed, it is based on it. Any aesthetic theory that is structured along the principles of physiognomy, topology, melancholia and allegory will at some stage stumble across the concept of gender and its differentiation. Whether psychoanalytically, anthropologically or structurally, this encounter needs to take place. The fact that it has not taken place already is more historical than purely theoretical. The theory/theoria of the *Trauerspiel*, like that of speculative philosophy, demands a reading of gender. The proposition put forward here is that the inclusion of Greek tragedy within this context leads to the incorporation of gender not only on the level of theme but also on those of structure, rhetoric and discourse.

This introduction of gender to the study of *theoria* is also fraught because tragic form does not directly and unproblematically represent gender; it is based on a queer reading of gender, where the feminine is absent but endlessly represented through the masculine. In turn this function is linked with homosexual male desire and anxieties of female reproduction. This contradictory aspect, particularly in regard to the position of the feminine, is inherent in and fundamental to tragic form. It is also crucial for the understanding of speculative philosophy in general.

Woman may be considered to be artistic, but she is rarely the artist. Representing falseness and theatricality, she needs to be endlessly mimicked by the male so that he too can learn how to make consciously what woman does in and of her own 'nature'. The male result, however, is art and not mere histrionics or neurosis. Through this process of copying the woman and creating art, the male gives birth to his greatest creation: himself. What the male is not aware of during this gestation is that he is copying a copy of a copy. As theories of performativity clearly show, the male creation, artistic or otherwise, is in the end plagued by the same structures of falseness and theatricality, making the process itself more obvious and self-referential, and undermining the assumption of a core essence, male or otherwise. This interaction, with its anthropological and psychoanalytical echoes, is clearly demonstrated by the acting convention of men-playing-women. Furthermore, it is the focus on this and its repercussions that helps to gender the thinking of Benjamin and to queer the thinking on *theoria* and speculation.

Trauerspiel and Tragedy: Atossa and Pentheus

The first tragedy we have from the Athenian canon, *The Persians*, is also the most difficult.[43] It is difficult to place in the Aristotelian model and it is notoriously difficult to stage. The whole play is one long song of mourning by Atossa, the Persian Queen, and the chorus of old men of Susa. It is also the only tragedy we have that is directly based on history rather than myth. This historical dimension of the play is paralleled by the equal emphasis, as both theme and theatrical convention, placed on mourning and lamentation. Indeed, Nicole Loraux claims that *The Persians* marks a shift in the way that the Athenians understood tragedy. It is the first and last historical play; it is also the last play where mourning is so unashamedly and overwhelmingly present. It is not disguised. It is physically present in its all its feminising and othering aspects. The stage is taken over by the mournful Persian Queen who is lamenting the fall of the Persian army to an all-Athenian audience. Reading the history of the Persians wars in this manner, through the guise of the defeated enemy, is extraordinary in any respect. The tensions between alterity and identification, distance and empathy, that this play examines are all heavily inflected by the modes of mourning that help structure it. Reading *The Persians* through the workings of the *Trauerspiel* and through the lens of Euripides (rather than the more Sophoclean character-based model), might help view it not as the exception – the sole historical/mournful tragedy – but as a precursor of Euripides himself. *The Persians* could be read as pre-echoing in its themes and in its form some of the traits that later were to mark the work of the stage philosopher Euripides. Its fascination with the 'barbarian' female protagonist, its reliance on mourning both in its theme and structure, and the ambivalent relationship it sets up with the Athenian audience are all traits that mark the works of Euripides. Atossa, the Queen of the Persians, and Pentheus, the mournful King of Thebes, might be read as mirroring each other, one at the start of Athenian tragedy and the other at the end. Both 'characters' are embodied through the workings of mourning, where an encounter with otherness and a gender reversal is significant. However, the journey from the first to the last mournful character of Athenian tragedy is not a straightforward one.

A few years before *The Persians* was presented (472) another tragedy by a little-known tragedian called Phrynichus was performed. This was *The Siege of Miletus* and it referred to the destruction of Miletus, an Ionian colony of Athens, by the Persians. What it also drew attention to was the fact that Athens had abandoned its colony, sacrificing the Ionian city to the

Persian invaders. Significantly, the play had brought the audience to tears, arousing feelings of remorse and shame, and in Platonic terms triggering the fear of an epidemic of uncontrollable grief. According to Herodotus, Phrynichus was fined a thousand drachmas and a law was passed prohibiting the performance of the play. Phrynichus himself, as a corrective gesture, wrote *The Phoenician Women* twenty years later. *The Persians* needs to be read in the shadow of that extraordinary ban. Nicole Loraux writes:

> When *The Persians* was presented in 472, the Athenian audience received it with enthusiasm and Aeschylus won the prize for tragedy. Was this simply because, from *The Capture of Miletus* to *The Persians*, victory had changed sides and mourning had changed its sign . . .
> If the formula of *The Persians* was such a good one, why was it not imitated?[44]

I would claim that this formula, which allowed for the safe rendering of mourning, was not so much imitated as intertextually reworked. Excessive female mourning is mediated through the *hypocrisis* of the male actor (where *hypocrisis* etymologically refers both to a mode of acting and to the ideas of judgement/crisis/critique); the Athenians are allowed to identify with their enemies while also being asked to take pride in their victory; they are allowed to cry for their victims but also for themselves. Loraux's answer to the problem posed by *The Persians* reworks the opposition between *andres*, Athenian citizens and soldiers, and *anthropoi*, humans. She claims that the text shifts between the two (or rather uses the epithets *brotos* and *thnetos*, both meaning mortal) in a movement that finally subsumes the political category of *andres* under the general humanist term of *anthropoi*. This, she claims, makes for an anti-political (as opposed to apolitical) reading of mourning, as the specific mourning triggered by the historical event dissolves into an all-encompassing humanism:

> Once again, through the evocation of mourning, despite the forgetting prescribed by the city-state, the spectator will be overcome, and purgation will arouse him to transcend his membership in the civic community and to comprehend his even more essential membership in the race of mortals. This has always been the final word sung, not so much to the citizen as to the spectator, by the mourning voice of tragedy.[45]

The transcendental reading of tragedy is restored through the function of mourning. In many ways, this book tries to restore mourning's metaphysical dimension through the primary separation of the categories of the citizen and the human. As we have seen, however, the categories of *andres* and *anthropoi* are sometimes conflated (as was the case in *Antigone*). The etymological ambivalence of *anthropoi* does not allow it to dissolve into an all-embracing humanism but might be marked by gender as well (in yet another conflation of *andres* and *anthropoi*). The emphasis on aspects of performance might further help to investigate how this conflation comes about.

Atossa, the Queen of the Persians, is central to our reading of the play. In an inversion that will always mark a court in crisis – that of a female ruler surrounded by a chorus of old men – Atossa becomes the kaleidoscope through which the audience is asked to encounter the Persians and the historical reality of their defeat. The actor playing her may have been a soldier as well and, according to legend, it may have even been Aeschylus himself. Atossa seems to embody, in a wonderfully seamless mergence, the various kinds of citizenship: soldier, actor and poet. The fact that these categories are all filtered in a double take through the feminine and the barbarian is also significant. At once it points to the interdependency of these two categories, gender and otherness, and in turn to the constitutive relationships between the categories of citizenship and their exclusions. The figure of Atossa becomes an allegorical trope through which all these issues are enacted on the stage. Through her mourning she invites the audience to occupy all these positions, possibly stressing the fact that no single position can be taken unless its exclusions are also occupied. This might prove an impossible task; it may also be why the first rendition of the feminine barbarian we have of the Athenian stage is also the first mournful one.

If 'allegories are, in the realm of thoughts, what ruins are in the realm of things', as Benjamin states, then Atossa presents us with such an allegory. As it is enacted, physically embodied, the ruins in the realm of thoughts and those characterised by their 'thingness' merge into one. It is not as if Atossa simply and directly represents the historical loss of the Persians. She becomes the formal, performative mechanism through which this loss is transformed into knowledge and critique. Terry Eagleton writes in his book on Benjamin:

> The mortified landscape of history is redeemed, not by being recuperated into Spirit, but by being raised, so to speak, to the second power – converted into a formal repertoire, fashioned into certain enigmatic emblems which then hold the promise of knowledge and possession.[46]

Atossa presents us with such a formal device. Rather than asking the audience of Athenian citizens to identify with the Persians through their common membership of the race of mortals, she invites them to identify through a series of differences. The allegorical trope allows her to do this.

Instead of the seamless closure of the symbol, whose impact would have been to recuperate the historical loss in terms of a shared humanity and a common mortality, the reliance on allegory and emblem propose a different relationship to the historical process. In other words, instead of representing ruins, Atossa is one herself. It is as if, in the words of Benjamin, 'history has physically merged into the setting'. Furthermore, like the princes of the *Trauerspiel*, Atossa has visionary dreams. In what is probably the first dream sequence in European theatre, Atossa says:

> Dreams haunt me.
> Night after night they come,
> Since my son drummed up his army
> Marched on Greece. Dream after dream –
> And none so clear as in this last night.
> Two women came: well-dressed,
> One in Persian elegance, one Dorian.
> In bearing both belittled us today:
> In beauty flawless sisters;
> In race identical. Their native lands?
> One Greek, one . . . not-Greek.
>
> (172–86)

This dream bears all the signs that define the play. These two women, although sisters, civically belong to different lands, to different states. Their difference is marked politically and not metaphysically. The markers of Persian and Dorian do not appear as fixed and transcendental categories but appear in the way they are dressed. This emphasis on dress and clothing sets up another opposition in the play, as the Persians are presented as indulgent and overdressed, marking exteriority, while the Greeks, the inventors of the 'golden mean', are modest, always a sign of a rich inner life. Towards the end of the play, Xerxes tears his clothes off, in a gesture that mimics mourning ritual. The vision of a king almost naked, divested of the symbols of power, verges on the obscene. Yet this is the image that ends the play. Before the audience reaches this end, they are asked to occupy a number of impossible positions, including the one occupied by the actor himself who plays Atossa.

It is the image of the King in rags, presented by Euripides in *The Bacchae*,[47] that supposedly angered his host, the King of Macedon, and led to his legendary death, according to which he was torn apart, limb-by-limb by dogs. Pentheus, the King of Thebes, whose name is etymologically linked with mourning, is the last tragic character of the Athenian stage. Although written in exile and never seen on that stage in the playwright's lifetime, I would claim that the figure of Pentheus is intertextually connected with the first tragic role of the canon, that of Atossa. The mournful Queen of the Persians and the King of Thebes, whose name means mourning, mark a trajectory of performance practice that constantly renegotiates the role of mourning in relation to the city-state, to gender differentiation and to theatrical representation itself. Euripides, in exile and in fear of his life, creates in the role of Pentheus, a ruse through which he re-examines mourning in the democratic *polis*. Rather than doing this through the mask of the barbarian, as is the case with Atossa, he does this through an extraordinary reworking of the Theban cycle. Away from the city of Athens, which would have provided him with the collective interpretative framework that would both produce this drama and receive it, Euripides creates a figure that intertextually is in dialogue with the original mourning character: Atossa.

There is evidence that Euripides is in dialogue with Aeschylus. His *Electra*, for example, consciously rewrites the recognition scene between Electra and Orestes from *The Oresteia*, and it is no coincidence that Aristophanes in *The Frogs* brings back Aeschylus and Euripides from Hades in an attempt to resurrect a poet who could save the city. In this debate Aeschylus is presented as the conservative traditionalist and Euripides as the somewhat decadent innovator. Surely Euripides, who severs the supposed organic link between his theatre and the democratic *polis*, is aware of the role he occupies in relation to his predecessors. I would like to propose a reading of Pentheus that sees him in conjunction with Aeschylus' Atossa. Through the Theban King (with Thebes functioning as the mirror to Athens) and from the ostracised position of another kingdom, a third kingdom, Euripides presents us with a character who both highlights and critiques the role of mourning in tragedy. Significantly, gender plays a crucial role in this dialogue.

Dionysus returns to the city of Thebes to prove that he is the son of Zeus. His genealogy is contested, as through various mythic technologies of reproduction he is one of the hybrid creatures who occupy both worlds. His divine status has been challenged so he returns to Thebes, where he was born from Zeus' lightning bolt and the mortal Semele. The women of Thebes, who initially doubted his divine lineage, have all been driven mad, 'homes abandoned they all roam the mountains, out of their senses, deranged: every last woman in Thebes, up there amongst the rocks and the trees, witless and homeless, Cadmus' daughters among them' (33–9). Indeed, Cadmus and Tiresias, as knowledgeable representatives of the old world order, want to join in these orgies. The only one to resist Dionysus is Pentheus. The King of Thebes and the stately power he represents are threatened by the arrival of this eastern god. And it is crucial to remember that Dionysus is the god of theatre. This god, however, was never fully accepted into the Olympian pantheon and occupied an ambivalent position even within tragedy itself. He is rarely referred to and almost never makes an appearance on stage. However, he is vital for the function of tragedy – something that the Euripidean text is glaringly aware of. This return of Dionysus to the stage prompts Nietzsche to state that it is Dionysus' revenge on Euripides for having abandoned him in his previous plays. This, in turn, has triggered the ritualistic and quasi-aestheticist readings of the play that see it as a corrective to the Athenian obsession with order, form and reason, epitomised by Apollo. It is as if *The Bacchae* charts the return of the repressed for the Athenian *polis*.

I would like to inflect the above reading by restating that *The Bacchae* is not simply a play that celebrates raw and unmediated violence (although it does this as well). It is not a case of Dionysus usurping Apollo in the collective sensibility of the audience. Too much reason, this reading maintains, only breeds madness in the end. Rather through a series of complicated rewrites and citations Euripides' play quite deliberately points towards the shortcomings of the Athenian *polis* but also its prime collective aesthetic expression: the tragedy. In rewriting tragic form through an emphasis on gender and mourning, *The Bacchae* appears as an unmediated paean to violence, but is also a subtle political critique of both the city and the institution of tragedy. The comparison between Pentheus and Atossa might prove helpful in proposing a reading of *The Bacchae* that is not only ritualistic and orgiastic but also political and historical.

It is Dionysus that usually receives most of the critical attention in this play. Pentheus, however, is equally interesting. This mourning king, whose name prophesies his end, is fascinated with Dionysus and the orgies he inspires. After trying to restrain him, he finally gives in and decides he wants to take part in these orgies outside the city. However, he can only do so by dressing as a woman:

> Dionysus: You will have to put on a dress. Linen, something like that.
> Pentheus: A dress? What do you mean? Dress like a woman?
> Dionysus: They would murder a man if they saw him, now wouldn't they?
> Pentheus: Yes, of course. You are right. You have thought it all out.
> Dionysus: Call it inspiration. From Dionysus.
> Pentheus: A clever idea. Now what?
> Dionysus: Come indoors. I will help get you dressed.
> Pentheus: Get dressed. I don't think I have the nerve. Not like a woman.
> Dionysus: Do you want a peep at the Maenads, or do you not?
> Pentheus: A dress, you say? What sort of dress do you have in mind for me?
> Dionysus: The dress should be full length. And a wig, a long one.
>
> (821–31)

This is an extraordinary sequence. Atossa, the mournful Persian Queen, would have been played by a male actor. Pentheus, the King of mourning, dresses up as a woman just before his *peripeteia* is about to commence. Indeed, it is the reversal of gender roles that signals the end of the kingdom itself. This complex set of relationships between gender, representation and theatrical convention, I would claim, is problematised in this play through the use of constant citation and meta-theatricality. This is further heightened through the use of mourning as both theme and structure of the play. From Atossa, male actor playing the Persian Queen, we reach Pentheus, a king cross-dressing on stage. This at once nods towards this 'grand' convention but also exhibits its shortcomings. From the heightened grandeur of the mourning Queen, we are thrust into a world that is distressingly similar to what we would today recognise as misogynist drag. And this is how this scene is usually performed, drawing out the comedic elements in the cross-dressing. However, the Euripidean text uses this comedic aberration to comment on the convention itself. If a king cross-dressing on stage generates laughter, or at least a reluctant smile, then this is what the Athenian actors are doing all the time, it seems to be saying. Furthermore, this excursion into the feminine, which at the same time signals social exclusion, seems to come at a price. The state of Thebes starts to collapse when Pentheus cross-dresses on stage. The blurring of gender roles (also refracted in the play through the oppositions of city/country, Hellene/barbarian, new/old and so on) brings about the collapse of the city-state. Pentheus' desire to look, 'to peep', as the text states, also comments on the function of the audience. Interestingly, the act of seeing is also structured as phallic, as the following sequence clearly shows:

> Messenger: . . . Then I saw the foreigner do an extraordinary thing. He took hold of a soaring ranch from one of the pines, and he pulled it, pulled it right down to the dark earth. He bent it over like a bow or the curved felloe on a wheel. Just so did this strange man take that tree in his two hands, and bend it to the ground. No ordinary man could have done it. His strength was superhuman. He sat Pentheus astride the branches, and let the tree slowly straighten, taking care not to unseat him. Up it went, up towards the sky, my master on its back, for all the Maenads to see, plainer than he saw them.
>
> (1063–73)

The power invested in the act of seeing here turns against the viewer, leaving him exposed, prey to the hunt of the Maenads. Pentheus' feminine clothes are ripped into shreds as he is hunted down and significantly beheaded by his mother, Agave, who mistakes him for a lion. This is also how Pentheus comes to enact his name. The end of the King and the end of the Kingdom come about through gender reversal and through close scrutiny of the function of viewing itself, which has turned into a quasi-pornographic activity. This is a damning critique that Euripides voices against both the Athenian *polis* and the institution of tragedy.

Reading Atossa and Pentheus in tandem this way, as allegorical characters rather than as symbolic or psychological ones, allows us also to focus on mourning. If *The Persians* can be read as a *Trauerspiel*, a play based on fact that negotiates historical loss through mourning, then *The Bacchae* could be read almost as a modern tragedy, where mourning has become cited and theatricalised, revealing the particular anxieties that the form conveys towards the feminine. As noted earlier, this allegorical site formally conveys similar anxieties about the feminine. These are paralleled, as Nägele claims, with anxieties about cannibalism and dismemberment (all present in *The Bacchae*). As is the case with Plato's anti-theatricalism, Goethe's and Hegel's worries about allegory (as feminising, barren and as a grammatical index) might contain a grain of truth. However, for all these reasons and not in spite of them, allegory becomes an appropriate trope in approaching the figures of Atossa and Pentheus.

Notes

1. Walter Benjamin, *The Origin of German Tragic Drama* (1928), trans. John Osborne (London: Verso, 1998), p. 235.
2. See Lutz Koepnick, *Walter Benjamin and the Aesthetics of Power* (Lincoln and London: University of Nebraska Press, 1999); Michael W. Jennings, *Dialectical Images: Walter Benjamin's Theory of Literary Criticism* (Ithaca: Cornell University Press, 1987), pp. 121–211.
3. For an insightful analysis of these sections, see Rainer Nägele, *Theatre, Theory, Speculation: Walter Benjamin and the Scenes of Modernity* (Baltimore: Johns Hopkins University Press, 1991), pp. 108–34.
4. For an account of Benjamin's relationship with Gershom Scholem and Theodor Adorno, see Richard Wolin, *Walter Benjamin: An Aesthetic of Redemption* (Berkeley: University of California Press, 1994) and Bernd White, *Walter Benjamin: An Intellectual Biography*, trans. James Rolleston (Detroit: Wayne State University Press, 1991).
5. See Benjamin, *The Origin of German Tragic Drama*, pp. 188–9.
6. See Olga Taxidou, *The Mask: A Periodical Performance by Edward Gordon Craig* (Amsterdam: Harwood Academic Publishers, 1998).
7. Gunter Berghaus, *Fascism and Theatre: Comparative Studies on the Aesthetics and Politics of Performance in Europe, 1925–45* (Oxford: Berghahn Books, 1996).
8. See John Willet (ed. and trans.), *Brecht on Theatre* (London: Methuen, 1978) and Walter Benjamin, *Understanding Brecht*, 1966, trans. Anna Bostock (London: Verso, 1983).

9. Friedrich Nietzsche, *The Birth of Tragedy*,1872, sect.4, in vol. 1 of A. Tille and T. Fisher (eds), *The Works of Friedrich Nietzsche* (London: Unwin, 1899). For the impact, see Patrick Bridgwater, *Nietzsche in Anglosaxony: A Study of Nietzsche's Impact on English and American Literature* (Leicester: Leicester University Press, 1972); M. S. Silk and J. P. Stern, *Nietzsche on Tragedy* (Cambridge: Cambridge University Press, 1981); for the impact on modernist dramatic theory, see Laurence Senelick (ed., and trans.), *Russian Dramatic Theory from Pushkin to the Symbolists* (Austin: University of Texas Press, 1981).
10. Benjamin, *The Origin of German Tragic Drama*, p. 103.
11. For a critique of Benjamin's aesthetisation thesis, see Boris Groys, *The Total Art of Stalinism: Avant-garde, Aesthetic Dictatorship and Beyond*, trans. Charles Rougle (Princeton: Princeton University Press, 1992).
12. Friedrich Nietzsche, *Basic Writings of Nietzsche*, trans. and ed. Walter Kaufman (New York: Princeton University Press, 1971), p. 52.
13. See Philippe Lacoue-Labarthe, 'Hölderlin's Theatre', in Miguel de Beistegui and Simon Sparks (ed.), *Philosophy and Tragedy* (London: Routledge, 2000), pp. 117–36.
14. It is interesting to note that most scholars now call 'Greek' tragedy 'Athenian' tragedy, which is historically correct. See Pat Easterling (ed.) *The Cambridge Companion to Greek Tragedy* (Cambridge: Cambridge University Press, 1997).
15. Benjamin, *The Origin of Tragic German Drama*, p. 29.
16. See Nägele *Theatre, Theory and Speculation*, p. 2.
17. Benjamin, *The Origin of Tragic German Drama*, p. 27.
18. Friedrich Hölderlin, *Essays and Letters on Theory*, trans. Thomas Pfau (Albany: SUNY, 1988), p. 83.
19. Ibid. p. 101.
20. Ibid. p. 101–2.
21. See Nägele, *Theatre, Theory and Speculation*, p. 39.
22. Benjamin, *The Origin of German Tragic Drama*, p. 178.
23. Although *The Origin* was written before Benjamin's strictly Marxist period, it is during the time that he is writing it that he meets Asja Lacis and is introduced through her to Marxist theory. See Bernd White, *Walter Benjamin: An Intellectual Biography*, pp. 68–88.
24. See Benjamin, *The Origin of German Tragic Drama*, p. 109.
25. See Nägele, *Theatre, Theory and Speculation*, p. 90.
26. Ibid. pp. 90–1.
27. Hegel, *Werke*, vol. 13, *Vorlesungen zur Asthetik* (Frankfurt am Main: Suhrkamp, 1970), pp. 511–13. Quoted in Nägele, *Theatre, Theory and Speculation*, p. 21, his translation.
28. See Edward Braun, *Meyerhold on Theatre* (London: Methuen, 1986).
29. For a feminist reading of Benjamin, see Rey Chow, 'Benjamin's Love Affair with Death', *New German Critique* 48 (1989): 63–86; and Eva Geulen, 'Toward a Genealogy of Gender in Walter Benjamin's Writing', *German Quarterly* 69.2 (1996): 161–80.
30. Hegel, *Phenomenology of Spirit*, trans. A. V. Miller (Oxford: Oxford University Press, 1977), pp. 18–19.
31. See Nägele, *Theatre, Theory and Speculation*, p. 92.
32. See Benjamin, *The Origin of German Tragic Drama*, p. 191.

33. Nägele, *Theatre, Theory and Speculation*, p. 93.
34. Benjamin, *The Origin of German Tragic Drama*, p. 139.
35. Nicole Loraux, *The Invention of Athens: The Funeral Oration in the Classical City*, trans. Alan Sheridan (Harvard: Harvard University Press, 1992), p. 328.
36. Thucydides, *The History of the Peloponnesian War*, trans. Robert Crawley (London: Everyman, 1993), pp. 87–88.
37. In the case of Pericles' funeral oration this is used to define Athenian democracy. This ends with: 'And where the rewards for merit are greatest, there are found the best citizens', ibid. pp. 88–94.
38. Benjamin, *The Origin of German Tragic Drama*, p. 121.
39. Judith Butler, *The Psychic Life of Power: Theories in Subjection* (Stanford: Stanford University Press, 1997), pp. 145–6. Also see her chapter on 'Melancholy Gender/Refused Identification', pp. 132–51.
40. Benjamin, *The Origin of German Tragic Drama*, p. 49.
41. See note 29 above.
42. Walter Benjamin, *Gesammelte Schriften*, ed. Rolf Tiedemann and Herman Schweppenhauser (Frankfurt am Main: Suhrkamp, 1971–89), vol. 4 p. 438. Quoted in Koepnick, *Walter Benjamin and the Aesthetics of Power*, p. 88.
43. Euripides, *The Persians*, trans. Frederick Raphael and Kenneth McLeish, (London: Methuen, 1991), pp. 1–36.
44. Nicole Loraux, *The Mourning Voice: An Essay on Greek Tragedy*, trans. Elizabeth Trapnell Rawlings (Ithica and London: Cornell University Press, 2002).
45. Ibid. p. 93.
46. Terry Eagleton, *Walter Benjamin or Towards a Revolutionary Criticism* (London: Verso, 1981), p. 20.
47. Euripides, *The Bacchae* trans. J. Michael Walton (London: Methuen, 1988), pp. 111–47.

CHAPTER FOUR

Euripides and Aristotle: Friends in Mourning

This study, so far, has been Brechtian in its aspirations. With its emphasis on distance and speculation, on form and convention, it attempts to question the sometimes given familiarity with which we greet Athenian tragedy. When we approach the work of Euripides, however, familiarity and sameness seem to be the dominant modes. Indeed, in terms of late twentieth-century production and reception, Euripides is seen to be the 'modern' of the three tragedians. Psychological character, suspicion of the gods, emphasis on women and slaves are all categories which contemporary scholars invoke to present us with a playwright who is at once part and parcel of the Athenian miracle but also deeply sceptical of it. Euripides is seen as having severed the supposed organic relationship between the playwright and his society that was inaugurated by Aeschylus and fully embodied by Sophocles. Euripides is the radical, the outsider, the poet who is forced to leave Athens itself, the unpopular one at the contests who dares to show the Athenians and their democracy their shortcomings. He questions the limits of Athenian democracy to such an extent that he has to leave the *polis* that has helped to create and nurture his very art form. In this sense Euripides introduces a new model of the playwright or poet, shattering the myth of the organic coupling between the theatre and the *polis* and proposing a view of the artist as an outsider, as critical of the society in which he works. The harmonious unity of the aesthetic and the political, for example, that is enacted through the work and persona of Sophocles (and his relationship with Pericles) is once and for all broken through the work and life of Euripides. What Euripides quite emphatically brings to the stage of Athenian drama is the category of critique and constructs a new identity for the notion of the playwright in the process.

Without diverting from this reading of Euripides as the most radical of the three playwrights, the approach proposed here wants to question whether the supposed modernity of Euripides can be read through the categories of character and psychology that are usually presented as arguments for his 'contemporaneity'. Instead, I suggest that the category of character is closely scrutinised and undermined in the works of Euripides. His modernity lies less in the fact that he presents us with recognisable characters than in the way he formally and thematically questions the role of character and individuality within the limits of the democratic *polis*. What we as moderns recognise in Euripides is a formal experimentation, very close to modernist experimentation itself, rather than a humanist version of the individual. Indeed, Euripides, the most quintessentially meta-theatrical of all the tragedians, introduces a critique of tragic form and experiments with its limitations.

It is fascinating to note that, despite his modernity, Euripides is the one tragedian who is the least attractive to the philosophies of modernity. In a long tradition instigated by Aristotle, Sophocles is the favourite among philosophers. The German Idealist and Romantic tradition, for example, which is crucial for re-theorising tragic form, almost ignores Euripides. This is particularly striking in the cases where the aesthetic, invariably read through the tragic, seeks to encompass the category of critique. Euripides should provide the ideal model but he is practically ignored in discussions that try to reconcile the aesthetic and the political. There are many reasons for this, ranging from Nietzsche's damning of Euripides as having brought about the death of tragedy[1] to the formal and experimental complexities of the plays themselves. Ironically, the 'stage philosopher', as he was called in his time, gets very little attention from philosophy.

Aristotle and Aristotelianism on the one end of the spectrum and Nietzsche's impact on the other have created a version of tragic poetics that relies almost solely on Sophocles[2] and is by analogy defined against Euripides. In a somewhat arbitrary manner I would like to introduce a Stanislavskian 'what if?' into the equation. Together with the unlikely partnership of Brecht, this imaginary scenario would like to investigate the possibility of a tragic poetics that gets its inspiration from Euripides rather than Sophocles. At the same time, the notion of tragedy as speculative philosophy will be approached with a Euripidean aesthetic in mind. The ideas of loss, fragmentation and melancholy, together with concepts of gender and power, will inform this approach to Euripides, which also tries to encompass formal elements of performance. The whole homosocial dimension of tragedy will be read through the particular lens of Euripides. The play-texts chosen to exemplify this experiment are *Helen* and *The Madness of Hercules*. Helen and Hercules, the epitome of femininity and masculinity respectively, are seen as emblems of a Euripidean aesthetic that interrogates the structural relationships among gender, power and the state, while also introducing a critique of theatrical convention and tragic form.

It is a commonly held assumption that Aristotle's preference for Sophocles is primarily based on their shared understanding of the function of tragic character. Furthermore, the whole Sophoclean world-view seems to be endorsed by the morality proposed in the *Poetics*. Martha C. Nussbaum comments on this parallel:

> It seems to me that Aristotle's characterization of the good person in adversity fits very well with Sophoclean tragedy – in which the hero's nobility does 'shine through' in calamity, and in which his or her unshaken disposition to do the best is a source of honor, even if he is not, finally, *eudaimon*... On the whole Sophoclean tragedy is dedicated to the assertion of unbending virtue in the fact of a hostile and uncomprehending world, and dedicated, too, to manifesting that human virtue has not in fact been altogether extinguished by the obstacles that menace it.[3]

This reading of Aristotle tends to privilege the category of 'character' and sees it as separate and distinct from 'action'. It then proceeds to focus on the ability of that character to differentiate itself initially from the communal and then in turn to stand in for the general good. We, the community, the audience, can then learn through identifying with this character. Their suffering becomes our suffering. Their response of pity and fear helps cause our *katharsis*. It is a reading that presupposes that the audience reacts as individuals. Indeed, in many ways, it constructs the audience as a group of distinct and separate individuals. Or, as Brecht would have it, it creates the illusion of individuality, while emotionally manipulating the audience's reaction.

This reception of Aristotle, however, as Nussbaum acknowledges, 'does not fare well with Dionysus'. Dionysus represents the quintessentially anti-humanist view of character, where the relationship between the individual and the communal is seen as inextricably bound, where one cannot really exist without the other. Dionysus, the shape-shifter, the transformer, the bisexual, is at the same time central to tragedy both in terms of themes and form. Although traditionally Dionysus is identified with the 'ritualistic' and unrational side of the tragic, in approaching Euripides I would like to introduce a reading of Dionysus that goes against the reading that sees him/her as representing flux, amorphous matter, pure otherness. Instead, this analysis claims that the Dionysus enacted in Euripides, particularly in *The Bacchae*,[4] is one that breaks down the binary between self and other, between the individual and the collective, between man and woman. Through the meta-theatrical use of Dionysus, Euripidean tragedy, contra to the reading that sees Apollo as the form giver, introduces a *critical* version of the god and his/her myth. Indeed, this view of Dionysus as providing not the matter but, more importantly, the form of the tragic constructs a version of the god not only as shape-shifter but also as shape-giver.

The self-referential use of Dionysus that we find in the work of Euripides fits almost too neatly the reading of tragedy as speculative philosophy. The speculation that Dionysus represents is enacted through tragic form itself. The fact that this is done in Euripides, the most sceptical and philosophical of all the tragic poets, creates a kind of poetics that is at once anti-Aristotelian and anti-humanist. This anti-humanism, however, does not rely solely on a version of otherness that defines itself against reason, linearity and progress. The Dionysus of the Euripidean stage is at once the same and other, reason and unreason. Euripides provides us with a way of turning myth into philosophy while still maintaining the power and impact of both categories. This coexistence is possible because of the formal properties of tragedy itself. The Euripidean Dionysus is both ritualistic and critical, both spectacular and speculative. This approach changes both tragic form and philosophy in the process. Indeed, this reading of Dionysus is possible in and by Euripides because he is working and citing tragic form. The 'stage philosopher' manages to spectacularise and theatricalise philosophy. At the same time, the stage, the *skene*, not only becomes the platform for the enactment of critical ideas, but also provides the language and the conventions that help create them. In this way theatre, tragic form, becomes philosophical.

This notion of tragic form as spectacular philosophy, embodied crucially by Euripides, is not as anti-Aristotelian as it initially may appear. If we shift the emphasis from character to action, as many readings of the *Poetics* propose, then we arrive at a very different view of tragedy. Elizabeth Belfiore writes on some of the problems derived from this character-centred view:

> This character-centered view has important consequences for studies of Greek tragedy, and for interpretations of the *Poetics*. For one thing, it often leads scholars to attempt to find a psychological realism in Greek tragedy that the dramatic conventions of this genre did not allow and that the extant plays do not display. The inappropriateness of the view that characters in Greek drama are psychological entities much like their real-life counterparts is now widely recognized . . .
>
> Another consequence of the modern character-centered view of tragedy, however, is less well understood. This is the tendency of many scholars to incorporate character into plot.[5]

Although Aristotle claims that 'without action there could be no tragedy; without character there could be' (6.145a 23–5), the predominant view is that tragedy is character-based or, as Stephen Halliwell puts it, 'agent-centered'.[6] Despite the significant difference between character and agency, action still determines tragic form. Indeed, it is a very specific type of action; it is a mimesis of praxis. Without delineating the complexity of the debates surrounding mimesis, for example, its claim to realist representation and its relevance to theories of narrative in general, it is important to stress that Aristotelian mimesis is essentially dramatic in nature. It is a form of dramatic enactment that relies on the body of the actor, on the one hand, and on the physical presence and reception by an audience, on the other. Indeed, it could be read as a formal equivalent of the performative – it relies on showing rather than telling while also depending on the interpretive re-enforcement of an audience.

This reading of mimesis that privileges the showing over the telling presupposes a particular theoretical perspective and raises a number of intriguing questions for further analysis. At first glance it should prove attractive to philosophers of modernity, as it seems to offer a way of reconciling philosophy and tragedy under the rubric of narrative. Indeed, this approach would have to assume that both forms of discourse are in fact that – discourse – and manifest themselves in varying narrative forms. However, this reading would deprive philosophy of its discursive hegemony. This issue, together with the undeniable fact of the love affair between philosophy and Sophocles, with its overall emphasis on the category of character, has left this aspect of mimesis relatively unexplored until quite recently.

There is, however, a body of work that redefines mimesis as enactment. This approach locates Aristotle's use of the term within the general philosophical discussions between himself and Plato.[7] Indeed, as some recent scholars have noted, Aristotle writes about tragedy as a philosopher.[8] Rather than seeing this as a negative aspect, I would like to examine the possibility that Aristotle's mimesis is equivalent to the philosophical notion of the performative. Plato himself in the *Republic* draws a distinction between two tropes of *lexis*:[9] one is *haple diegesis*, simple or direct narration, and the other, which he calls mimesis, involves the poet taking on the *persona* of someone else. In the case of *haple diegesis*, 'the poet himself speaks, without attempting to turn our attention elsewhere as though someone else other than he were the speaker'.[10] This act of assuming a *persona*, or a psychological character, makes *mimesis*, as Plato defines it, potentially corrupting both towards the world (or truth) that is being represented and towards the actor undertaking the act of mimesis. Indeed, in Platonic terms, mimesis is chiefly located in the notion of the *persona*. Here, for Plato, lies its danger. It is fascinating to note that this debate takes place in a *dramatic dialogue* between Socrates and Adeimantus. It is, however, a dramatic dialogue that is narrated rather than enacted. It is as if philosophy itself appropriates drama in order to voice a quintessentially anti-theatrical argument. The act of imitation is achieved through writing alone, not through physical and bodily enactment. The particular narrative and rhetoric of the dramatic dialogue on the page and its relation to drama on the stage merits a study that is, however, beyond the scope of this analysis. This act of ventriloquy is part of a long-standing philosophical tradition that takes on the voice of the drama, imitating it in order to declare its own discursive superiority. As is the case with the debate between Plato and Aristotle, this is always a political argument as well.[11]

In this context Aristotle's use of the term mimesis could be read as an attempt to reclaim the term and, in the process, to restore the political usefulness of tragedy. Rather than locating mimesis in *persona*, or character, as Plato would have it, Aristotle applies a more general use of the term, describing tragedy as mimesis of an action. The action itself must be *spoudaios* (serious) and must be complete after a duration of time (*teleias megethos ekhouses*). It is delivered through *hedysmeno logo* (sweetened language) and, most importantly, *dronton kai ou di apangelias* (through acting and not through narration).[12] In other words, tragedy involves mimetic action; it does not simply describe action. This notion of mimesis does not rely on persona, or character. It relies primarily on enactment. Indeed, we might suggest that this notion of enactment helps carry or even construct the idea of the dramatic character. What is clear, however, in Aristotelian terms, is that action and its mimetic re-enactment, the drama, is at the core of tragedy, not character. Aryeh Kosman makes the following comments on the use of the term *dronton*:

> This word is an inflected form of *dran*, which Aristotle has earlier reminded his readers is the Doric for *to act*, equivalent to Attic *prattein*.
> To describe a tragedy thus as acted is to make clear that the medium of the mimesis of an action is itself an action. But in using a term which is equivalent to but distinct from the standard Attic term for action Aristotle makes clear that it is an action of a special and peculiar character. It is an action which is an instance not of *prattein* or praxis, but of *dran*. We may describe such action using a scholastic distinction as *formally* a drama and *objectively* a praxis . . . it is a drama because it is the mimesis of a *praxis*.[13]

In emphasising the crucial role of action over character, Aristotle is also proposing a reading of tragedy that allows for a rather dispassionate experience on the part of the audience. Against the Platonic view of tragedy as potentially corrupting for both actors and audience, this view of the tragic as performative enactment dissolves the fixation with ideas of psychology and identification. The pity and fear that traditionally help bring about *katharsis* need not necessarily involve psychological identification. If anything Aristotle's general reworking of the term mimesis, contra Plato, adds a level of self-reference that underlines the iconicity, the fictional mechanisms of all artistic representation. Rather than create an illusion of closeness it endows the stage with a quality of strangeness, of otherness, which requires that we experience pity and fear dispassionately. Kosman comments on this:

> The deep ontological otherness of the fictional thus enables us to experience these emotions, as it were, *dispassionately*. Our awareness that we are not to rush down the aisle to prevent Hamlet's stabbing of Polonius, an awareness which is an important element in our grasp of the mimetic, has its emotional counterpart in our ability to experience pity and fear in the context of the theatre without the affective consequences and connections that accompany fear and pity in the contexts of, as we say, real life.[14]

However, given the ontological awareness that a play is a play and that members of the audience are always aware that they are at the theatre, there are still schools of theatre whose intentionality and very reason for existence lie in the fact that they try to elide that difference. Most of the schools of theatre that see art as a mirror of life, as a direct and unmediated representation, and most of the debates on realism and naturalism in the theatre or otherwise claim Aristotle as their predecessor. But they rely on a misreading of the mimetic function in Aristotle. Hence the abuse that the term 'Aristotelian' has suffered in recent critical and literary theory. It came to stand for verisimilitude with an emphasis on psychological character and linear development of plot. In this way a direct line has been drawn from Aeschylus to Ibsen.

Brecht's supposed anti-Aristotelianism further polarised and schematised this debate. Aristotle and tragedy came to stand for empathy, psychology and identification – a process of making and receiving art that for Brecht was basically anti-historical and relied on the aura of the bourgeois subject. Instead his epic theatre, as opposed to Aristotle's dramatic theatre, would rely on abstraction and distance, on historical process and the collective rather than the hero or the individual. As mentioned elsewhere in this book, this is a historical debate that has generated a very useful body of work, which is crucial for contemporary performance theory. However, the fact that this historical debate relies on a fundamental misunderstanding misses other potential readings of this creative and argumentative dialogue.

The quasi-structuralist analysis of Aristotle's definition of tragedy proposed above, with its stress on action as citationality, on distance rather than identification, finds very exciting parallels with the Brechtian project. As has become apparent at various stages of this analysis, Brecht's and Benjamin's search for a mode of theatre that is political and non-representational, that relies on type rather than character and that uses *gestus* as its mode of representing rather than verisimilitude, finds an unlikely ally in Aristotle's effort to rehabilitate tragedy as a socially useful art form in the face of the criticisms launched against it by Plato. As with Brecht and Benjamin, who seek to use theatre for the workings of a revolutionary project within modernity, Aristotle might be read (together with his artistic narrative partner Sophocles) as attempting to create a space for theatre within the democratic *polis*. Both these projects encompass 'theoretical' writing on theatre that elide the distinction or opposition between philosophy and tragedy (or theatre in general). One is seen as the double of the other, as Artaud would have it. And both narrative couples, as it were, are writing within a philosophical tradition that is essentially anti-Platonic.

The term *katharsis* is pertinent in this context. Allegedly it is the impact of *katharsis* on an audience that Plato and Brecht, to a certain extent, find repulsive. Both seem to agree that it is the fact that it is achieved through pity and fear that make Aristotle's *katharsis* unacceptable. The term *katharsis* itself receives little attention in the works of Aristotle as a whole, but has generated a wide-reaching and sophisticated debate within classical scholarship and literary theory as it pertains to important issues of reception and understanding of tragic form, or the work of art in general.[15] Indeed, if *katharsis* refers to the audience at all and not simply and directly to the tragic protagonist – an issue which is never resolved in Aristotle – then it is a case of a theory of poetics that has already inscribed a theory of reception. In view of the emphasis we have been placing on the civic and political but also on the purely physical and bodily impact of tragedy, the term acquires particular significance.

The main concern of these debates is with the issues of purgation and/or instruction or correction. Do the feelings of pity and fear bring about an emotional purgation, in a manner similar to psychodrama, and parallel to ritual? Does the protagonist enact them on behalf of the audience, both representing them and safeguarding them from the potentially dangerous impact of these strong emotions? Is this notion of relief that the audience experiences contained within the theatre? And does this social and individual purgation replace critical understanding or is it accompanied by it? In other words is *katharsis* an enactment of extreme emotions in an attempt to manage them and cleanse them, offering a type of social safety valve, or does it introduce an intellectual component that implies alienation and distance and results in scepticism rather than reconciliation?

Despite the stress placed by scholars on either side of this argument, most seem to arrive at a reading of *katharsis* that restores its therapeutic capacity to bring together and reconcile opposing elements in society. Note the conclusions presented by two leading scholars in the field. These are conclusions that have been arrived at by taking completely different, even opposing, methodologies. Aryeh Kosman writes:

> Through the ritualized and formalized action of tragic poetry, we as audience are thus enabled to participate in the restorative capacities of human society to forgive and thus to heal the guilty sufferers of tragic misaction. And in so far as we are able to identify with Oedipus, for example, and to do so by the very fear and pity we experience at the witnessing of his fate and which is the occasion of his theatrical purification, we are at the same time relieved of the more painful (and potentially paralyzing) aspects of the general fear we feel at the possibility of that identification: we achieve, like Orestes, a salvation through purgatory, a *soteria dia tes katharseos*.[16]

This identification of *katharsis* with purgation and the emphasis on the regenerative and restorative powers of tragedy echo a Christian if not simply humanist interpretation. Such a reading sees in tragedy the *pharmakon* of social and personal malaise. Indeed, that may be the case, but it is also important to remember that *pharmakon* is both the poison and the cure. Jonathan Lear reaches similar conclusions:

> Even in his humiliation and shame, Oedipus inspires our awe and admiration. In the *Rhetoric* Aristotle says that those who have already experienced great disasters no longer feel fear, for they feel they have already experienced every kind of horror. In tragedy, we are able to put ourselves imaginatively in a position in which there is nothing further to fear. There is consolation in realizing that one has experienced the worst, there is nothing further to fear, and yet the world remains a rational, meaningful place in which a person can conduct himself with dignity. Even in tragedy, perhaps especially in tragedy, the fundamental goodness of man and world are reaffirmed.[17]

This slightly triumphalist, all-affirming aspect of tragedy incensed Brecht and urged him to define his own theatrical project against it. It is a view that sees in tragedy an all-encompassing ideology that hails the power of the individual and reinforces the great humanist ideals of goodness, harmony and maleness (note the paradigm of Oedipus once again). At the same time an organic relationship is reproduced between the individual and the collective, which also reflects on the relationship between the aesthetic and the political. As scholars never fail to point out, these regenerative, purgative and reconciliatory effects of tragedy are achieved through the human institutions, which are part of the Athenian state. Tragedy is called upon to act as the great school of Athenian democracy and citizenship. If Aristotle was striving to reinstate the civic dimension of theatre, to cleanse from it all the unsettling elements that Plato had pointed out, then this view of tragedy certainly achieves its aim.

In the unlikely alliance that we have set up between Plato and Brecht, this use of the emotions of pity and fear is seen as manipulative and reliant on people's basest fears and desires. What if there is a grain of truth in Plato's view of mimesis as inherently corrupting, of his view that the stage can carry contamination? After all, this view is reiterated by Christianity and makes for the difficult relationship between Christian doctrine and theatrical practice in general. What if there is some truth to Plato's view that the very act of representation through enactment is potentially dangerous? It is precisely this potentially dangerous and subversive aspect of all theatrical representation that is taken up by Brecht in his epic theatre. It is not for nothing that theatre was banned from Plato's *Republic*. However, he too has room for the uses of *katharsis*.

In the *Phaedo* Plato uses a group of words all related to *katharsis* to describe the soul's search for knowledge in a process that separates this activity from the murky influence of the emotions, these having been castigated in the *Republic* as obstacles to intellectual activity.[18] The terms that he uses are *katharos*, *katharsis*, *katharmos*, all related to the general meanings of 'clearing up', or 'cleaning up', or 'clarifying'. This use of *katharsis* as an activity separate from emotions or indeed helping to foreground and 'frame' those emotions that are seen to impede intellectual clarity is significantly different from the use made by Aristotle. M. C. Nussbaum claims that Aristotle's use of the term *katharsis* is a response to Plato. She writes:

> It is also clear that the idea of a *katharsis* produced, as in the *Poetics*, 'through pity and fear' would have been deeply repellent to Plato. Indeed, it would sound to his ears close to an oxymoron . . . It is, to him, tantamount to saying 'cleaning by mud', or 'clearing up through disgusting mess.' For Aristotle, however, these emotions can be genuine sources of understanding, showing the spectator possibilities that are there for good people. Therefore, what more succinct summary of his difference from Plato could there be, than to speak of a 'getting clear through pity and fear'? This interpretation . . . does not require denying that *katharsis* takes place through the emotions themselves. In fact, it insists on this. Once we notice their cognitive dimension . . . we can see how they can, in and of themselves, be genuinely illuminating.[19]

This very useful approach to the definition of *katharsis* cannot in the end resist a 'happy ending'. It stresses the positive, uplifting and moralising rewriting of the term by Aristotle. This intertextual relationship between the uses of the term, however, may generate, intentionally or unintentionally, a type of negativity, which would rely on the oxymorous nature of the concept of '*katharsis* through pity and fear' and not simply exist despite it. Rather than denying the potentially dangerous and corrupting emotions, it places them in tandem with a kind of critical activity initiated by the 'clearing up', or 'sorting out' dimension of the term. This critical activity would be infused with negativity as it relies on an impossible coexistence of opposing forces. This dialectical coexistence and interdependence allow for a less than triumphalist and anti-humanist reading of tragic form. The possibility of 'clearing up through mud', through the very elements that tragedy is supposedly trying to be rid of, might be a real one. Just as *pharmakon*[20] is both poison and cure, *katharsis* through pity and fear might instigate a process of emotional and intellectual immunisation that relies on the poison being accepted by the body of the actor, the audience and the community at large.

This reference to the medical genealogy of *katharsis* usefully reminds us of the 'murder or sacrifice' that is said to be at the core of cultural production. Indeed, tragedy's lineage in fertility ritual probably entailed human sacrifice. This is turned into a type of 'taboo' on the tragic stage as murder of any sort becomes, quite literally, 'obscene', never performed in front of an audience. Aristotle's attempt, as read by Nussbaum, to humanise *katharsis*, to turn it into a passage towards goodness might not be as successful as he may, or may not, have wished. Death, violence, dismemberment and lamentation might not be elements that are successfully purged through 'pity and fear'. Rather they might quite literally become incorporated by the body of the actor (as Plato would have it) and then transferred by a process of contamination on to the audience. Rather than achieving relief, at least initially and for the duration of the performance event, this audience will experience the unease and discomfort that accompany exposure to an illness.

If we venture away from Sophocles and particularly Oedipus, there are many tragedies that do not conform to the 'happy ending' scenario proposed by a reconciliatory reading of Aristotle's famous definition. Indeed, Nussbaum herself concedes to this view when talking about Euripides' *The Bacchae*:

> This strange and transfigured world does not seem easy to reconcile with Aristotle's categories of analysis – either with his demand for causal intelligibil-

ity or with his assumption of firm character ... I do not think his mode of analysis impoverishes our understanding of many major dramas, including most of those of Sophocles; but it is not complete, and does not fare well with Dionysus.[21]

But, as we know, tragedy is not possible without Dionysus. If we reintroduce, however, a critical, meta-theatrical Dionysus, then we might have a number of interpretive possibilities that make up for the proposed 'incompleteness' of Aristotle's analysis. This view of Dionysus would stand for all the elements of negativity that are not so much purged as embodied by the stage. Indeed, as the god of transformation and, in many ways, representation and mediation itself, Dionysus bears the traces of all the negativity he carries. He is the poison without which there can be no cure. The *katharsis* that is proposed, including the Dionysian elements, would be one that is at the same time critical, intellectual and emotional; where each of these categories is structurally linked, keeping *katharsis* from collapsing into either pure rhetoric (or philosophy), on the one hand, or into pure ritual, on the other. What emerges from this oxymoronic reading of *katharsis* (from the cleaning by mud, as Plato would have it) is a mode of reception that is both emotional and intellectual, both physical and spiritual.[22] It implies a negative critique that may be uplifting and reconciliatory in the end but is usually and definitely alienating and unsettling.

This could not be more true than when discussing the dramas of Euripides. Hailed as the 'stage philosopher', Euripides occupies the position of dissent within the canon of Athenian tragedy. His critical stance towards the Peloponnesian War, his endorsement of the problems of women and slaves and his overall critique of the contradictions within the democratic project itself make him particularly attractive for modern and modernist stagings. However, his overall aesthetics, as I argued earlier, has received very little attention in discussions about tragic form in general. This is somewhat surprising because, if we move away from the Oedipus-obsessed approach to tragedy, Euripides might provide us with a useful paradigm where action rather than character is privileged, and where the critique voiced does not derive from a hero-character (against the gods or fate) but from a historico-political perspective on the world.

Surprisingly enough, Aristotle's other favourite tragedy was Euripides' *Iphigenia in Tauris*. His analysis of this tragedy, however, has not received nearly as much attention. *Iphigenia in Tauris* at first glance does not seem like an obvious choice. Like many a Euripidean drama, it presents us with structural problems. Neither a tragedy nor a comedy, it has been classified as a problem play. Some scholars see it as the precursor to the modern melodrama. Here is how Aristotle presents the 'universal' of the Iphigenia:

> A certain girl after being sacrificed and disappearing from the view of those sacrificing her was settled in another land where the custom was to sacrifice strangers to the goddess, and she came to hold that priesthood. A while later, it happened that the brother of the priestess arrived. The fact that the oracle commanded him to go there. For some reason that is outside the universal, and his purpose [in going], are outside the plot. He arrived, was seized, and when about to be sacrificed, he made himself known, either as Euripides or Polyidos wrote it, saying, as was plausible, that not only his sister but himself had to be sacrificed. Thence is salvation.[23]

This analysis is plot-driven. A famous girl from the house of Atrides gets abducted. The abduction, however, is perpetrated by a goddess, Artemis. The fact that Euripides chooses this version of the myth of Iphigenia is interesting in itself, as it acts as a comment on the actions of Agamemnon, her father, who decides to sacrifice his daughter for the purposes of war. The sacrifice of Iphigenia has been called the first *pro patria* sacrifice, performed for the good of the state and not necessarily to appease the gods. Instead of burning at the stake, Iphigenia is rescued by a female goddess and taken to a female domain, where she becomes a priestess. This separation between feminine and masculine worlds is common and in some cases can be read as an inflection of the supposed shift from the world of the mother to the world of the father, or of the transition from myth to history. Iphigenia is rescued from certain death, from a male world, and is transported into a female zone. It is also significant that the world is overseen by Artemis, the huntress, the goddess most associated with the Amazons. There she acts as a priestess until the arrival of a stranger, who unbeknown to her, is her brother, and whom, according to custom, she should sacrifice to the goddess. The *anagnorisis*, the recognition between Iphigenia and Orestes, between brother and sister, avoids the sacrifice. (The duo of brother and sister, is another reference to a matriarchal order, where the sibling relationship stands in for heterosexual marriage, as in Isis and Osiris or Medea and her brother.) Sacrifice, which is a taboo on the Athenian stage and in tragedy in general, is averted. In its place the new order of things reasserts the role of the brother, and Iphigenia enters another male world, where human sacrifice is no longer hailed either as a way of communicating with the gods or as a way of solving political problems. Iphigenia left the war-torn world of her father (and, according to Heraclitus, 'war is the father of all things' – *Polemos panton men pater esti* [24]), lapsed momentarily into a type of feminine Utopia (or dystopia), then was rescued by the more benevolent male presence, of the brother.

Her relationship with her brother deserves particular attention. This is not a grand brother/sister duo as we see in the matriarchal/barbarian tradition of Medea and her brother (who gets killed by her so she can enter the world of the Greeks); rather it is a bonding of *philia*, of friendship, that imitates the male-to-male relationships of *philia*. What makes this tragic plot particularly strong, according to Aristotle, is the emphasis placed on *philia*. Elizabeth Belfiore writes on the centrality of *philia* to Aristotle's definition of tragedy:

> Thus, the best tragic plot, in Aristotle's view, is not just an exciting story. It is instead a story, with the compelling force of probability or necessity, that concerns *philia* relationships.[25]

There is an on-going discussion on the relationships between kinship and *philia*. Most interpretations agree that kinship is seen as a form or aspect of *philia* and does not precede it as a category. Indeed, relationships of fraternity, *adelphoi*, are seen as part of *philia*. That the concept of the 'sister' is merely a female inflection on the word *adelphos*, turning it into *adelphe*, is noteworthy in and of itself. If *adelphos* is seen as a subcategory of *philos* and *adelphe* is its female version, grammatically at least, then it might be safe to assume that the brother–sister relationship (like the one we also find between Antigone and her brother) mirrors the male-to-male homosocial relationship of *philia*. Émile Benveniste writes of this relationship between *adelphoi* and *philoi*:

> Similarly in Greek it was necessary to distinguish two types of kinship, and *phrater* now being used solely as a classificatory term, new terms for consanguineous 'brother' and 'sister' had to be forged.
>
> These lexical creations often overturn the ancient terminology. When Greek used for 'sister' the feminine form (*adelphe*) of the term for brother (*adelphos*), this instituted a radical change in the Indo-European state of affairs. The ancient contrast between 'brother' and 'sister' rested on the difference that all the brothers form a phatria mystically descended from the same father. There are no feminine 'phatriai'. But when, in a new conception of kinship, the connection by consanguinity is stressed – and this is the situation we have in historical Greek – a descriptive term becomes necessary, and it must be the same for brother and sister. In the new names the distinction is made only by morphological indication of gender (*adelphos, adelphe*).[26]

In his critique of Benveniste, Derrida claims that this transformation also impacts on the category of *philia*, since fraternity is one of its main characteristics. Either way, this etymology touches upon some of the issues surrounding *philia* and gender that are central themes of most tragedies: the relationships between ties of blood, nature, the law and the state. In this context it is worth underlining the fact that the brother–sister duo, a blood tie, imitates a male-to-male *philia*, a cultural tie, or as Benveniste states, a bond that is mystically forged.

Whether mystically, naturally, or ideologically forged, the centrality of *philia* to tragic form seems crucial. As we shall see in studying Euripides, *philia* not only forms a vital theme in the workings of most tragedies, but is vital to tragic form itself, so much so that it is a constitutive element of tragic form, helping to shape relationships between protagonists, helping to move the narrative, and setting up a pattern of communication with the audience. The male-to-male *philia* presents a model of interaction and communication that provides most tragedies with theme, form and, in many cases, their ethics. If we consider that the ultimate *philia* is *philosophia* itself, the friendship of wisdom (where *sophia* is feminine), then the complex position that the concept of *philia* occupies in discussions about tragedy also might impact on the relationships between tragedy and philosophy.

In *The Politics of Friendship* Derrida constructs an inspired genealogy (or rather anti-genealogy) of the term starting with classical Greece and moving through the Enlightenment to modern philosophers, particularly Heidegger.[27] His reading of Diogenes Laertius' citation of Aristotle's aphorism, '*O philoi, oudeis philos*' (O my friends, there is no friend)[28], traces a lineage that sees the term *philia* as parallel to the establishment of our received understanding of *democratia*. In his search for the political dimension of *philia*, Derrida unravels a history of the term which he uses to define its potential for contemporary democratic politics. In the process, however, he also unravels the difficult but structural relationships between *philia*, fraternity, homosociality, virility and autochthony. The story of universal fraternity also appears to be a story of phallocentrism. This economy of friendship sets up a discourse that excludes of a number of issues that contemporary democratic politics need to confront. Derrida writes on this elevation of *philia* to a universalising political *schema*:

> On the one hand, fraternal friendship appears essentially alien or rebel to the *res publica*; it could never found a politics. But on the other, as we have proved, from Plato to Montaigne, Aristotle to Kant, Cicero to Hegel, *the great philosophical and canonical discourses on friendship* will have explicitly tied the friend-brother to virtue and justice, to moral reason and political reason.
>
> The principle question would rightly concern the hegemony of a philosophical canon in this domain: how has it prevailed? Whence derives its force: how has it been able to exclude the feminine or heterosexuality, friendship between women or

friendship between men and women? Why can an essential inventory not be made of feminine or heterosexual experiences of friendship? Why this heterogeneity between *eros* and *philia*?[29]

If we see tragedy, as Nicole Loraux suggests,[30] as one of the ways in which the city of Athens discursively and imaginatively invents itself, then the centrality of *philia* needs to be highlighted further. This theorising of *philia*, both in philosophy and on the stage, helps construct a version of democracy whose trajectory we still inhabit. Indeed, it seems impossible to think through this democratic lineage without considering its exclusions. Derrida writes:

> What relation does this domination maintain with the *double exclusion* we see at work in all the great ethico-politico-philosophical discourses on friendship: on the one hand, the exclusion of friendship between women; on the other, the exclusion between a man and a woman? This double exclusion of the feminine in this philosophical paradigm would then confer on friendship the essential and essentially sublime figure of virile homosexuality.[31]

And he continues further on:

> The Greek model of *philia* could never be 'enriched' otherwise than with that which it has violently and essentially attempted to exclude.[32]

The use of the word 'attempted' is, I believe, significant, particularly when we are discussing the role of *philia* on the Athenian stage. Tragedy is not philosophy, and the types of *philia* it enacts rely less on the workings of *sophia* (wisdom) than on the workings of the body and the emotions. This is not, in and of itself, an anti-intellectual activity, but one that poses the question of the contingency of the workings of *sophia* (wisdom, knowledge). It is true that the homosocial and virile homosexual sublime is at work in tragic form. The heterogeneity between *eros* and *philia* that Derrida emphasises above is only true in relationships between men and women. The ambivalence towards heterosexuality is also present; its tendency to reproduce being one of the main aspects that was seen as impossible to reconcile with a homosocial and homoerotic view of the private and the public. Anxieties about fatherhood also are deeply rooted in tragedy (the 'legal fiction' as Joyce put it in *Ulysses*[33]). The almost certain absence of women in the audience adds to the homosocial dimension of the tragic event. In general the centrality of the male-to-male *philia* model must be one of the great unexamined areas of tragedy.

Of course, one of the reasons this has escaped scrutiny is primarily due to the fact, as Derrida stresses, that it can disguise itself as universal; *philia* is one of the great humanising discourses:

> The concept of democracy is confirmed in the *Eudemian Ethics* (1236–ab): it is politics of friendship founded on an anthropocentric – one could say humanist – concept. To man alone, in so far as he is neither animal nor god, is appointed the primary and highest friendship, that from which all the others receive their name ... There is no friendship, at least *in this primary sense*, with animals or with gods. There is no friendship, either, between animals or gods. No more so than democracy, fraternity, law, community, or politics.[34]

The ways in which *philia* helps shape tragic form and its subsequent impact on notions of democracy is not necessarily straightforward and direct. The homosocial world that tragedy both derives from and helps construct establishes a relationship of reciprocity which forges notions of citizenship but also helps to create a particular aesthetic that we associate with tragic form. The convention of all-male acting, for example, needs to be read in this context. However, again, theatre is not philosophy. The fact that the *philia*, so central to tragic form, is also staged through the use of performance conventions and the presence of an audience might offer possibilities, and open up gaps that philosophical *philia* leaves hermetically sealed.

The notion of 'playing the other' on the Athenian staged introduced by Froma Zeitlin has fuelled many feminist approaches to tragedy.[35] The fact that an all-male stage plays to an all-male audience creates a great synecdoche of the male-to-male concept of *philia*, where friendship is thematised, formally enacted and echoed throughout the great Greek auditoria. It seems like the perfect venue for the principle of Aristotle's primary friendship, *e prote philia*, to parade itself, constantly folding over and into the perfect audience, who are already *philoi*. However, this excessive application of the concept, in theme, in form, in convention, in the structure of the space itself might in the end act as a subtle reminder of its artificiality, its status as a 'legal fiction'. The fact that this fiction is in turn enacted and not simply narrated stresses the self-referentiality involved: men playing women, playing animals playing gods: the very categories that Aristotle posits to be outside the scope of *philia*. In the liminal world that tragedy occupies, *philia*, so crucial to its existence, might be both reinforced and critically undermined.

If in turn we read Aristotle's famous exclamation, 'O friends, there is no friend', as a piece of drama rather than as a philosophical axiom, a different set of propositions arise. The use of the vocative case sets up a quasi-dramatic context that presupposes the use of a mask (as the use of persona might be anachronistic), the reading of lines and the existence of an audience. The audience to which it is being addressed would already be an audience of friends. The oxymoronic and contradictory nature of the phrase might point to the very exclusions that Derrida mentions. There can be no friend since all these factors are denied presence in this economy of friendship. Indeed, like the philosophical plays of Euripides (the problem plays) to a modern audience, the tone of this aphorism might bear the ever-so-slight tinge of melodrama.

However tempting this proposition may appear to a contemporary audience the very use of the term 'melodrama' would imply anthropomorphism and humanisation, categories that, as Derrida claims, are alien to the Greek sense of philosophy. They are, however, as can be inferred through the rest of his analysis, forged through the very concept of *philia* (among other things). Whenever the term 'melodrama' springs to mind and particularly in the work of Euripides there is some formal experiment with the traditions and conventions of lamentation. This is obvious in plays like the *Alcestis* or *Helen* (as will be examined in the following chapter). In the *Alcestis*, a wife stands in to save her husband from Hades, and in *Helen*, Helen fakes the funeral of her husband Menelaos in order to trick the King of Egypt and eventually escape. In both cases death ritual is perverted and the result is a problem play that can be classified as neither tragedy nor comedy. In both cases, a *philia* relationship is enacted. In *Alcestis* it is the friendship between Hercules and Admetus, and in *Helen* the spousal relationship between Helen and Menelaos mirrors that of the male-to-male *philia* (indeed one in which Helen has become the man and Menelaos the woman). This perversion of death ritual usually involves 'male tears', men pretending to mourn. It also involves women as 'traffic' between male-to-male relationships. This concept of the 'lamenting man' is somewhat ambivalent within tragedy. If tragedy at once relies on death ritual and attempts to purge it of its excessive, female associations, then the image of 'male tears' is at best a 'melodramatic' one. Charles Segal writes on this notion of 'male tears':

> For the Greeks after Homer, even more sharply than for us, tears were a gendered category. Although men wept, tears were particularly characteristic of women. Women's 'love of lamentation' and 'love of tears' were a commonplace of Greek thought, often reiterated in tragedy. Like all intense emotions, weeping was associated with the female and with irrationality, and thus required social regulation. According to Plutarch, Solon established for women's expression of grief (*penthesi*) a law that restrained its 'disorderly and unbridled quality' (*to atakton kai akolaston, Life of Solon 21.5*). He also restrained 'breast beating and lamentation' (*threnein*) at burials; and Plutarch adds that even in his time the *gunaikonomoi* could

punish those who indulged in 'unmanly and womanly expressions of emotion in grieving'.[36]

This fear of feminisation, I would argue, is sublimated through the workings of *philia*, where one of the functions of the male-to-male relationship is seen as the impossibility of mourning. Derrida is very insightful on this matter:

> In any case, *philia* begins with the possibility of a survival. Surviving – that is the other name of a mourning whose possibility is never to be awaited. For one does not survive without mourning. No one alive can get the better of this tautology, that of the stance of survival [*survivance*] – even God would be helpless . . .
> Hence surviving is at once the essence, the origin and the possibility, the condition of possibility of friendship; it is the grieved act of loving. This time of surviving thus gives the time of friendship.[37]

Within the context of Greek tragedy, however, this 'time of friendship' allows for mourning. It is a safe space where men are allowed the pleasures of lamentation with all the fears of feminisation that these pleasures carry with them. When *philia* is transferred to the Athenian stage, with all its homosocial associations of fraternity and autochthony, it is as if the excluded feminine or 'other' returns with a vengeance. This can either lead to full-blown 'tragedy' like Klytemnestra or Pentheus or, where flirtation with lament is concerned, it usually leads to 'problem plays', plays that we today recognise as having melodramatic elements. Melodrama is primarily associated with some sort of threat to notions of manliness and virility.

The *philia* of the Athenian stage, so central to Aristotle's view of tragedy, has to be read in conjunction with mourning and with that other great male concept of Greek thought, *philoxenia*, hospitality. When read in relation to mourning it allows for possibilities that were probably alien within the terrain of philosophy. Charles Segal writes:

> One of tragedy's functions may well have been to display and demonstrate that women's proclivity to excess grief was every bit as bad as it was supposed to be. But, paradoxically, it simultaneously gave expression to that release of tears, including male tears, that the Greeks from Homer on regarded as a 'pleasure' . . . But tragedy can explore the exceptional situations where it is permissible, thereby both validating the norm and also providing the occasion for indulging in its relaxation, at least vicariously. A male audience could enjoy identifying with the cathartic release of tears without suffering the stigma of 'womanliness'.[38]

Although the safety-valve of the stage is present, the fear of 'womanliness' would always be there as well. This adds a quality to the discourse of *philia* that allows for the exception to manifest itself on the stage. This manifestation would always be in a 'portrayed', enacted form – never the real thing, as it were. It does, however, impact on the self-referential, artificial and imagined nature of the real thing. So the impossibility of mourning, the condition of survival for *philia*, does not seem so impossible on the Athenian stage. It does, however, always carry with it the threat of feminisation. It is this threat, together with the general 'otherness' that the stage enacts, that helps to create tragic form and to undermine it, in the same way that it validates *philia* and subverts it.

The image of 'male tears' is at once sacred and profane. It is tragic and comic. It touches upon the notion of a genre that would appear later, that of the divine comedy. The attempt of *philia* to mourn its own absence might now be reread into Aristotle's 'O my friends, there is no friend'. It could be read as a form of lament, or even as its male equivalent, in Greek terms, a funeral oration (*epitaphios logos*) – in the way that Derrida himself used the quotation after Foucault's death[39] – about the impossibility of friendship. Indeed, as form requires, it is a staged lament. The quotation itself is merely attributed to Aristotle. It always appears masked and ventriloquised. To this long history of the performance of this aphorism we can add the ritual conventions of lament, like 'male tears', the beating of breasts and the tearing of hair. In this dramatised version of the aphorism it no longer sounds like an anguished cry in the wilderness, or rather it sounds like a melodramatic, slightly camp, 'cry in the wilderness' that, yes, laments the true absence of *philoi* but through the masks of those that this economy of *philia* excludes. It is at once a sacred – almost totemic – use of this exclusion, and a blasphemous and profane one.

Philoxenia, hospitality, is another domain where the impossibility of primary friendship (*prote philia*) is tested and contested. The offering of hospitality from a male friend to another male friend (usually both from famous aristocratic households) forms another great theme of the tragedies. Derrida approaches this theme stressing the Latin version *host–hostis*, meaning both host and enemy. The concept of *philoxenia*, in many ways the ultimate friendship, the friendship of the foreigner, again examines the limits of the private and the public, the autochthonous and the heterogeneous. The end of *Oedipus at Colonus*, as Derrida underlines, presents a fascinating model of *philoxenia*:

> What happens at the end of *Oedipus at Colonus*? As we were saying, Oedipus illustrates this strange law of hospitality: you die abroad and not always as you would have wanted it. In this tragedy of written and unwritten laws, before living the experience of the last duty to render one of her dead brothers, Antigone endures and names that dreadful thing: being deprived of her father's tomb, deprived

above all, like her sister Ismene, of the *knowledge* as to the father's last resting place . . .

He [Oedipus] is going to deprive them of their mourning, thereby obliging them to go through their mourning of mourning. Do we know of a more generous and poisoned gift?[40]

By his gesture Oedipus brings together *philia*, *philoxenia* and his 'poisoned gift', and so underlines the impossibility of mourning. He makes his friend Theseus accept an oath (*orkos*) never to reveal to anyone the place where he will be buried.

> Son of Aegeus, what I have now to unfold
> Is a thing that your city shall keep in its secret heart
> Alive to the end of time. Soon I shall take you,
> None guiding me, to the place where I must die;
> And no one else must know it. Tell no man
> The region where it lies concealed from sight,
> That it may be for you henceforth for ever
> A source of strength greater than many thousands
> Of yeoman shields or allied spears. What follows,
> A holy mystery that no tongue may name,
> You shall then see and know, coming alone
> To the place appointed. There is no one else
> Of all this people to whom I can reveal it;
> Not my children, though I love them well.
> You are to keep it for ever, you alone.[41]

The denial of mourning, however, is not without political consequences. In breaking away from his 'family' and denying his daughters/sisters the right to mourn, Oedipus, in many ways, rewrites his family history, his primary relationships, and turns them into those between *philoi*. In stressing the impossibility of mourning that this act of hospitality initiates, Derrida's analysis fails to see the act of redemption that is also taking place. Oedipus – the first philosopher, the first man – has a propensity to invent himself even in his death. In trying to disassociate himself from the bad blood that his relationships with his daughters/sisters carry, he reinvents himself through the workings of *philia* and *philoxenia*. It is not uncommon for Theseus especially, the founder of democratic Athens, to be called upon to provide this solution (as also happens at the end of *The Madness of Hercules*). A world of blood/nature identified with the monstrous mother is rewritten through the 'legal fictions' of the male-to-male world. Theseus' final act of hospitality towards Oedipus also redeems him as it turns him into a type of protector of the city of Athens, buried at its outskirts at Colonus. Oedipus calls him *philtate xenon*, dearest of strangers or foreigners, while he himself is the foreigner about to be buried in a strange land.

> Dark day! How long since thou was light to me!
> Farewell! I feel my last of thee. Death's night
> Now ends my life for ever.
> Your land and all that serve you, and yourself,
> My best-loved friend; and in your blessedness,
> That it may be yours for ever, remember me.[42]

> Now I am going to hide my last light in Hades. But dearest of strangers, to this country, to all those who follow you, may you be happy, and in your good fortune remember me in my death, forever blessed.[43]

Oedipus might think he is being buried in a strange land, but surely there is a level of irony at play here as the audience and Theseus knew very well that this land (*chora*) is Athens. Athens and Thebes in myth and tragedy have an interdependent relationship, Thebes usually standing in for the other of Athens, for all the things of which the democratic state wants to rid itself. However, like the Furies at the end of *The Oresteia* (also buried at Colonus), some things can never be totally forgotten. Oedipus makes sure of that. He turns himself into a 'lucky charm' for the city of Athens. But this gift that he has to offer is not without its own exchange value. As Derrida rightly claims, he takes 'hostages': 'everyone is a hostage to the dead man, beginning with the favourite host, linked by the secret he has been given'.[44]

Usually such a transaction of gifts between *philoi* involving *philoxenia* would also involve some kind of traffic/exchange of women (Orestes–Pylades, Ademdetus–Hercules, Hercules–Theseus and so on). We could say that Antigone is implicated in this economy of gift exchange. More precisely the right to mourn is the secret gift that Oedipus takes away from Antigone and passes on to the city of Athens. The debates between written and unwritten laws and the right to mourn will be enacted by Antigone herself, as she comes to stand in for and represent her brother. Having been denied the right to mourn her father/brother Oedipus, she attaches herself to her brother and tries to reclaim her right to mourn. However, in some ways, Oedipus' gesture of offering himself to the Athenian state and denying funeral rights and mourning to his daughters has already resolved the issue. Mourning as a domain, in the democratic *polis*, falls within the jurisdiction of *philia* and *philoxenia* (when it involves foreigners). It no longer belongs to the world of the household and of women. The tragedy of Antigone lies in the fact that she is asked to enact an argument that has already been resolved by Oedipus.[45] In this way she will always be his hostage, and also a hostage to the Athenian state. Her own drama at Thebes will act as a test of the limits of the democratic state; however, this is a state that has lost the power of mourning, or, rather, has converted it into political *logos*, through the workings of *philia*. All she can really do, particularly since 'she' is a male actor, is pretend to mourn:

> She weeps at not weeping, she weeps a mourning dedicated to saving tears. For she does, in fact, weep, but what she weeps for is less her father, perhaps, than her mourning, the mourning she has been deprived of, if we can put it like that. She weeps at being deprived of a normal mourning. She weeps for her mourning, if that is possible.[46]

It is certainly possible; and a whole tragedy is based upon that premise. What this analysis overlooks, however, is that the reason this weeping is repetitive and histrionic is due to the fact that she is weeping 'male tears'. In doing so she also allows the audience to weep 'male tears'. This is weeping between *philoi*, between friends, which, of course, is contained within the theatre and restored within the *polis* by the *epitaphios logos*. But mourning and *epitaphios logos* are not interchangeable and reducible to each other. The impossibility of mourning, as the ultimate expression of *philia* and *philoxenia*, is once again enacted.

Furthermore, mourning shows itself to be central to tragedy. It impacts on form and content. It results from the various interactions and transactions outlined by the aesthetic I have been proposing. This aesthetic would bring together all the themes touched upon above. This would happen not in a programmatic, prescriptive manner, but, to borrow another Benjaminian term, in terms of the constellation or the mosaic. The imagined conversation I have been outlining between the stage philosopher Euripides and the philosopher of tragedy Aristotle might perhaps yield a poetics that could work towards the reconciliation of tragedy and modernity.

The shift from an Oedipal/Sophoclean obsession with tragedy and the focus on Euripides, and Aristotle's alternative proposition of *Iphigenia in Tauris* as a paradigmatic tragedy, opens up critical possibilities for the study of tragic form and its relevance for modernist aesthetics in general. Brecht's vehement anti-Aristotelianism is somewhat diluted if we see in tragic form a historical precursor to the politics and aesthetics of epic theatre.

Moving away from a humanist, character-centred reading of tragic form has allowed us to concentrate on the importance of action and narrative. This emphasis, always already present in the writing of Aristotle, also radically rewrites the notion of mimesis, hinting at its potential to be read as a function of the performative. As an attempt to render the power and impact of enactment as both aesthetic and political phenomenon, the concept of performativity proves pertinent to this analysis as it stresses both the civic and the psychoanalytical dimensions of the event of tragedy. Indeed, this forms yet another dialogue in the long-standing debate between philosophy and tragedy. It does not necessarily follow that mimesis is identical to the performative, but the concept of the performative might help us to read the physical, bodily, spatial and communal aspects of the tragic event. It offers a way of reading theatrical praxis as not simply 'embodying' a written text. It reconciles the apparent opposition between the discursive aspect of a dramatic text and the material nature of theatrical production. The unique aspect of tragic form is that it is at once material and discursive, with an aesthetic (unlike naturalism for example) that makes no attempt at hiding this fact. In this context the Brechtian category of *gestus* also proves useful when approaching tragic form.

The main content or mask of this imaginary *gestus* would be one of mourning. The possibility or impossibility of tragedy acting as a *pharmakon* is constantly tested and contested on the Athenian stage. This would be a *pharmakon* that at once purges and contains those elements that are considered dangerous and contagious for Athenian democracy. Moreover, the constitutive relationship between mourning and gender and how it pertains to the recurring themes of *philia* (and *philoxenia*) is of vital importance in this reading.

The constellation or mosaic formed by the heterogeneous voices (Aristotle, Plato, Brecht, Stanislavsky) in this imaginary conversation hints at the possibilities of speculation and critique that tragic form may offer. At once embracing the spectacular and the intellectual, the sacred and the profane, an essentially Euripidean poetics of tragedy might help to 'rescue' it from 'the abyss of aestheticism' that Benjamin accused Nietzsche of creating, and restore to tragic form its civic and political power.

Notes

1. See Friedrich Nietzsche, *The Birth of Tragedy*, trans. Walter Kaufmann (New York: Random House Vintage Books, 1967). Nietzsche writes of the relationship between Socrates and Euripides, which supposedly brought about the death of tragedy, 'Socrates, the dialectical hero of the Platonic drama, reminds us of the kindred nature of the Euripidean hero who must defend his actions with arguments and counterarguments and in the process often risks the loss of our tragic

pity; for who could mistake the *optimistic* element which, having once penetrated tragedy, must gradually overgrow its Dionysian regions and impel it necessarily to self-destruction – to the death-leap into the bourgeois drama. Consider the consequences of the Socratic maxims: "Virtue is knowledge; man sins only from ignorance; he who is virtuous is happy." In these three basic forms of optimism lies the death of tragedy' (*Birth of Tragedy*, sec. 14). For a discussion of this misunderstanding see Walter Kaufmann, *Tragedy and Philosophy* (Princeton: Princeton University Press, 1992), pp. 242–6.
2. Although Aristotle also presents an analysis of *Iphigenia in Tauris* by Euripides in his *Poetics* most commentaries focus on Sophocles and the Oedipus plays. See *The Poetics of Aristotle*, trans. and introduced by Stephen Halliwell (London: Duckworth, 1987). Also see Stephen Halliwell, *Aristotle's Poetics* (London: Duckworth, 1986) for an analysis of the impact of the *Poetics*.
3. See Martha C. Nussbaum, 'Tragedy and Self-sufficiency', in Amelie Oksenberg Rorty (ed), *Essays on Aristotle's Poetics* (Princeton: Princeton University Press, 1992, pp. 261–90, p. 285. Also see M. C. Nussbaum, *The Fragility of Goodness* (Cambridge: Cambridge University Press, 1986).
4. Although *The Bacchae* is the only tragedy to be exclusively about Dionysus, the approach put forward here wants to explore the possibility of Dionysus not only providing the theme but also helping to constuct the form of Euripidean drama.
5. See Elizabeth Belfiore, 'Aristotle and Iphigenia', in Rorty (ed.), *Essays on Aristotle's Poetics*, p. 363.
6. See Halliwell, *Aristotle's Politics*, p. 146.
7. For an elaboration of this discussion, see Halliwell, *Aristotle's Poetics*, p. 2, n. 2.
8. See Michael J. Walton, *Greek Theatre Practice* (Westport, CT: Greenwood Press, 1980); David Wiles, *Greek Theatre Performance* (Cambridge: Cambridge University Press, 2000).
9. Plato, *Republic* III, 392D. Quoted in Aryeh Kosman, '*Acting*: Drama as the Mimesis of *Praxis*', in Rorty (ed.), *Essays on Aristotle's Poetics*, p. 52, Kosman's translation.
10. Plato, *Republic* III, 393 A6 f. Ibid.
11. See Aryeh Kosman, 'Silence and Imitation in the Platonic Dialogues', in J. C. Klagge and N. D. Smith (eds.), *Methods of Interpreting Plato and his Dialogues* (1992 Supplementary Volume to *Oxford Studies in Ancient Philosophy*) (Oxford: Clarendon Press, 1992), pp. 73–92.
12. Aristotle, *Poetics*, 6, 1449b 24–7 (Oxford: Clarendon Press, 1968), introduced by D. W. Lucas; for a recent translation of Aristotle's definition of tragedy, see Stephen Halliwell, *The Poetics of Aristotle*, p. 37.
13. See Aryeh Kosman, '*Acting*: *Drama* as the Mimesis of *Praxis*', in Rorty (ed.), *Essays on Aristotle's Poetics*, p. 58.
14. Ibid. p. 63.
15. See Leon Golden, 'Catharsis', *Transactions and Proceedings of the American Philological Association* 93 (1962): 51–60; 'Mimesis and Katharsis', *Classical Philology* 64, (1969): 145–53; 'Katharsis as Clarification: An Objection Answered', *Classical Quarterly* 23 (1973): 45f.; 'The Purgation Theory of Catharsis', *Journal of Aesthetics and Art Criticism* 31 (1973): 473–9; 'The Clarification Theory of Catharsis', *Hermes* 104, (1976): pp. 437–52.
16. See Kosman, 'Silence and Imitation', p. 68.

17. See Lear, 'Katharsis', in Rorty (ed.), *Essays on Aristotle's Poetics*, pp. 315–40, p. 335.
18. For a discussion of the uses of *katharo* word group, see M. C. Nussbaum, *The Fragility of Goodness*, Interlude 2.
19. See M. C. Nussbaum, 'Tragedy and Self-sufficiency', p. 281.
20. For a discussion of the term *pharmakon* in Plato, see Jacques Derrida, 'Plato's Pharmacy', in *Tragedy: A Reader*, ed. and introduced by John Drakakis and Noami Conn Liebler (London: Longman, 1998), pp. 338–60, reprinted from *Dissemination*, trans. and introduced by Barbara Johnson (Chicago: University of Chicago Press, 1981).
21. See Nussbaum, 'Tragedy and Self-sufficiency', p. 286.
22. The term 'spiritual' is used here in an attempt to avoid the use of 'psychological' as it implies character and subjectivity.
23. Aristotle, *Poetics*, 1455b3–12.
24. Heraclitus, fragment 53, my translation.
25. See Elizabeth Belfiore, 'Aristotle and Iphigenia', in *Essays on Aristotle's Poetics*, p. 367. Also see *Nichomachean Ethics*, 1155a4–6; *Eudemian Ethics*, 1234b32–33 for Aristotle's views on *philia*.
26. Émile Benveniste, *Indo-European Language and Society*, trans. Elizabeth Palmer (London: Faber and Faber, 1973), p. 179.
27. Jacques Derrida, *The Politics of Friendship* (London and New York: Verso, 1997). In this book, as well as in other more recent ones (*Of Hospitality: Anne Dufourmantelle Invites Jacques Derrida to Respond*, trans. George Collins (Stanford: Stanford University Press, 2000); *On Cosmopolitanism and Forgiveness*, trans. Mark Pooley and Michael Hughes (London and New York: Routledge, 2001)), Derrida traces a genealogy of concepts in an attempt to investigate the future of the political.
28. As Derrida notes, there are two possible grammatical renditions of this phrase. The first using the vocative O, yields the received translation (O my friends, there is no friend); the second relying on the O being a dative would produce a different translation (To him who has many friends, there is no friend).
29. Derrida, *The Politics of Friendship*, p. 277. Derrida continues, 'Why cannot such a history of the canon be reduced to a history of philosophical concepts or texts, nor even to a history of "political" structures as such – that is, structures determined by a concept of the political, by this concept of the political? Why is it a matter of a history of the world itself, one which would be neither a continuous evolution nor a simple succession of discontinuous figures? From this vantage point, the question of friendship might well be at least an example or a lead in the two major questions of "deconstruction": the question of the history of concepts and (trivially) so-called "textual" hegemony, history *tout court*; and the question of phallocentrism. Hence *qua* phallocentrism,' p. 278.
30. Derrida heavily relies on Loraux's work in order to read the 'Greek' model of friendship. See notes to the chapter 'The Phantom Friend Returning (in the Name of "Democracy")', in Derrida, *The Politics of Friendship*, pp. 75–111.
31. See Derrida, *The Politics of Friendship*, p. 279.
32. Ibid. p. 300.
33. This phrase is often quoted by Derrida as well in the above book *The Politics of Friendship*.

34. Derrida, *The Politics of Friendship*, p. 198.
35. See Froma Zeitlin, *Playing the Other: Gender and Society in Classical Greek Literature* (Chicago: University of Chicago Press, 1996).
36. See Charles Segal, *Euripides and the Poetics of Sorrow: Art, Gender and Commemoration in Alcestis, Hippolytus and Hecuba* (Durham and London: Duke University Press, 1993), p. 63.
37. Derrida, *The Politics of Friendship*, pp. 13–14.
38. See Segal, *Euripides and the Poetics of Sorrow*, p. 64.
39. For another meditation on Foucault's death, see Jaques Derrida, 'Michel Foucault (1926–1984) – To Do Justice to Freud', in *The Work of Mourning* (Chicago and London: The University of Chicago Press, 2001), pp. 77–90.
40. Jacques Derrida, *Of Hospitality: Anne Dufourmantelle Invites Jacques Derrida to Respond*, trans. George Collins (Stanford: Stanford University Press, 2000), p. 93.
41. Sophocles, *Oedipus at Colonus*, in *The Theban Plays*, trans. and introduced by E. F. Watling, (London: Penguin Books, 1974), lines 1515–30.
42. Ibid. lines 1590–5.
43. Derrida's translation of the same lines, *Of Hospitality*, p. 105.
44. Ibid. p. 107.
45. In this context it is interesting to note that *Antigone* was the first play from the Theban trilogy to be performed in 442 BCE, followed by *Oedipus Tyrannus* in 425 BCE and *Oedipus at Colonus* in 406, after the poet's death in the same year.
46. Derrida, *Of Hospitality*, p. 111.

CHAPTER FIVE

The Heroism of Hercules and the Beauty of Helen

The Heroism

> Chorus: Let us go then, full of tears and sorrow,
> Since we have lost the best of friends.
> (*steichomen oiktroi kai polyklautoi
> ta megista philon olesantes*)

These are the closing lines of *The Madness of Hercules*, in many ways a tale of friendship gained, lost, regained and then commemorated. I would like to suggest a reading of this play that focuses on the centrality of male-to-male *philia* both to Euripides' rereading of the myth of Hercules, and to the overall aesthetics proposed. Indeed, in this play, which sets out to examine the role of *philia* in the democratic *polis*, *philia* is linked structurally to notions of heroism, familial responsibility and masculinity in general. If primary friendship (*e prote philia*) is impossible with gods and animals (and women), then this play tests this supposition by reworking myth through tragedy. Hercules, a demi-god himself, a hybrid creature, becomes the most suitable candidate to enact the transition from the world of the gods (where friendship is impossible) to the civic world of the democratic *polis*. His journey, chartered in this play, from Hades, through Thebes to Athens, also becomes a journey from darkness to light. It is a journey that starts from the underworld, passes through the world of the Theban 'stage', where all fears and desires are enacted, and ends up on the road to Athens, where everything that Hercules has suffered will be redeemed, turned into knowledge and finally recuperated. Of course, it is a journey he could not undertake without the help of his friend Theseus. As is the case with the ending of *Oedipus at Colonus*, Theseus, the representative of Athens, appears centre stage to provide the eventual solution.

The Madness of Hercules was performed between 421 BCE and 415 BCE and belongs to Euripides' late period. Some scholars make it contemporary with *Oedipus at Colonus*, making the parallels between the two plays even more striking. Both display a contemplative mood and both end up in Athens through the intervention of the friendship of Theseus. However, Euripides' relationship to the Athenian *polis* was at best strained and this play was probably written while he was a guest at the court of the King of Macedon in self-imposed exile. Like most of his plays, it exhibits the formal innovations that he introduced to tragedy: the use of an extended prologue and the (*apo mechanes theos*) *deus ex machina*. The prologue allows him to frame the action and to outline his version of the myth. Since Euripides almost invariably either chooses an obscure version of the myth or radically rewrites it, the function of the prologue is crucial. The *deus ex machina* is his gesture towards the gods. He turns them into a theatrical convention. These are gods that no longer have an organic relationship with the world of the humans. They quite literally need a technology of production in order to become visible. They are clearly represented and theatricalised. They become part of the mechanics of the stage. In an interesting meta-theatrical rewriting of his own innovation, in *The Madness of Hercules*, the role of the *deus ex machina* is taken up by Theseus in a gesture that recasts the relationship with the sacred through the male-to-male *philia*.

According to the myth, madness strikes Hercules and he kills his wife and children before he takes on his famous tasks. In this way the tasks themselves and all they presuppose and engender become a form of cleansing for Hercules, and a way in which he can construct his identity. In a typical rite of passage, he leaves the world of the monstrous female and enters the new order of things (in a journey not unlike the one undertaken by Oedipus – although, as we have discussed, Oedipus' journey is that of the mind, whereas Hercules' involves physical labours). However, in Euripides' version we have a crucial inversion. Hercules encounters Lyssa (mania) not before but after he has completed his labours. So there is nothing left to provide him with a *pharmakon*. He kills his wife and children as a result of his heroism. The murderous act is read as a symptom of the rite of passage itself, in a way that renders it at least problematic, if not totally meaningless. The only thing that can save Hercules in the end, since he has no heroic feats left to accomplish, is his relationship of *philia* with Theseus.

A summary of the plot of the play might be useful at this point. Hercules is in Hades on a task given to him by Eurustheus to bring back Cerberus, the dog. While he is away his father, Amphitryon, his wife, Megara, and his three children are being looked after by Creon, Megara's father and King of Thebes. There is a conspiracy against Creon and he is usurped by Lykos from Euboia, who kills Creon and takes over the kingdom. He decides to kill all the members of Hercules' family so no one can challenge his reign. While Lykos is planning this, Hercules suddenly arrives from Hades, kills Lykos and saves his family. However, Hera, Hercules' sworn enemy, sends Iris and Lyssa to visit Hercules. Under their spell, he falls into a frenzied madness and kills his wife and children, mistaking them for the wife and children of his enemy Eurustheus (the one who gave him the labours in the first place). In the end his friend Theseus (whom he had previously rescued from Hades on another task) comes from Athens to take him away and rescue him from his shame. Amphitryon, his earthly father, stays in Thebes to bury the dead.

In the prologue Euripides gives us a genealogy of Hercules and explains how he was assigned his famous labours. Amphitryon sought refuge at Thebes and was given it by Creon, despite the fact that he had killed his uncle Electryon, albeit unknowingly. While at Thebes Amphitryon marries Electryon's daughter, Alcmene, and is urged by her to avenge the deaths of her brothers in an earlier struggle involving the kingdom of Mycene, where he originally came from. While Amphitryon was away, Zeus, taking his appearance, sleeps with Alcmene and from this encounter Hercules was born. Hera, Zeus' wife, was enraged by this act and persecuted Hercules for the rest of his life. Hence his assignment of the twelve labours. When the play opens, Hercules already has completed eleven of these. The remaining labour is to go to Hades to bring back Cerberus. As mentioned earlier, the function of this prologue is vital as it presents us with an inverted order, whereby Hercules, counter to the received myth, already has fulfilled his tasks and completed his rites of passage when the tragedy occurs. The labours themselves no longer offer a consolation. They seem completely unjustified and arbitrary. Their only function seems to be to build up the heroic foil that is Hercules. His ultimate heroic gesture, saving his family, turns into a murderous act. The prologue also establishes a fraught relationship with the gods. Most of the hybrid creatures in Athenian tragedy that result from *hierogamy* (holy rape) inhabit such liminal spaces. Neither divine nor earthly, they are trapped between the two worlds and this somehow makes them more susceptible to both murder and madness.

The play itself can be roughly divided into two sections, separated by the arrival of Lyssa (mania). The first part, including the prologue, establishes the difficult relationship with the gods. Their power and influence is under scrutiny as it is challenged by the human relationship of *philia*. Amphitryon accosts Zeus over the evils that he and his family are about to suffer in the absence of Hercules:

> Oh! Zeus, we shared the same bed
> and had the same son, all in vain!
> I considered you to be a great friend,
> but you weren't.
> Even though I am a mortal
> I am more virtuous than you, a god.
> I have not betrayed the sons of Hercules.
> Secretly creeping into other men's beds,
> and taking women that do not belong to you,
> is something you do well;
> saving friends is something
> you do not know how to do.
> You seem to be an ignorant god rather than a just one.
>
> (338–47)

This is certainly a damning accusation against Zeus. Amphitryon seems to be under the impression that because he has shared the same woman with Zeus, he can in turn rely on his friendship. This, however, is not the case. A similar traffic of women, would act as a seal and pact for *philia* in the world of the mortals.[2] Indeed I would claim that the traffic of women in the human world mirrors the transactions initiated by *hierogamy* in the worlds between god and man. This bridge to the world of the gods (and the holy rape it presupposes) is one axiom of the mythic world that Euripides sets out to criticise. In accusing Zeus of 'bad friendship', Euripides is preparing the way for the male-to-male *philia* that is to take its place. The opposition set up is between the 'old', the mythic world and the 'new' world of the democratic *polis*. For Euripides the time when gods roamed the earth, in disguise, in search of unsuspecting female bodies to transmit their desires to man is over. This relationship between god and man is going to be replaced by the end of this play by the male-to-male *philia*, a relationship that will be reinforced, conceptualised and celebrated by the institutions (discursive, textual, imaginative and material) of the *polis*. Of course, tragedy is one such institution. In the Euripidean world-view man can no longer rely on the gods; the only relationship on which he can rely, for knowledge and power, is that with another man. Neither Amphitryon nor even Hercules, the demi-god, are able to rely on the gods.

However, the new world of male friendship that is heralded by the end of the play is foreshadowed in tones rather less triumphalist and heroic. The dominant narrative throughout this play is that of lamentation, again underlining the crucial relationship between mourning and friendship,[3] and its centrality for tragic form. The build-up to the arrival of Hercules is full of premature lamentations for the forthcoming deaths of Hercules' family. Megara, like Medea and in lines that echo hers, mourns her children while they are still alive:

> Everything is lost; fortune has turned her back on you
> and instead of brides she has given you the Kires of death.[4]
> and to me, whose mind has been lost to sadness,
> she's given endless tears instead of your wedding baths.
> And your father's father is laying your wedding feast
> thinking Hades is your father-in-law.
>
> (480–5)

These lines encapsulate very traditional conventions of female lament, where the wedding ceremony and the funeral rite are conflated. The mention of the baths (*loutra*), as in Medea, is a double reference to both wedding and burial custom: to the sprinkling of the bride with holy water and to the washing of the dead body.

This female lamentation is mirrored by the chorus as they enumerate the feats that Hercules has already accomplished in the style of the official funeral oration. In anticipation of his arrival he is praised in the discourse of the funeral oration as if he already were dead. The tasks that he has completed are described in detail in the style of a eulogy. His heroism, undermined later in the play, is praised not through a heroic, epic narrative but through the words of lamenting old men. And since the chorus is made up of old men anyway,[5] the fear of feminisation through lament collapses as the official discourse of the funeral oration breaks out into full-blown lamentations. They end with: 'I am so miserable that I cannot contain the flood of tears that spring from my eyes' (448–50). The image of male tears is again significant in this context. If this is a play about the crisis of heroism and masculinity, then one of the ways in which the relationships between genders is inverted is through the use of the conventions of lamentation. This acts as both a comment on the heroic discourse that preceded it and as an introduction to Hercules, who is about to appear. In turn, the audience is allowed momentarily to observe male tears, possibly even experience them themselves. This again foreshadows the tears that Hercules himself will shed later in the play after he has committed the horrific act. The various modes of lament, official and oral, that are presented in this section comment on each other and display the interdependency of the excessive mourning of women and the strict, stately orations of men. It is quite common for Euripides to ask his audience to identify or recognise various forms of 'womanliness', some of them in men themselves. Few plays, however, display such a fixation on different styles of lamentation. After this section Heracles arrives on the stage. It is as if he walks in on his own funeral, or the funeral of his masculinity, particularly since he is returning from Hades. He finds his household steeped in excessive mourning and says:

> In front of my house I see
> my children with burial decorations on their heads,
> my wife standing amidst a group of men,
> and my father crying. What grief!
> I have to get closer
> to find out.
> Wife, what is the evil that has
> besieged our household?
>
> (525–30)

The image that greets Hercules on his arrival, right on his doorstep, on the threshold between private and public, cries out for masculine reordering. It projects threatened masculinity all round: the children dressed for a funeral, the wife surrounded by other men and the father steeped in tears. Indeed, Hercules' arrival acts as a corrective not only to the real threat of death that awaits his family but also to the aesthetics of the image on the stage. The indulgence in public mourning that has taken place, and the audience's permission to partake of it, will quickly be stopped by the arrival of our hero, Hercules. Typically he reads the ills that have befallen his household as being a result of the absence of friends, 'I have left and friends have abandoned us' (558). It is interesting that, while he urges his family to 'Get rid of those deathly decorations and look up at the light' (562–3), he implies that he will rescue them as a friend, *philos*, and not necessarily as a father or husband. Of course, the main issue at play here is whether that is at all possible.

After explaining his late arrival,[6] Hercules proceeds to fulfil his mission and kills Lykos. Off stage he can be heard summoning the chorus: 'Old men, the transgressor no longer exists/The palace is now silent, let's all dance/The friends that I love are happy' (760–3). But he is not allowed to revel in his triumph. All the celebrations are brought to an abrupt end as Iris and Lyssa appear on the roof and once again 'we are overtaken by the same fear' (816). Iris is symbolised by a rainbow in mythology and acts as a bridge between the world of the mortals and the world of the gods. She transmits messages to humans and is primarily in the service of Hera. She is there to herald the arrival of Lyssa. Lyssa herself belongs to the daughters of the night. Like Hecate, she hunts with a herd of wild dogs from hell at her side and, like the Furies, she too inspires madness and frenzy.[7] This dynamic duo – one a messenger, the other the message itself – forms yet another incarnation of the monstrous female that Hercules has already encountered on his previous labours. In the traditional rites-of-passage mode these monstrous females would be slain by the hero and the road to full adulthood and masculinity would be open. It is interesting that Iris, in her introduction to Lyssa's appearance, says that while Hercules was fulfilling his tasks they could not touch him as he was protected by Zeus. Now, however, right at the moment when he thinks he has successfully completed his labours, they are here to undo them. Traditionally, once the hero has killed the monstrous female, he can wed the bride, the 'good' female, who will help him continue his line. Hercules' reward, however, is a horrific inversion of this pattern. Rather than reap his trophy and enter the world of the fathers as a patriarch in his own right, with his wife and children, he is now made to cut his own line short. The trials of heroism that he successfully fulfilled through his labours were supposed to prepare him for this entry into the patriarchal family. He could rightfully claim the 'legalised fantasy' of fatherhood. Instead of all this, and in a radical rereading of this structure, Hercules is driven to kill his wife and children, in a stroke undoing everything that preceded this moment. Iris urges Lyssa to get on with her final task:

> Come now, unwed virgin, daughter of the darkest night,
> shut the sadness out of your heart,
> and chase this man with child-murdering frenzy
> and with nerve-shattering shudders and wild rushes,
> drive him to madness.
> Drop the blood-wrenched rope of murder
> into the river Acheron,
> together with a beautiful wreath
> for the children
> butchered by his own hand.
>
> (833–9)

After this introduction Iris leaves and Lyssa enters the house as she is being described by the chorus as yet another birth-child of the night, a Gorgon,[8] again drawing parallels between this 'feat' and the ones that Hercules has already completed. Dionysus is called upon at the crucial moment of the murder of the children. The god of dismemberment, transgression and ecstasy is invoked to oversee the undoing of the heroism of Hercules.

> *Paizei pros emas despotes e mainetai;*
> Is the master playing with us, or is he crazy?
>
> (952)

In an extraordinary speech the messenger describes the murders committed by Hercules off stage. He tells us using reported speech (something that I believe is vital to this account and its reception) that Hercules confused these murders with the previous ones he committed during his labours. This sets up yet another mirroring effect between the heroic murders and the un-heroic, frenzied ones, between the sacred killings and these supposedly blasphemous ones. Like an actor, Hercules goes through the gestures of the violence that he has previously committed and through a pattern of divine repetition is doomed to enact once more. The confusion between the ritual and the drama, between the real and the enacted, was such that those watching for a fleeting moment thought that Hercules might be bluffing. As the messenger says about this stage within a stage, 'the slaves were shaking with fear and laughter at the same time and as they exchanged glances, someone said, "Is the master playing with us, or is he crazy?"'. In a wonderful meta-theatrical moment, Euripides manages to fold over the impact of the murder (with the repetition, the conflation of the divine and the profane) and project it on to the audience itself. To play, of course, means child's play but it also means to act. It is not for nothing that Dionysus, who is mentioned at this point in the text, was called upon to preside over this murderous frenzy, where playing, acting, laughter and tears are all conflated.

Like *The Bacchae*, the interdependency between theatre and ritual, acting and madness, is explored and exposed. Whereas in *The Bacchae* this is achieved through an exploration of the feminine, in *Hercules* it is approached through a detailed deconstruction of masculinity. However, it does not follow from this conflation that the 'sacred', 'madness' and 'ritual' are privileged at the expense of logic and reason. This is not an uncritical celebration of ritual and madness. It is, however, a type of sacred madness that acts as a *pharmakon*, a kind of corrective to the acts of violence that it mirrors. Whether playing/acting or performing for real, the violence that Hercules is asked to enact once more manages to undo, or cure, the previous acts of heroism to which he was subjected in his labours. In turn the audience is asked to repeat this mirroring effect and contemplate the impact of the acting itself. Twice removed now, the act of watching (with the proximity of laughter and tears that it induces) becomes implicated in the violence on the stage.

When Hercules recovers from this violent undoing of his heroism, he is shocked and bewildered. Indeed, it is not just his heroism that gets torn apart but his very subjectivity. When he recovers, he recognises nothing. He, too, like many a tragic role, becomes a stranger to himself. The only remedy to such a loss is friendship:

> I am dazed. I have no idea where I am.
> Is there a friend nearby or further away
> who can cure my confusion?
> Everything that was once familiar
> is now strange.
>
> (1105–8).

If we were to attempt a quasi-Oedipal reading of Hercules, as odd as this may seem, Hercules might surface as a quintessentially anti-Oedipal character. Indeed, if hysteria is the great unexplored of Oedipal/Freudian psychoanalysis,[9] then Hercules (as he appears in this play) begs to be read as a hysteric. Rather, the building up and then gradual dismantling of his masculinity makes for a very subtle reading of male hysteria. Hercules, along with a group of numerous tragic roles, forms a formidable study in hysteria (Cassandra, Medea, Klytemnestra). Indeed, if we stop reading Greek tragedy through the Oedipal lens of Freudian psychoanalysis, there is fertile material for such a reading. As Chapter 2 on Oedipus suggested, there are also grounds for reading elements of hysteria in the role of Oedipus himself.

The narrative of *The Madness of Hercules* could be read as such an anti-Oedipal proposition. The hero, through an attack of Lyssa (mania), which is manifested on both his mind and body, proceeds ritualistically to dismantle his own subjectivity, while murdering those who would have provided him with identity (family, lineage). In many ways it is the rite of passage undertaken by Oedipus himself, as he murders the Sphinx (he drives her to suicide through his reason) and then proceeds to give birth to himself by sleeping with his mother. Oedipus' reward for his troubles is knowledge and insight. He becomes the first philosopher and his grave is faithfully guarded by his friend Theseus. The same friend rescues Hercules by bringing him to Athens. However, his previous adventure seems totally illogical and unjustified. What it does present us with is an astute study of male 'hysteria'.

Despite the complex issues involved in the anachronistic use of this term, I would like to suggest that this play could be part of a trajectory of thinking about hysteria at the time. In the Hippocratic writings the symptoms of what we today call 'hysteria' were difficulties in breathing and a sense of suffocation, symptoms very close to those of mania. They were associated with lamenting women, mainly widows. The womb deprived of satisfaction, since the husbands were dead, left its usual place and would start wandering around the body exerting pressure on the organs, which would result in breathing difficulties, and so on. The link with conventions of lamentation and the fascination with the female body and particularly its reproductive aspect make for interesting analogies with the tragic form in general. The complex anxieties expressed about reproduction and lineage and their association (or disassociation) with the female body that form a crucial theme in Athenian tragedy are also fruitful ground for hysteria (in the version of the theory that identifies it with the female womb). Compounded by the fact that the primary mode of hysteria is imitation (mimetic behaviour), this area of study deserves further detailed research.

In her book on hysteria entitled *Mad Men and Medusas*, which also works well as a subtitle for the Hercules play, Juliet Mitchell charts the untold story of hysteria in the west. She claims that it has been written out of the history of psychoanalysis due to the impact of the Oedipal complex. She attempts a genealogy of the term while also defeminising it. She traces a history of male hysteria:

> At least in Western societies until the seventeenth century, hysteria was mostly linked to women and its etiology either thought to reside in the womb or in the seductions of the (male) Devil. Although observations of male hysteria were made from time to time throughout history this was rarely problematic. Certainly it was not the impossible contradiction which it was thought to be in the nineteenth century. Prior to this, men could behave like women in certain contexts.[10]

Athenian tragedy certainly forms one such context, and *The Madness of Hercules* might just be a study in male hysteria. As Mitchell claims, one of the manifestations of male hysteria in the twentieth century is what we call shellshock, the effect of experiencing great violence during war. Hercules might be said to be suffering from such a shock once he has completed his labours. As with the sufferers of shellshock, this situation is compounded by an intense homosociality experienced on the battlefield. The tendency to dramatise, exaggerate and in general be histrionic (i.e. feminine) is also a trait of hysteria. All these features are present in this play. Furthermore, the conventions they are using for such enactments are those of funeral rites and lamentation, both seen as the origins of female hysteria in the Hippocratic writings, as the triggers for the wandering of the womb.[11] The physical breaking down of Hercules is just as crucial as his mental collapse in this context:

> Ancient Greek Hippocratic medicine did not distinguish in the same way as its twentieth-century equivalent does between the physical and the imaginary movement of the uterus (*pnix hystericus*) . . . But this lack of distinction between the physical and the imaginary does not mean that the condition described was not therefore what we would understand as hysteria; all it indicates is that this particular distinction between organic and non-organic was alien to Greek modes of

thought... In the movement of passion through the mind and the body, Greek thought resonates more with that aspect of hysteria than does our own.[12]

I would suggest that this play also resonates with such aspects of hysteria. The intense homosociality, the impact of violence and the breaking down of Hercules' masculinity are all traits of hysterical behaviour. Indeed, this analogy could be taken even further and we could venture to suggest that the Athenian stage itself might function as fertile ground for hysteria. The emphasis on femininity (always imitated), the fascination with reproduction, the physicality of presence and the constant reference (either reinforced or subverted) to death ritual might all be read as symptoms of hysteria. However, such a reading would have to pathologise the stage and see it as the site of some sort of archetypal psychic conflict. Without reinstating this trope, and viewing the Athenian stage as the great 'laboratory' of the human psyche, as the Oedipal reading tends to do, it might still be possible to put forward a hysterical reading. If we introduce hysteria as a *sine qua non* of tragic representation, then the potency of the Oedipal stage is severely threatened. Furthermore, if hysteria has been there all along, implicated in the very workings of Oedipal representation, then it creates a version of 'Oedipality' that is almost too heterogeneous to sustain itself.

The case of *The Madness of Hercules* is especially interesting in this context as it creates a version of male hysteria at the time when hysteria was mostly feminine. Indeed, it is this feminised hysteria (historically synonymous with femininity itself) that has been inherited and reproduced in the medical literature of the west. What Euripides undermines is this received interpretation of hysteria. Men are just as prone to it as women. However, men are always feminised in the process. This reintroduction of the feminine (albeit represented, enacted), through the specific conventions of mourning, acts as an antidote to the Oedipal drive that deals with male subjectivity. *The Madness of Hercules*, like *The Bacchae*, which also deals with anxieties of gender differentiation, flirts with a type of aestheticised hysteria. Here Euripides establishes one of the oldest (and most problematic) connections between hysteria as symptom and hysteria as aesthetic practice. In a meta-theatrical context these two plays might be said to examine the links between hysteria and creativity, as this is manifested in theatrical representation. In fact, the dangers of pretending, enacting (especially pretending to be another gender), are explored in ways which prove very exciting for contemporary performance theorists. However, this analysis does not intend to construct a model of the hysterical stage as opposed to the Oedipal stage,[13] although such a genealogy of the stage would include, possibly even start, with a play like *The Madness of Hercules*.[14]

Whether frenzied or hysterical, Hercules is rescued from his madness by his friend Theseus. As he recovers from the horrific account of his deeds and just as he contemplates suicide, he sees Theseus on the horizon:

> Ah, here is Theseus, my friend and relative[15]
> he comes to put a stop to my deadly thoughts
> What a horror! His eyes will see me,
> the child murderer,
> he who is the friendliest of foreigners.
>
> (1153–6)

Philtato xenon is also what Oedipus calls Theseus when he is about to entrust him with his burial place. Just as he is about to rely on his hospitality, Hercules calls him a foreigner. Again the host, Theseus, is about to become a hostage to the guest, as the guest carries with him a miasma. The exchange that follows between the two men is also a meditation on the workings of *philia*. Hercules yet again enumerates his labours. For the third time they are narrated utilising tropes of the funeral oration. As Theseus also gives accounts of Hercules' bravery he manages to turn the previous funeral decorations into wreaths of heroism. He says that Athens would be proud to receive such a man:

> For them it will be like wearing a bright wreath of glory,
> for the Greeks to claim that
> they have helped a brave man.
> This is how I will repay you
> for saving me.
> It is now that you need friends.
> You do not need friends
> When the gods are willing to stand by your side.
>
> (1334–8)

As we know, the gods no longer stand by his side. Instead there is the male friend who owes him a favour. This economy of friendship is not without exchange value. Hercules rescued Theseus from Hades, where he went with his other friend, Perithous. When Hercules went to Hades to abduct Cerberus, the dog, he met Theseus and Perithous there. They were chained by Hades because they tried to rescue Persephone. Hercules freed Theseus, but Hades demanded that one of them stayed behind. So Perithous, who had had a long, glorious and adventurous *philia* with Theseus (killing the Minotaur and so on), remained in Hades. In many ways, Theseus' new friendship with Hercules is in exchange for his old one with Perithous. However, this new *philia* shares none of the quasi-mythological traits of the old one. This one will be forged within the institutions of the democratic *polis* itself. The wreath that has had so many transformations throughout this play – from funeral wreath on the heads of the children, to both heroic and un-heroic wreath on Hercules – now sits proud on the temple of Athens itself. It has been redeemed and glorified. It is now a symbol of *philia* within the workings of the *polis*.

Within the democratic polis, male-to-male *philia* can act as a surrogate for family and blood relations. What surfaces is a reworking of a familiar theme in tragedy: that of legally forged relationships prevailing over blood ties. Not surprisingly, this debate between 'natural' and 'cultural' bonds is also gendered. After a long discussion that Hercules has with his armour, dramatised in a monologue (a histrionic gesture that also signals his not-so-complete recovery), he is urged by Theseus to follow him to Athens:

> Hercules: If only I could be turned to stone and have no memories.
> Theseus: Calm down, give your hand to a friend and servant.
> Hercules: Beware the blood might stain you.
> Theseus: Wipe your tears, don't be sad.
>   I am not worried about that.
> Hercules: Now that I've lost my sons, I can have you as one.
> Theseus: Give me your hand and I will guide you.
> Hercules: Two friends, one in sorrow. Old man,
>   you should have a friend like this man.
> Amphitryon: What good children the fatherland breeds.
>
> (1398–1405)

As the last line of the above quotation suggests, this *philia* has the ability to rebirth both men within the notion of the 'fatherland'. The blood of Hercules' children, slain by his own hands, normally would ignite its own cycle of vicious revenge (through the appearance of the Furies or similar female creatures/monsters). This is overtaken by the function of *philia*, but not before this *philia* manages to render both friends born again: first, one as the son of the other, and, finally, both as sons of the fatherland. When Hercules slightly hovers over the bodies of his dead children, Theseus warns him, 'You won't gain any respect if you act like a woman' (1412). Both men, hand-in-hand, head for Athens, leaving Amphitryon to bury the dead bodies. In this play which resonates with conventions of lament, either directly referred to or inverted, the only real funeral that needs to take place does so after the action is complete. This way, Hercules avoids the fear of feminisation that performing the funeral of his wife and children would entail. They are left to be buried by an old man, Amphitryon. Hercules' last lines are, 'Only a fool values wealth and power over good friends'.

The Madness of Hercules is not a very popular tragedy. It is hardly ever performed and it has only been adapted once.[16] Indeed, it is a difficult tragedy. I would suggest that its poor performance history is linked to the difficulties that the text presents. These difficulties, however, only manifest themselves if we view it through the Oedipus-obsessed, Sophoclean model of tragedy. But this play, like many others by Euripides, suggests a way of making tragedy that is neither character-centred nor humanist. Taking our lead from Aristotle, we might say that it exhibits the centrality of *philia* for both the theme and form of tragedy. *The Madness of Hercules* can be read as a study of male-to-male *philia* and its significance for the democratic *polis*. *Philia* is seen as constitutive of notions of masculinity, and in turn this masculinity manifests itself first on the stage then in the audience. Mourning is crucial even in negative terms for the function of *philia*. The inability to mourn is itself seen as something that strengthens the power and the political impact of the male-to-male relationship.

The play has a happy ending. But this ending, signalled by the arrival of Theseus as a *deus ex machina*, is not reached without pain, violence and loss. The whole meta-theatrical dimension of the play and the speculation that it arouses in the audience creates an ambivalence regarding the very issues it supposedly sets out to reinforce. This is not a direct and unmediated celebration of male heroism and *philia*. It is also about the violence and loss that this economy of friendship engenders. In many ways the play can be read as a mourning of masculinity, as oxymoronic as that may sound in Greek terms. Hercules, whose received perception is that of a farcical figure, clumsy and awkward, is turned into a tragic role by the use of some of the main conventions of tragic form: dismemberment, mourning and feminisation. He might in the end be redeemed through *philia*, but conventionally Euripides' use of the *deus ex machina* is usually a mere theatrical gesture that has lost its conviction. It is more of a machine than a *pharmakon*. In this sense Hercules' advent in Athens carries with it the miasma of his predicament. Despite Theseus' triumphalist rhetoric of redemption Hercules still carries within him the curse of the murder of his wife and children. It is this legacy that he brings to the democratic *polis*. The male-to-male *philia* which manifests and reproduces itself within the *polis* – and through tragedy – is never absolutely clear of the blood and violence created by its exclusions. In turn, this loss and violence become constitutive of the democratic *polis* itself.[17]

The Beauty

Another rarely performed play is Euripides' *Helen*. Traditionally received as a light comedy, it hovers on the margins of any discussion about tragic form and aesthetic theory in general. It is yet another problem play, a *hiralotragoedia*, blending genres and confusing the audience. Despite the fact that it deals with Helen, one of the main protagonists of the Trojan War, it has attracted little critical attention. Philip Vellacott writes in his introduction to the Penguin edition of the play:

> It is possible to enjoy a work of art for the succession of moving or delightful moments it provides, together with a vague impression of design and a strong sense of atmosphere, without troubling to acquire that knowledge of detail, association, and source which was assumed by the author as necessary to its full comprehension . . . In this way a reader may find great enjoyment in *Helen*, while allowing numerous questions to remain unanswered. It is impossible to miss the attraction of Helen herself – her grace, wit, lightness of touch . . . It was written in a good humour which is infectious, and in a poetic mood which quickens both eye and heart.[18]

The awkwardness with which the play is greeted, I would suggest, is due to the fact that we are dealing with yet another play that does not comply with the received notion of tragedy. Like *Iphigenia in Tauris*, Aristotle's 'other' model for tragedy, it is a somewhat experimental play. The confusion that this play arouses could be due to the anxiety of form that Euripides is trying to portray. Of all his plays this is the most self-referential one, with most scenes explicitly drawing on other plays previously performed. It is also the play that is parodied by Aristophanes in *Thesmophoriazusae*, performed a year after the public production of *Helen*. Helen herself, a character who is mostly mediated, becomes the vehicle for a play that is basically a pastiche, a compilation of other plays by the same poet.[19]

The version of the myth that Euripides chooses is significant. Rather than accept the mainstream view of Helen, he chooses the tale invented by Stesichorus a few generations earlier. According to this version, Paris went off to Troy with a phantom Helen, while the real Helen spent seventeen years in Egypt. This story immediately sets up a critical rereading of the Trojan War, the war that supposedly was fought for the beauty of the 'face that launched a thousand ships' was all in vain. Helen was never there in the first place. It also scrutinises the relationship between war and romance. The Greeks might like to think that this war was fought for honour and love, but colonisation and expansionism was the true goal. Furthermore, the metaphorical relationship between the female body and the concept of nationhood is also examined. The Trojan War was the war that united *all* the Greeks indeed, it was one of the historical events that helped construct the very notion of Greekness. What the play *Helen* examines in this context is the structural relationships between concepts of nation and formations of gender. If, in fact, Helen was in Egypt all the time, then what did the Greeks fight for? Her phantom, her replica seems to have provided the Greeks with an imaginative and ideological excuse for the atrocities they committed.

The Trojan War has been read as the 'original sin' in European history. It is also one of the first instances where the body of a woman is abducted and then used as the metaphorical and literal excuse for war and expansionism. It is this complex network of interdependencies that the play sets out to examine. It forms part of the cluster of Euripidean anti-war plays, but this one has an interesting twist. In its almost obsessive preoccupation with originals, replicas, phantoms and images it examines the power of representation, especially as this manifests itself on the Athenian stage. Hence its constant mirroring of tragic conventions and its explicit references to other plays by Euripides. The confusions and misunderstandings created by mixing up originals and phantoms, on the one hand, might be classically farcical, but, on the other, they also generate an ambivalence and an uncertainty which undermines tragic form itself. It is this that helps to create the overall formal anxiety. The swapping of the two Helens might be the source of light comedy, but it has also generated, as the play never fails to remind us, one of the bloodiest chapters in the history of Europe.

The play opens with Helen in Egypt providing her own prologue in which she narrates her freakish genealogy. She is interrupted by Teucer, who arrives with practically no explanation at all, other than giving Helen the news that the Trojan War is over and Menelaos has vanished, lost at sea. This, in fact, she could have found out from the priestess Theone all along. What Teucer provides, however, is a series of interesting exchanges in which he cannot quite believe his eyes, as what he encounters is, he believes, the spitting image of Helen. After another soliloquy by Helen and an anti-war exchange with the chorus, Menelaos arrives. He is dressed in rags (again Euripides is parodying himself) and again cannot believe his eyes as he encounters Helen. This is followed by the *anagnorisis*, prefaced by the messenger who announces that Helen, whom Menelaos had rescued from Troy and kept in a cave, has vanished. Now Menelaos has to concede that the real Helen is standing before him. After the *anagnorisis*, the priestess Theone arrives to tell Helen what she already knows: that Menelaos has arrived and that he has lost Helen's phantom. Helen wants to be reunited with Menelaos, but there is a slight problem. After all these years of hospitality, the King of Egypt, Theoclymenus, has claims on her. He wants to marry her. Helen asks Theone for her help to trick Theoclymenus. Theone complies. Helen and Menelaos agree to trick Theoclymenus by saying that Menelaos is dead, and that Helen, as a dutiful Greek wife, will need to perform the funeral rites. Since he died at sea, those rites need to be performed on a boat out at sea. Theoclymenus agrees to provide them with a boat for the performance of these death rites. They take the boat and escape to Greece, leaving Theoclymenus behind looking like a fool. The Dioskouri appear as *deus ex machina* and provide a quasi-moralist ending. They even manage to stop Theoclymenus, the King of Egypt, from feeling betrayed and bitter.

Even this rudimentary outline of the plot reveals how whimsical and arbitrary the narrative is. In many cases it seems that the arrival or disappearance of characters happens simply to draw attention to the dramatic device that they might be embodying or to other Euripidean plays to which they may be referring. The meta-theatrical quality of the play works on the level both of theme and form. In a play about the power of representation, the function of pastiche and 'citationality' appear to be more important than the logical progression of story-line. The ending of the play spoken by the chorus appears like an unconvincing reiteration of many other tragic conclusions:

> The Gods reveal themselves in many forms,
> Bring many matters to surprising ends.
> The things we thought would happen do not happen;
> The unexpected God makes possible:
> And this is what happened here today.
>
> (1685–92)

At best this could be read as ironic. The gods had very little to do with what preceded this ending and the appearance of the Dioskouri presiding over it only compounds the irony. Everything that came before, rather than leading to this conciliatory outcome, experiments with tragic form and perverts tragic conventions. This it does through the theme and form of one of tragedy's most notorious roles, Helen.

The genealogy of Helen, which she outlines in the prologue, is crucial to this. Like Hercules, she is a hybrid creature, born of *hierogamy*, when Zeus, disguised as a swan raped her mother, Leda. For most of her life Helen is a trophy, standing in for something else. Initially, this is beauty. The three goddesses Hera, Aphrodite and Athena asked Paris to judge who was the finest. Hera tempted him with the art of government, Athena with war, and Aphrodite with beauty, embodied in Helen as the final prize. Putting aside the arts of politics and war, Paris chose the aesthetic, manifested in the body of a woman. However, the aesthetic is also the art of illusion, as Helen points out, continuing her story:

> She gave the royal son of Priam for his bride – not me, but a living image compounded of the ether in my likeness. Paris believes that he possesses me: what he holds is nothing but an airy delusion.
>
> (30–5)

From traffic among the gods and the mortals, Helen becomes traffic among men, as she is used as the excuse for war 'to ease the swarming earth of her measureless burden of men' (38–9). The beauty of the prize is immediately followed by the outspoken condemnation of the violence of war. The story of her birth, the exchanges she partakes in and the violence they exert are all interwoven as she draws up the separation between herself and her image: 'Helen was not I, only my name.'

Furthermore, it is a name that generates its own power invested with the ideology that the Greeks infuse into it. So much so that when Teucer arrives he simply cannot believe the image he encounters. Having imagined Helen for seventeen years, the strength of that imagining cannot be ousted by the real image in front of him. In a fascinating sequence in which Helen speaks of herself in the third person, the image of Helen is finally disembodied from her as the actors discuss its potency and its fate during the Trojan War. As Teucer says that the final image he has of Helen is that of Menelaos dragging her off by the hair, she responds:

> Helen: Poor woman! Did you see her? Or are you telling me what you heard?
> Teucer: I saw her as plainly as I see you now.
> Helen: Is it not possible that the gods made you all imagine this?
>
> (141–5)

Or to put it another way: is it not possible that man has made you imagine all this? The simple and direct experience granted by the senses is undermined. In a masterly ironic twist the same eyes that fail to see Helen standing on the stage also failed to see her during the war. These lines reiterate one of the main themes of the play. The assumption that there is an unmediated relationship with reality is questioned; the eyes are unable to see. The senses cannot have a one-to-one relationship with experience. And the aesthetic is primarily the sensory mode. This is a play about the relationship between beauty and power. Through this deconstruction of the image of Helen, the play challenges the privileged position of the aesthetic in general and of its claim to truth. All these references to seeing and viewing are also a comment on the function of the theatre (*theatro, theoria*, where the verb *oro-* (to see) – is *a* component of *theoria*). What starts out as a genealogy of Helen ends up confusing the audience. She quite literally retells her life and almost enacts her death, shouting out that she 'will not be seen dangling in a noose'. This is the convention that is reserved for female suicide in Greek tragedy. In drawing attention to the convention itself, and not simply to the act of dying, she is being overtly theatrical and histrionic. However, the audience has already been warned not to trust such representational conventions. And this play is full of them.

Aristophanes, in his criticisms of Euripides, calls him *ptochopoion*, a moulder of poverty, and *rakiosyrraptaden*, a weaver of rags. This, of course, refers to the prominent position he grants on his stage to slaves, women and the disenfranchised in general. On another level we can read it as exposing the poverty of the stage itself, as a deliberate remoulding and weaving of theatrical convention once he has stripped it of its representational certainty and its spectacular glamour. For example, the appearance of Menelaos is typical of how Euripides undermines and subverts tragic conventions, even if it is one he himself had previously used. Menelaos appears dressed in rags, and these rags are highlighted, referred to and mocked throughout the play. The appearance of a king in rags is indeed flirting with blasphemy (and, according to legend, may even have cost Euripides his life), but it is also reworking the convention shaped by the poet himself in his earlier plays. As mentioned earlier, *Helen* is full of references to other plays by Euripides, which is fitting for a play that analyses the mechanics of representation.[21] In reworking theatrical convention, in some cases quite literally 'to death', this play, like many others by Euripides, exposes the poverty of tragic form itself.

The main convention scrutinised in this play is also the one that provides the solution, the narrative trick at its centre. It is the obsession with funeral rites and ritual lament that Helen draws on in order to orchestrate her and Menelaos' escape. Like a stage director, she uses one of its most prominent conventions, not necessarily to add gravitas and depth, but to deceive and confuse. She mocks conventions that Euripides himself took very seriously in plays like *Medea* and *Trojan Women*. According to Charles Segal, this 'poetics of sorrow' is quintessentially Euripidean and it ties in well with the poet's political affiliations. He writes:

> Drawing on the traditions of ritual lament and choral song, Euripides' tragedies are in a sense songs of sorrow – sorrow for the suffering that seems an inevitable part of being human, and sorrow for the hatred, bitterness, folly, and error that make life even harder than it need be. They are also songs of the sorrows that would otherwise be hidden away, uncommemorated because they are endured in the

privacy of the secret world where the larger part of Athenian women's lives unfolds.[22]

This 'poetics of sorrow', however, fulfils a dramatically different function. Rather than reinforce the inevitability and the universality of the pain of being human, it tends to politicise and historicise that pain. In constantly rewriting the conventions that constitute such pain and exclusion, Euripides' poetics attempts to expose the very 'conventionality' (as in, artificiality) of these categories. In dealing with the mechanics of their representation, it highlights the fact that they are 'man-made' and not 'natural' and 'inevitable'. Rather than simply performing an act of recuperation and visibility in a quasi-feminist and slightly anachronistic manner, it sets out to examine the interdependency of these categories: of sorrow and celebration, of exclusion and visibility, of man and woman, of private and public. It also implicates tragic form in the creation of these categories of exclusion. By examining the limitations of tragic form, this 'poetics of sorrow' opens up possibilities for critique and change, both of the form and of the world-view it helps create.

Helen could not be a more appropriate role to enact such a critique of tragic convention. Although she is presented as the most feminine of all women, her life could not be more incongruous with that image. She is the most public of women. One could say that she has a solely public life as opposed to the traditional private domain that most women occupy in tragedy. As she comes to present 'pure representation' and mediation, she really could only exist in the public, the male sphere. This already grants her an androgynous quality (something she shares with most Euripidean female protagonists). Helen, who is created, exchanged, turned into a gift and trophy, becomes the perfect agent to scrutinise the conventions of this economy of representation. Here is her exchange with Menelaos as she perverts lamentation conventions to forge their escape:

> Helen: Listen, Menelaos – a woman's plan might succeed: will you let me invent a story that you are dead?
> Menelaos: It may invite ill-luck; but if there's something solid to be gained, I'm willing to die – in fiction.
> Helen: Good; then I will appear before this pagan king in mourning for you, and weeping –
> Menelaos: How will that help our escape? This plan of yours seems a bit old-fashioned.
> Helen: I will tell him you were drowned at sea, and ask his permission to make a cenotaph for you.
> Menelaos: Suppose he agrees; giving me a cenotaph won't save our lives without a ship.

Helen: I will ask him to provide us a ship, from which we may drop your burial-offerings into the lap of the sea.
Menelaos: It's a good plan, except for this: if he tells you to perform the rites on land your story will be no use.
Helen: But I'll tell him it's against Greek custom to bury on land those drowned at sea.
Menelaos: Yes, that will do; then I'll go on board with you to help in the ritual.

(1040–58)

In this exchange Helen assumes a masculine role and Menelaos typically becomes the woman. Like a *chorodidaskalos*, or director of the chorus, she plans and will later execute every movement and gesture of this story. Her use of terms like 'cenotaph' means she is familiar with the discourse of the official funeral oration. The idea of the cenotaph would be useless in the world of female lamentation, where the presence of the dead body is required. Menelaos' questioning of the usefulness of the cenotaph in the female position he occupies is also a more general comment on its function. His plea that Helen's plan is 'a bit old-fashioned' could be read as an indication that funeral rites in general tend to be overused in tragedy. However, Helen intends to use them with a twist. Once she has mockingly underlined the artificiality of funeral rites themselves, in a discourse that blends modes from the oral female tradition with the official male one, she then proceeds to tackle the whole category of 'Greek custom': 'I'll tell him it's against Greek custom'. She is inventing traditions and customs and undermining the category of 'Greekness' in the process. If 'Greek custom' can be drawn on in such a manipulative way, then what does this say about notions such as autochthony that the Greeks were using at the time to differentiate themselves from the 'barbarians'?

This reference to custom connects this use of lamentation with ones used previously in the play. In a more somber mode Helen has already used the funeral oration in lamenting the ills of war. Lest we forget that this is also an anti-war play, or a play where the violence of war and the violence of representation are read as parallel, Helen has long soliloquies where she interchanges the Greeks and the Trojans and presents them both as victims of war. 'Weep for the tears of Troy' (330) and 'Through Hellas too the same river of weeping runs' (400) are uttered by her in a gesture that equates Greek loss with Trojan loss. It also draws a connection that is crucial in this play, that of the interdependency between private, female lament and official, male funeral oration.

After Helen has convinced Menelaos to enact these mock funeral rites she says: 'I will go in now, change this white dress for mourning black, cut my hair short and tear my face with my nails till the blood runs' (1090). Menelaos protests slightly at the mention of blood, but is convinced at the end that such an act of deception requires blood. The blood of Troy, the blood of the Greek soldiers and now the blood on Helen's cheeks are brought together in this gesture that connects private and public, male and female weeping, and, through the inversion/perversion of death ritual, comedy and tragedy. After a sequence which for all purposes appears to be comic, the audience is once again confronted with the possibility of real blood. It is this ambivalence and unease that make this play experimental.

The perversion of funeral rites also draws on the connection between marriage and funeral. According to this convention, the marriage ceremony is equated with the funeral, in so far as the young bride's entrance into marriage also signifies her ascension into death (Iphigenia, Cassandra, Antigone). This is turned inside out as Helen escapes marriage through her mockery of funeral rites. She says to Theoclymenus, the King of Egypt, who wants to marry her:

> My husband-to-be, duty insists that I honour my first husband, and the memory of our marriage; and for love of him I would even die with him. But what pleasure could it give him, that I should share his death? No; let me go myself, and give my gifts to the dead; and may the gods grant to you everything that I wish; and to this man too, for his help in what I am doing. You shall find in me such a wife as your goodness to us both deserves; for all this leads to a happy end. Now, complete your generosity by commanding a ship to be given us, to carry these gifts.
> (1328–39)

The marriage ceremony, funeral rites and the laws of hospitality (with the exchange of gifts) are all mocked in this sequence. Helen and Menelaos manage to escape as a result, although we have grave doubts as to the kind of new marriage they are entering. As for Theoclymenus, the King of Egypt, he is made a fool. He has not only been tricked by a woman, but towards the end of the play he is even challenged by a slave:

> Theoclymenus: Am I to take orders from a slave?
> Messenger: Yes, because I am right!

Even though this exchange mocks a foreign king and not a Greek one, it still flirts dangerously with blasphemy. This play has exchanged the positions of men and women, it has perverted tragic conventions, and it also appears to be inverting the positions of slaves and masters. Indeed, the play draws parallels between the treatment of women and the treatment of slaves. Moreover, it is concerned with the regime of representation that creates the names 'woman' and 'slave', where both categories are seen to expose the 'poverty' of such a system. Aristophanes' accusation of Euripides as *ptochopoion* comes to mind once more. The presence of slaves is crucial in this play. They are there not only as foils for their masters, but to question the 'nature' of slavery itself. There is a fascinating exchange between Menelaos (who is dressed in rags) and the slave-messenger early on in the play:

> Messenger: I'm a slave by birth, I know; but there are slaves who are noble, who have the mind of a free man, if not the name: I want to count as one of them. It's the best way; otherwise you've a double misfortune – you take orders from every one all round, and you feel like as slave as well. (690–700)

Just as Helen refused to identify with the image created for her, this messenger refuses to consider himself a slave. This constitutes a radical gesture given that the Greeks believed people were born into slavery, unless, of course, they were captured at war. And this is a play that questions war and all its ramifications, both imaginary and material.

As even this rudimentary reading of *Helen* hopes to show, we are dealing with a complex and sophisticated experiment with tragic form. With the general thematic context of the so-called Trojan cycle of myths, Euripides presents us with a narrative that questions war, the violence of representation, and its implications in the historical reality of war. Through the theme of gender differentiation and its two civic domains – marriage and death – the play opens up a subtle but insightful critique of Athenian democracy. Far from being a light comedy, or a tragi-comedy, it surfaces as one of Euripdes' most political plays.

The play was performed in 412 BCE, less than a year after the disastrous Sicilian expedition led by Athens. It forms part of the overall criticism of the Peloponnesian War – in the shadow of which most of Euripdes' work takes place. Ironically, according to legend and Plutarch's *Lives* (*Life of Nicias*, 29), Euripides may have actually helped to save some of the Athenian prisoners-of-war at Syracuse. His poetry was so highly regarded that when it was recited by the Athenian prisoners their guards yielded to its beauty and could not refuse them food and drink. Some of these prisoners managed to escape and on their return to Athens hailed Euripides as their saviour.

Unlike most tragedies which would have been performed at the Great Dionysia Festival of Athens, this play was shown at the small festival of the Thesmophoria. This was a women's only festival in honour of Demeter and her daughter Persephone. This venue raises a number of questions regarding performance. In many ways, it seems appropriate for a play that so explicitly deals with the mechanics of 'femininity' and with the political dimension of this category to be shown to a women-only audience. If in addition to the rare presence of women in an audience there were also women actors, then this is indeed a unique play. It could be one of the few plays written with women actors in mind. It seems to be asking the actors to question the performativity of their gender. In separating the image of Helen from the body of the actor Helen, it also creates a distance between the functions of role, character and actor. This is a kind of distance that estranges rather than familiarises, even though, and possibly especially since, it was enacted by 'real' women.

The Madness of Hercules and *Helen* present us respectively with readings of masculinity and femininity. Both texts are concerned with how such a differentiation in gender has implications for more general issues of representation and power. They are exemplary of a Euripidean aesthetic that, far from being celebratory and humanist, acts as a critique of the Athenian project. The formal strategies that this aesthetic utilises are classically tragic but, more importantly, they push tragic form to its limits. It engages with tragic form, while also exposing the exclusions and the violence that constitute it. Its *gestus* is not one of triumph, hope and progress, but that of melancholy and speculation.

Notes

1. Euripides, *The Madness of Hercules*, lines 1427–8; my translations used throughout this chapter.
2. For an insightful analysis of the systems of exchange and gender in Greek tragedy, see K. W. B. Ormand, *Exchange and the Maiden* (Austin, TX: University of Austin Press at Texas, 1999); V. J. Wohl, *Intimate Commerce: Exchange, Gender, and Subjectivity in Greek Tragedy* (Austin, TX: University of Austin at Texas Press, 1998).
3. For a more detailed analysis of this relationship, see Jacques Derrida, *The Politics of Friendship*, trans. George Collins (London and New York: Verso, 1997) and the previous chapter of this book.
4. The Kires of death are demons mentioned in the *Iliad* and are associated with *Moira*, fate, and the Furies.
5. A chorus of old men almost always signals a kingdom in crisis as is also the case in *The Persians* and *The Oresteia*. See Edith Hall, 'The Sociology of Athenian Tragedy', in Pat Easterling (ed.), *The Cambridge Companion to Greek Tragedy* (Cambridge: Cambridge University Press, 1997), pp. 93–126.
6. Hercules was delayed in Hades as he was rescuing Theseus, a fact that will be crucial for the ending of the play.

7. In the fragments of an Aeschylean tragedy called *Xantriai* she appears to incite the Mainades. Virgil in the *Aeniad* seems to equate the 'hounds of Lyssa' with the Furies.
8. The epithet *marmaropos* is attributed to the Gorgon Medusa because she had the ability to turn people into stone through her glance alone. And this epithet is used here as well.
9. See Juliet Mitchell, *Mad Men and Medusas: Reclaiming Hysteria and the Effects of Sibling Relations on the Human Condition* (London: Penguin Books, 2000).
10. Ibid. p. 10.
11. This lineage is, however, disputed. See H. King, 'Once Upon a Text: Hysteria from Hippocrates', in S. L. Gilman, H. King, R. Porter, G. S. Rousseau and E. Showalter (eds), *Hysteria Beyond Freud* (Berkeley: University of Berkeley Press, 1993). King argues that the link with Hippocrates was a Renaissance invention in order to create a credible and 'classical' heritage to justify that period's own definition of the illness.
12. See Juliet Mitchell, *Mad Men and Medusas*, p. 119.
13. In this case the structure of *philia* would act as a parallel for the all-important sibling relationships. Mitchell writes in *Mad Men and Medusas*, 'the relationship between hysteria and psychoanalysis has been haunted since its inception by a crucial omission: that of sibling relationships', p. 19.
14. Such a genealogy would also have to cover the fraught relationship between psychoanalysis and the stage.
15. In the *Children of Hercules*, Euripides explains the blood ties between Hercules and Theseus. His mother, Alcmene, and Theseus' mother, Ether, were first cousins and Pelops was their grandfather.
16. The only adaptation I am aware of is by Heiner Müller, the German playwright. He rewrites in *Hercules 13*, the play and adds a thirteenth labour, where Hercules liberates Thebes from the Thebans.
17. It might be interesting in this context to draw attention to the legend of Euripides' fate. He left Athens in self-imposed exile and arrived in Macedon as a guest of King Archelaos. According to myth, when the King found out that he had dressed a king in rags in his play *The Bacchae*, he supposedly turned his hounds on him and they dismembered him. This is a typically tragic death, one that mirrors the fate of Dionysus himself. It is also a tale of *philia* and *philoxenia* turned inside out.
18. See Philip Vellacott's introduction to Euripides, *The Bacchae and Other Plays* (London: Penguin Books, 1973), p. 24.
19. For a very insightful analysis of this play as an '*anodos*' drama, see Helen P. Foley, *Female Acts in Greek Tragedy* (Princeton and Oxford: Princeton University Press, 2001), pp. 303–30. She writes, 'I shall borrow the term "*anodos* drama" from Jean-Pierre Guepin to describe those Euripidean plays that are plotted against the mythical story pattern most familiar both to ourselves and, I think, to the Athenian audience, in the story of the rape and descent (*kathodos*) of the goddess Kore/Persephone and her subsequent ascent (*anodos*) to the upper world,' p. 304. She then proceeds to reread this myth in terms of the implications it has on death/funeral rites, marriage and the relationships of gender.
20. All translations of Euripides' *Helen* are from Philip Vellacott's *The Bacchae and Other Plays*.

21. Vellacott states in his introduction to *The Bacchae*, 'Its plot is largely modelled on that of *Iphigenia in Tauris*, with an opening taken from *Andromache*, a lyric strophe and an entrance from *Hippolytus*; there are also very many echoes, mainly from *Iphigenia*,' p. 24.
22. See Charles Segal, *Euripides and the Poetics of Sorrow: Art, Gender and Commemoration in Alcestis Hippolytus and Hecuba* (Durham and London: Duke University Press, 1993), p. 233.

CHAPTER SIX

Mourning and Tragic Form

> Tiresias: Oh, you fool, you do not realise what you are saying. Witless before, you are now stark mad. Cadmus, we must go, do what we can for the man, whatever his savagery: do what we can for our city, god preserve it . . . Son of Zeus, Dionysus must be served. Pentheus' name means grief. That is not a prophecy, Cadmus. It is a fact. A foolish man. Foolish words. May he never bring grief upon your house.[1]

Throughout Athenian tragedy, from the first play we have, *The Persians*, to *The Bacchae*, allegedly the last, the aesthetics and politics of mourning are central to the way tragedy is worked out, both as a specific language of performance and as a civic institution. Atossa, the Queen of the Persians, a male actor dressed in excessive eastern garb, and Pentheus, a Greek king dressed in women's clothing, present two pivotal moments in what I would hesitantly call an epistemology of mourning. *The Persians*, one of the primal texts and theatrical events through which the Athenian state imaginatively and discursively creates itself in conjunction with its barbaric other, presents us with a lamenting barbarian queen. Through this lament, the Athenians are asked to identify with and mourn for their eternal enemy, the Persians. The intricate set of relationships set up between Athenian and Persian, man and woman, soldier and citizen, barbarism and civilisation, and the inversions implicated, are all enacted through the processes of lamentation and mourning. Through this somewhat contradictory and ambivalent process, as Nicole Loraux suggests, Athens starts to invent itself.[2] Since *The Persians* is seen as the first extant tragedy, it is also read as one of the foundational elements both of tragedy as an aesthetic mode and civic institution and of the democratic *polis* itself. At the end of this trajectory, after the devastating Peloponnesian War and the critique of this experiment mounted by Euripides himself, Pentheus represents the state in pieces, gender roles reversed and an excessive sexuality unleashed. Mourning, which in Atossa is associated with femininity and otherness, its two crucial modes of representation, in Pentheus turns into a name, not simply a prophecy, but a fact, as Tiresias mentions above. As such it is 'cited', performed and enacted. Its relationship to the founding of the state is turned inside out, as Thebes, the mirror of Athens, is portrayed as a dystopian landscape. Atossa and Pentheus can be read as mirror images, standing at the respective wings of the Athenian stage: one at the entrance and the other at its exit. Both, however, underline the formal and thematic significance of mourning for tragedy.

The discourse of mourning within which I attempt to locate tragic form is one that combines both the textuality and the materiality of this process. The use of the term epistemology tries to encapsulate this and to differentiate it from the ontological use of the term. Mourning as it is reconfigured with notions of attachment and loss through psychoanalysis,[3] together with historical readings of its relationships to the founding of law and the city-state, creates a very diverse and dense *topos* through which to approach tragedy. The psychoanalytical notion of mourning, in places conflating it with desire, sees it as central to the process of identity formation, and indeed, in more recent guises, as part of gender differentiation.[4] The issue of primary loss as central to the creation of the self will be read in conjunction with the political and civic function of mourning. This is done in a gesture that tries to read mourning not necessarily as part and parcel of the quasi-existentialist and metaphysical reception of tragedy. The evocation of mourning as constitutive of tragic form is also an attempt to formulate a theory of tragedy, a *theoria*, that sees it as speculative, critical, physical and civic. In the same gesture, it forms part of the dialogue of reconciliation between philosophy and tragedy. If mourning can be read as an aspect of material and materialist critique, as it appears in the work of Walter Benjamin, it may also provide a way of renegotiating tragedy and modernity.

The aesthetics and the politics of mourning are not things we readily associate with Brecht or the other theorists of modern performance. However, the anti-idealist reading of mourning proposed here and the mediation of Benjamin might prove fruitful for a discussion of tragedy as a form of speculative philosophy, as a performative philosophy that is engaged and engaging, that negotiates between strangeness and familiarity.

Plato, Aristotle and the Repudiation of Mourning

Unlikely parallels have already been drawn in this study between Plato's dislike of tragedy and Brecht's. We can read similarities in the way both approaches abhor emotional attachment and identification as part of the aesthetic experience. Both thinkers propose a 'theory of tragedy' against which they proceed to define their own philosophical projects. Before we proceed to evaluate the validity of these parallels, especially in conjunction with the idea of mourning, I would like to investigate Plato's 'sense of tragedy'. According to recent readings, what we identify as a 'sense of the tragic' in its metaphysical dimension can really only be glimpsed in the work of Plato and not, as we would presume, in Aristotle. This is fascinating in itself. Plato, the great anti-theatrical philosopher provides us with one of the first formulations of the 'tragic idea'. Aristotle, on the other hand, for all his specific writings in the *Poetics*, lacks that metaphysical dimension that would give us a 'tragic sense of life and art'. Stephen Halliwell writes in a recent study of this phenomenon:

> I take it, accordingly, as a necessary condition for a conception of the tragic that it should suppose tragedy (at least in its ideal form) to intimate some ultimate insight, of profound spiritual and moral consequence, into reality, even if the nature of such insight may have to be characterized as inherently mysterious. As that condition perhaps already implies, where the tragic is framed in metaphysical or quasi-metaphysical terms, the dramatic genre of tragedy will become subsumable under, rather than representing the exclusive carrier of, the larger vision or world-view.[5]

This is already a reading of tragedy that sees it in metaphysical and idealist terms. The search for profound insight has already been formulated in Platonic terms. If the notion of tragedy can only be read in mysterious and metaphysical terms (in ideal terms), then it cannot, almost by definition, be found in Aristotle. Halliwell says of Aristotle's work on tragedy:

> All the major features of Aristotle's treatment of the genre bear out the proposition that his interpretation of tragedy is independent of, and in some ways actually inimical to, what we might now deem to be a developed notion of the tragic. These features include an analytical framework (the 'six parts' model) which stems from a general theory of poetic art and could consequently be applied equally to comedy, as well as a fundamental concern for issues of structure, unity, and coherence which are likewise much larger than tragedy, or even than poetry, in their scope.[6]

Rather curiously, Aristotle transpires in this analysis as a formalist and Plato emerges as the great humanist who is concerned with the psychological and political dimension of tragedy. Edith Hall in 'Is there a *Polis* in Aristotle's *Poetics*' extends this argument by proposing that Aristotle's alleged formalism is what makes his writings on tragedy open to later universalist interpretations and appropriations. She writes:

> The *Poetics*' near total displacement of the *polis* from tragedy seems to me to be an astonishingly original innovation, which adumbrates the incipient and future status of tragedy as an international art-form. Tragedy was soon to be consumed

and appreciated by multifarious individuals, in widely disparate political locations at great distances from the Athenian theatre of Dionysus. The *Poetics*, the work of a non-Athenian and of an opponent certainly of *radical* democracy, enacts this divorce on the level of theory, a divorce which was to have a huge impact on the future of ancient literary criticism, quite apart from the direction taken by literary theory in later ages.[7]

The total absence of any cultural and historical specificity from the *Poetics* is what opens the text up to interpretation and misunderstanding. Aristotle's theory of tragedy, in the sense proposed here, lacks the 'world-view' that would provide us with a sense of the tragic. It is left to Plato, the great anti-tragic philosopher, to formulate the 'sense of tragedy'. Accused of what in modern terms would be equated with formalism, Aristotle cannot provide us with a philosophy of tragedy. Halliwell writes:

> The Platonic disavowal of the tragic reflects an awareness, paralleled in antiquity only by the later and partly platonizing views of the Stoics, that the tragic itself is a philosophy in embryo.[8]

It is a philosophy that is quintessentially anti-theatrical. Halliwell delineates the Platonic contrast between two 'ultimate hypotheses about the world':

> The first [is] that human lives are governed by external forces which are indifferent to, and capable of crushing, the quest for happiness; the second [is] that the source of true happiness is located nowhere other than in the individual soul's choice between good and evil. To embrace the first of these is to open the floodgates to (self) pity, and to interpret the world as a stage made for the tragedy of life. To follow, on the other hand, a belief in the soul's capacity to forge its own moral fate is to entertain hope which nourishes the psychological, ethical, and metaphysical aspirations of Plato's own dialogues.[9]

This distinction is primarily a Platonic one. The individual is either opposed to the cruelty of a metaphysical logic or he in a sense internalises it and acquires a 'soul', which makes him an individual in the first place. The only other way he can deal with the metaphysical dimension of reality is to turn it into a stage, to theatricalise it, but that, in turn, only incites pity or rather self-pity.

The notion that there could be a different way of dealing with the 'metaphysical cruelty' of the world, or the view that individuals themselves cannot ultimately be separated from the world or the process that helps construct them, is alien to Platonic thinking. Tragedy can only corrupt the ideal world and the world itself can only be viewed as a twice-removed stage. Mourning is only configured as self-pity, and as such it is base and corrupting in itself. The view that tragedy could propose a different relationship with the 'real' through the process of mourning is left unexamined. The main reason for this is that theories about the 'sense of tragedy' or 'tragedy as philosophy', from Plato onwards, have almost always inhabited the same metaphysical thinking that inspired the repudiation of tragedy in the first place. It is significant that the greatest anti-tragic philosopher, Plato, should also be the one to initiate the long and diverse trajectory of the understanding of tragedy as metaphysical and idealist. This legacy is elaborated on by the German Idealists and Romantics, and it is inherited by Brecht. He, too, bases his critique of tragedy on an idealist reading of the form. In this sense, Plato and Brecht form an unlikely narrative couple in their repudiation of tragedy.

Although beyond the scope of this analysis, it would be worth investigating exactly how Aristotle is deemed to be concerned only with form and structure and Plato with the content and meaning of the tragic. Already the terms to which I am alluding draw on the great modernist debates about the politics of form and its relation to content. The fact that Aristotle does not specifically mention the *polis* does not mean it is not inscribed in the ways he conceptualises tragic form, and similarly Plato's altogether 'philosophical' reading of tragedy presupposes formal qualities. A discussion of their respective uses of the term *katharsis* might prove useful as it presupposes 'pity and fear', and different ways of identification and audience response. Such a discussion was outlined in Chapter 4. On the whole, however, it is noteworthy that Plato's views of tragedy are serious enough to amount to a philosophy whereas Aristotle's writing can be viewed as a type of handbook on tragedy, one that is open to interpretation and appropriation by later generations of literary critics. The founding philosopher of the anti-theatrical tradition, Plato, is the first to provide us with a philosophical definition of the 'idea of tragedy'.

This definition has reverberated across the centuries and forms the hallmark of most subsequent philosophical readings of tragic form. It is idealist and metaphysical, situating the individual on the brink of the abyss that is loss and death. Of course, even as I begin to describe this tradition I need to 'resort' to theatricalising and spectacular terms. This tradition usually figuratively and imaginatively manifests itself in histrionic and even slightly melodramatic modes. It is driven by a *thanatoerotic* impulse that is always gendered, as the mother is seen as the first and primary experience of loss (George Steiner fittingly calls the sense of tragedy a 'black hole'), and it is stubbornly ahistorical. It is based on an outright denial of mourning, as a discourse that might provide a different relationship to loss and death.

Plato's repudiation of mimesis is first and foremost a repudiation of mourning. In his famous critique of poetry as a double fantasy in *Republic* 10, he voices caution against the derangement of the soul and mind caused by excessive mourning:

> [T]the naturally best part of us, since it has not been properly educated by reason or habit either, relaxes the guard over this lamenting part, because it is a spectator of the sufferings of others; it feels no shame for itself in praising and pitying another man who, calling himself a good man, weeps and wails unseasonably.[10]

What a truly 'good man' is able to control in his private life is, through the function of mimesis, turned into a public spectacle. It panders to the lowest aspects of his existence. Watching the suffering of others who 'pretend' to be good triggers the process of self-pity. And self-pity, which for Plato is always the outcome of mourning, leads straight to unreason. For Plato, mourning is primarily bad philosophy. It is philosophy traversed, feminised and spectacularised. Henry Staten writes about Plato's difficulty with mourning in *Eros in Mourning*:

> What we begin to see in Socrates' critique of poetry, and specifically Homer, is that mourning, as the agitation that is set off in the soul by an illusion, deception, or untruth that magnifies the importance of losing what we love, is philosophical unwisdom in general.[11]

If mourning is 'philosophical unwisdom', then tragedy, which can be read as a new negotiation of mourning in relation to the political and the aesthetic, is total and utter folly, triggering the basest feelings in the individual and helping spread the epidemic of uncontrolled grief. The shift from Homer is significant and might be read as an appropriation of mourning by the newly founded city-state through the aesthetic and civic institution of tragedy. For the function of mourning in tragedy takes on dimensions far greater than those primarily described in Homer. Through the reintroduction of physical presence, both in the actors and the audience, tragedy returns this 'unwisdom' to the body, usually the eroticised body of the absent mother, which triggers the process of mourning.

Staten states that this view of *eros* as sublimated mourning is itself the origin of idealism. He cites the speech of the prophetess Diotima from the *Symposium*:

> First of all . . . he will fall in love with the beauty of one individual body . . . Next he must consider how nearly related the beauty of any one body is to the beauty of any other, when he will see that if he is to devote himself to loveliness of form it

will be absurd to deny that the beauty of each and every body is the same ... Next he must grasp that the beauties of the body are as nothing to the beauties of the soul ... And from this he will be led to contemplate the beauty of laws and institutions ...

And next, his attention should be diverted from institutions to the sciences, so that he may know the beauty of every kind of knowledge ... And, turning his eyes toward the open sea of beauty, he will find in such contemplation the seed of the most fruitful discourse and the loftiest thought, and reap a golden harvest of philosophy.[12]

By sublimating the specific and the physical *eros*, the philosopher can admire the beauty of laws and institutions; indeed, this sublimation results in the advent of philosophy itself. As Staten stresses, this love of ideas, this 'divine *eros* is rooted in mortal *eros*', but the 'ascent to the ideal' is also a 'liberation from the realm of the body'.[13] This eroticisation of philosophy, even in this extract from Diotima, also presupposes a certain theatricalisation, a certain enactment through the function of poetry. The phrase 'And, turning his eyes toward the open sea of beauty' already employs figures of speech that can be strictly called literary. This *eros* is also dramatised. It is, however, a fleeting moment, which under different circumstances might have filled the philosopher's eyes with tears. But weeping would lead to unreason as the philosopher is not allowed to mourn for the loss of the erotic object. The process from the physical *eros* to the divine and from the body to the realm of ideas can in no way include the act of mourning. It is too tempting and seductive, since its realm is always feminine. It might trick the philosopher, distort and traverse the ideal world, and land him right back in the physical, the bodily, and the particular from which he is trying to ascend.

In this sense, tragedy, as an aspect of a discourse of mourning, might be read as an anti-idealist philosophy, based not on the repudiation of mourning but on its celebration. Although straightforward celebration might be too strong a term, as mourning occupies an ambiguous *topos* within tragedy, it still remains one of the first attempts to inscribe or reinscribe the act of mourning into a literary/aesthetic genre. This mode is implicated in civic and political dimensions, it also proposes or rather constantly negotiates relationships between mourning and the state. The significance of these relationships were, of course, appreciated by Plato in his banishment of poetry as mimesis (i.e. tragedy) from the ideal state. In the idealising and transcendentalising tradition of Plato, mourning not only leads to bad philosophy, it also leads to bad politics, which aspires to the lowest instinct of man's existence: the physical, the bodily, the erotic and the feminine.

To begin to view tragedy as a discourse of mourning with all its ambiguities and contradictions is automatically to see Plato and his philosophy of tragedy as anti-mourning. As Henry Staten writes:

> And yet Platonism as antimourning would invade the generative system of Western poetry at a fundamental level, by the perversely brilliant doctrine of eros that holds its true nature to be not attachment to but transcendence of the object, and in fact of all objects.[14]

It would also invade the generative system that identifies the tragic with the 'idea of tragedy'. This metaphysical tradition sees tragedy as loss and transcendence; it is a tradition that is figuratively and imaginatively reconfigured as 'black holes', gaping absences, voids that need to be filled, with the individual constantly standing on the edge of an abyss. This is an abyss in which he is always in danger of being consumed, unless he can ascend from it. It is this, always failed, attempted deliverance from the object (any object) that tragedy is supposed constantly to re-enact. The already inscribed failure of this attempt is due primarily to the fact that he undertakes it not as a philosopher but as an actor. The kind of deliverance that mourning requires can only be achieved through philosophy, and tragedy, as we have ascertained, can at best be described as bad philosophy, if indeed it is philosophy at all. This metaphysical reading of tragedy would have the individual doomed to eternal repetition of the always-failed attempt to liberate himself from the object of desire. As it is an act that also always requires an audience, its dead-end can only trigger unstoppable grief. It can never incite reasoned thinking. Hence the fear of the political epidemic of uncontrollable weeping is induced by mourning through tragedy.

Ironically this 'idea of tragedy' – relying on this transcendentalising logic – is also deeply anti-theatrical. In many ways it is part of the tradition that *philosophises* tragedy without acknowledging that it is a performative event, with all the political, aesthetic and psychoanalytical dimensions that this may entail. It already reads it as part of the idealist philosophical tradition that it in turn uses for its analysis. This may also account for the long-standing but difficult love affair between philosophy, particularly in its transcendental and idealist schools, and tragedy. This tradition usually ignores the fact that tragedy comprises a theatrical event and proceeds to read it as if it were philosophy. The kind of philosophy it best resembles in this case is probably the Platonic dialogue.

It is not so much that tragedy is not philosophy as that it may be philosophy by other means. Rather than deliverance from mourning, tragedy might propose total and utter immersion in it. The discourse of morning presupposes attachment and loss. But rather than concentrating on the inescapable function of loss, mourning as tragedy might focus more on the process of attachment. Rather than viewing the eroticised object as always and forever lost and irretrievable, mourning tends to dwell on the attachment itself. As these attachments need to be eroticised before they take part within the economies of loss and transcendence, we need to investigate how this eroticisation comes about. How is the object of desire eroticised and does this process also account for gender differentiation? In other words, if mourning is part of the economy of the self, how does it impact on the formation of gender? This will lead us to question whether the function of mourning is itself gendered. A reading of tragedy as mourning might also account for both the absence of the female and for the ubiquitous position it occupies as the always represented and representable on the stage.

For the Love of Women: Mourning and Gender

> 'To philosophise is to learn how do die' – Montaigne

> 'Without a bent for melancholia there is no psyche, only a transition to action or play' – Julia Kristeva[15]

The philosophical slips very easily into the psychoanalytic interpretation of mourning. Both models in some way occupy the same transcendental trajectory. Mourning as bad philosophy can neither teach us 'how to die' nor can it, as always incomplete, occupy the place of melancholia in the creation of the psyche. As the primary 'transition to action or play' in both philosophy and psychoanalysis, it transpires as something fragmentary and unfinished. As a category it can neither be viewed as 'reason' in philosophical terms, nor can it be pathologised, like melancholia, in psychoanalytical terms. It cannot, therefore, be remedied by critique, nor can it be cured. Neither critique, nor pharmaceutical cure, it somehow fluctuates between both, and can probably assume the guise of both. And, as guise is the operative word, it always tries to mislead us, to seduce us.

Freud's classic essay 'Mourning and Melancholia' is one of the first attempts to include notions of attachment, loss and grief in the process of ego formation. As the incomplete process of grieving/mourning, melancholy is crucial to the identifications that help form the ego. Indeed, it is this emphasis on the 'unfinished' nature of mourning that needs to be highlighted. Incomplete grief, according to Freud, always incorporates the lost object and phantasmatically preserves it in the ego. Through the processes of attachment and cathexis, the ego-in-the-making manages finally to become the fully fledged ego through never really letting go of the lost object. This incorporation of the lost object always, as the word suggests, involves the body. It is, according to Freud, the body ego that is formed through the processes of mourning and melancholia. In this way mourning and melancholia also appear to be fundamental to the process of gender differentiation. Two recent readings of this web of relationships are significant for the thinking about the ways gender functions within both mourning and tragic form.

In *Black Sun: Depression and Melancholia*, Julia Kristeva talks of melancholia not so much as an illness but as an alternative way of understanding the world. In her psychoanalytical analysis of this discursive melancholia,[16] she states that women are more prone to it and that it informs certain types of artistic practices.[16] On the connection between women and death rites she writes:

> The unrepresentable nature of death was linked with that other unrepresentable – which for mythical thought is constituted by the female body. The horror of castration underlying the anguish of death undoubtedly accounts in large part for the universal partnership with death and the penis-lacking feminine.[17]

This connection of women with death may account for the orality and the 'femininity' of the lament and mourning traditions. More generally, melancholia is linked with the processes of representation and individuation. In her model, however, there is a crucial difference from Freud's: matricide rather than parricide is the crucial stage in the process of individuation. This aspect makes her approach essentially anti-Oedipal:

> Matricide is our vital necessity, the sine-qua-non condition of our individuation, provided that it takes place under optimal circumstances and can be eroticized – whether the lost object has recovered as erotic object (as is the case for male heterosexuality, or female homosexuality), or it is transposed by means of an unbelievable, the advent of which one can only admire, which eroticizes the *other* (the other sex, in the case of the heterosexual woman) or transforms cultural constructs into 'sublime' erotic objects.[18]

This analysis claims that the process of individuation is more complicated for women and bears different consequences. Heterosexual women have a further stage to undergo – one that transforms cultural constructs into the eroticised other. Since women have to identify narcissistically and erotically with the mother, the process of creating identity and acculturation poses further problems for women. Because matricide is more difficult for women, Kristeva claims that they might be prone to a type of melancholy that is manifested in the melancholic putting to death of the self rather than having to kill the mother. The next process is one of mourning, where the individual-in-the-making laments the loss of the body of the mother. Lament itself as a cultural practice entails these various stages of identifying with the dead body and of symbolically putting the self to death.

When this stage of mourning has been completed, the individual moves into the world of language and representation. The successful shift relies on two factors: the completion of the mourning for the dead mother, and the identification with the new object – the father. This acceptance of the new object/father is what helps overcome the melancholy:

> What makes such a triumph over sadness possible is the ability of the self to identify no longer with the lost object but with a third party – the father, form, schema. A requirement for a denying or manic position, such an identification, which may be called phallic or symbolic, insures the subject's entrance into the universe of signs and creation. The supporting father of such a symbolic triumph is not the oedipal father but truly the 'imaginary father', 'father in individual prehistory', according to Freud, who guarantees primary identification.[19]

This 'prehistoric' father also guarantees entrance into the symbolic and historical order. The smooth transition relies on the successful completion of the stage of mourning and the shift into melancholia. If this remains incomplete, however, then 'melancholia ends up in asymbolia, in loss of meaning', where an incomplete subject is 'no longer capable of translating or metaphorising'.

The drift towards asymbolia is also prevented by the inversion of the matricidal drive, which creates the image of the death-bearing woman. Kristeva claims that the process of representation itself relies on this inversion of the matricidal drive, which in turn creates the death-bearing woman for the purposes of representation. The process of representation, in this model, relies on the differentiation of gender and assumes the female to be the object of representation and the male the subject. She writes:

> Thus the feminine as image of death is not only a screen for my fear of castration, but also an imaginary safety catch for the matricidal drive that without such representation would pulverise me into melancholia if it did not drive me to crime. No, it is she who is death-bearing, therefore I do not kill myself – in order to kill her, but I attack her, harass her, represent her – For a woman, whose specular identification with the mother as well as the introjection of the maternal body and self are more immediate, such an inversion of matricidal drive into a death-bearing maternal image is more difficult, if not impossible. Indeed, how can she be that bloodthirsty Fury, since I am She (sexually and narcissistically). She is I?[20]

This theory claims that the process of individuation and representation is structurally linked with the specific representation of the female. Indeed, the female provides the inversion of the matricidal drive and the image of the death-bearing woman, without which representation would be impossible. This, of course, bears relevance to the process of theatrical representation. When theatrical rituals that are tied up with fertility rites or death rites become artistic conventions, women disappear from the scene. Furthermore, in most traditions where theatre is in some way linked to religious ritual we do not have women actors.[21]

The analogy with theatre is one that Kristeva herself touches upon, albeit indirectly. Because of its reliance on processes of identification and enactment, it provides her with a useful metaphor:

> Indeed, we sense the imaginary experience not as theological symbolism or secular commitment but as flaring-up of dead meaning with a surplus of meaning, in which the speaking subject first discovers the shelter of an ideal, but above all the opportunity to play it again in illusions and disillusion.[22]

This idea of playing it again 'in illusions and disillusion' is a basic theatrical function. The notion that theatre enacts semiotic processes is not new and is not without its problems. Kristeva's contribution lies chiefly in the fact that, in reading this process as structured through mourning, she also makes it gender-specific.

Judith Butler's work on the relationship between melancholia and gender formation in some ways follows through Kristeva's logic but seems to take it further. Both agree that the representation of the female, and the obsession with the feminine, is one of the main motors that propel the subject into being. More specifically, Butler maintains that the formation of gender is produced through melancholic identifications. This always presupposes at least in part the loss of certain sexual attachments, which are never fully grieved. Butler maintains that this is also the way that the subject enters a partly enforced heterosexual economy. Although Kristeva makes a similar point regarding the identifications and losses that a heterosexual woman needs to fulfil, the primary loss being always that of the mother, Butler takes this claim even further in suggesting that homosexual identification is indeed the primary one. The entrance into a heterosexual economy is accomplished through the function of the Oedipal complex, which, as she states, is already predicated on heterosexual desire. In this sense becoming a 'woman' or a 'man' both depend on the successful repudiation of femininity:

> Heterosexuality is cultivated through prohibitions, and these prohibitions take as one of their objects homosexual attachments, thereby forcing the loss of those attachments. If the girl is to transfer love from her father to a substitute object, she

must, according to Freudian logic, first renounce love for her mother, and renounce it in such a way that both the aim and the object are foreclosed . . . Only on this condition does a heterosexual aim become established as what some call a sexual orientation . . .

Becoming a 'man' within this logic requires repudiating femininity as a precondition for the heterosexualization of sexual desire and its fundamental ambivalence.[23]

Since such a melancholy formation of gender presupposes the incorporation of the lost object, this repudiation needs constant reinforcement. As mourning is also its primary function, this repudiation might be said to be always incomplete.

One of the most anxious aims of his desire will be to elaborate the difference between him and her, and he will seek to discover and install proof of that difference. His wanting will be haunted by a dread of being what he wants, so that his wanting will also always be a kind of dread.[24]

Read in this way the categories of gender emerge as the result of an ungrieved loss and are never fully successful.[25] Rather than seeing sexuality as the expression of fully formed gender, gender is said to be constituted of what is never fully articulated through such a notion of sexuality. The emphasis on the homosexual prohibition is crucial in this analysis as it is predicated on the original denied identification with the mother. Butler's reading of gender as a function of melancholy is also concerned with understanding the workings of a heterosexist economy of the self.[26]

The above psychoanalytical excursion into the workings of mourning, brief and schematic as it is, still serves to highlight its significance for the definition of the self, especially of the gendered self. However, all sorts of problems arise if we try to apply it to theories of tragedy. Indeed, it is a very attractive model as it seems to reinforce the centrality of mourning and the crucial role it plays in the process of gender differentiation. If tragic form deals, among other things, with the complexities involved in such a differentiation, then thinking of gender as a melancholy category might also prove useful. But psychoanalysis is notoriously ahistorical, or rather specific to the period of modernity with little understanding of history in general. The subject, as it is interpreted here, seems to be a stubbornly modern subject. The categories of gender and sexuality are also read within the context of modernity. More specifically, the category of homosexuality as it pertains to notions of gender is, as Foucault stresses, a modern creation. Butler's model in particular might seem problematic if transferred to the historical context of classical Athens, where male homosexuality seemed to be the dominant mode of desire.

Nevertheless, I still believe that there might be a useful critical interface between the proposed reading of tragic form as a discourse of mourning and psychoanalysis' handling of the same term. In many ways the life of the subject as it continues today results from the creative encounter between Athenian tragedy and modernity. Most metaphors applied by Freudian psychoanalysis derive from this encounter. This is a trajectory that sees the modern subject as originating, more or less, on the Athenian tragic stage. But it is a quintessentially anti-mourning and anti-theatrical reading of this subject that appears in the Freudian tradition, and it is in this way that Freudian psychoanalysis participates in the transcendentalist tradition of Plato. Adam Phillips writes in a fascinating interpretation of Freud's view of character:

> If, as Freud suggests, character is constituted by identification – the ego likening itself to what it once loved – then character is close to caricature, an imitation of an imitation. Like the artists Plato wanted to ban, we are making copies of copies, but unlike Plato's artists we have no original, only an infinite succession of likeness to someone, who, to all intents and purposes, does not exist. Freud's notion of character is a parody of a Platonic work of art; his theory of character formation through identification makes a mockery of character as in any way substantive. The ego is always dressing up for somewhere to go.[27]

Or, we might add, the ego is always dressing up as a woman with nowhere to go (taking on board concepts of melancholy gender and performativity). However, Phillips' reading of character as a parody of the Platonic notion is already a generous revision of the term. More traditionally, Freud's view of character relies on a more straightforward Platonic view. The notion of character as imitation of an imitation implies loss, violence and death, and it is this legacy of violence that propels the subject into being. The appearance of the law of the father puts an end to all the 'creative and artistic' activity that preceded it. The entrance into the 'real', which is the mirror image of Plato's 'ideal', depends on a repudiation of imitation, performance and enactment. In this sense, 'performative' theories of the subject also are anti-Platonic, as they reintroduce and highlight the crucial function of mimesis in the formation of the subject.[28] This emphasis on performativity is always a reintroduction of the concept of mourning as well.

Stressing the vital significance of mourning in the formation of the subject is a way of highlighting its theatrical life. If we propose a reading of tragedy as mourning we are instituting a revised relationship between psychoanalysis and tragedy. Rather than seeing the Athenian stage as enacting the origins of the modern subject, mainly through the function of the Oedipal story, this new encounter stresses that the very 'originating' moment might be fragmented at its source. It suggests, through a kind of negative dialectic, that the so-called 'story of the subject' might contain its own critique. Through an emphasis on the process of mourning that underlines narratives of ambiguity, playfulness, disguise and theatricality, we have a version of the subject that is anti-philosophical, leaning heavily towards the literary and the creative, as in, the theoretical (*theoria*). And it is an anti-idealist view of the subject proposed, which stresses its materiality, its historical and civic life as much as its psychic one. Whereas a melancholy philosophy might teach us how to die, a *theoria* of mourning, on the other hand, ironically might teach us how to live.

The dialogue between post-Freudian schools of psychoanalysis and tragedy that I am attempting to put forward radically reinterprets the process of gender differentiation as part of subject formation. The separation of the spheres of feminine and masculine, and their equivalent political dimensions, is inscribed in the themes and forms of tragedy. The attempt to reconcile the female reproducing body with an economy that is mainly homosocial and homoerotic (always male in this context) seems to generate much of the anxiety of the Athenian stage. At the same time, the shift towards a more patriarchal-nuclear type of family model creates a crisis in systems of kinship, lineage and inheritance. The tension between the necessity of women as child bearers, and the power that that may (or may not) bring with it, and the predominantly male function of desire create one of the most significant tensions within Athenian tragedy. This opposition seems to be the dominant one (not the one between homoerotic desire and heterosexual desire, as Butler suggests) and it thereby predicates the formation of the subject. But we are dealing with a predominantly male homosexual sublime one that manifests itself in other aspects of classical Greek literature as well, as we saw in the function of *philia*. The repudiation of the feminine remains central to this reading as well. The anxiety attached to heterosexual love was more or less absent from male homosexual attachments. As Foucault has argued, homoerotic love was considered philosophical love, whereas heterosexual love, the love of women, was tainted with the physical and the bodily. Staten writes:

> From Plato to the Pseudo-Lucian in the early centuries of the Christian era, pederasty was 'linked to philosophy, to virtue and hence to the elimination of physical pleasure'; in short, it was placed 'under the sign of truth'. The very existence of the powerful imperative to idealize homosexual love, an imperative that persisted for centuries (in its sublimated form – as the ideal of friendship for millennia) indicates a danger that is being kept at bay as much in homoeroticism as in heteroeroticism.[29]

This repudiation of the feminine appears as an obsession that always returns to haunt the Athenian stage. Women's absence from the civic life of the *polis*, including the institution of the theatre, is more than made up for by their dominant presence on the stage. However, this is a traversed presence, one that is always represented, enacted. It is in this context that Butler's work might prove useful in a reading of the cross-dressing aspect of tragic form, which also can be read as embodying notions of mourning. Butler writes:

> If there is an ungrieved loss in drag performance, perhaps it is a loss that is refused and incorporated in the performed identification, one which reiterates a gendered idealization and its radical uninhabitability. This is, then, neither a territorialization of the feminine by the masculine nor a sign of the essential plasticity of gender. It suggests that the performance allegorizes a loss it cannot grieve, allegorizes the incorporative fantasy of melancholia whereby an object is phantasmatically taken in or on as a way of refusing to let it go. Gender itself might be understood in part as the 'acting out' of unresolved grief.[30]

The melancholia that derives from this unresolved grief becomes part of the yearning for a philosophy that teaches us, in Montaigne's words, 'how to die'. For the melancholia that results from this albeit incomplete mourning in the end serves to fix and maintain gender categories. It is not as if the cross-dressing aspect can in and of itself be seen as voicing some type of critique. As Butler writes:

> Drag allegorizes some set of melancholic incorporative fantasies that stabilize gender. Not only are the vast number of drag performers straight, but it would be a mistake to think that homosexuality is best explained through the performativity that is drag.[31]

Butler's use of gender terms is decidedly modern. Despite this, I still think that her analysis pertains to the function of gender on the Athenian stage. The emphasis I would like to place on tragedy as a discourse of mourning rather than of melancholy might also be useful in viewing gender as a less fixed category. Indeed, this might prove more historically appropriate. The categories of gender were less rigid at the time and certainly different from our understanding of the terms. As mentioned earlier, the main reconciliation would be that between the reproducing female body and the male body as object of desire. Within this context of a homosexual sublime, Butler's analysis of drag could prove useful in reading the cross-dressing aspect of Athenian drama.

Rather than stressing the melancholia that results from this imitative process, mourning remains stubbornly artistic. It stresses the function of mimesis in the process of gender formation. As mimesis is always identified as theatrical and feminine, then to act is to behave like a woman, just as to mourn is to behave like a woman. These two functions, I would claim, come together on the Athenian stage in the conventions of men playing women. At the same time, these conventions also comment on the political and civic dimension of gender formation as well. The centrality of mourning at once comments on the process of gender formation and on the civic and political life of that gender. This is one of the first historical instances (as will be examined below) where mourning is legislated – that is, it literally becomes the law. In order for mourning to become the law, it, too, like philosophy, must be imbued with melancholia. This process from the oral tradition to the written is also a gendered one. The rituals and rites of mourning and lamentation are turned into the official, stately funeral oration and into the institution of tragedy. The physical bodies of the dead, the known dead that were mourned, are turned into the absent bodies of the cenotaph. When mourning becomes the law, and is finalised as such, it is always a melancholy law. However, the mourning that precedes it stresses the process of becoming itself. This is the space that tragedy occupies. In this sense, the convention of men-playing-women might also comment on the process of law formation and the exclusions it entails.

The Law, the State and Funeral Rites

Tragedy is littered with examples of female mourners. Where they are male their lamentations feminise them (Hercules) or serve to stress their barbaric identity (the chorus of *The Persians*). Either way, tragedy provides a strong platform for this feminising, barbaric and quintessentially theatrical discourse of mourning. Recent new-historical readings of this dominant presence of mourning on the Athenian stage tend to read it in conjunction with contemporary legislation against excessive female mourning.[32] In most readings the curtailment of public death rites brings with it the rise of the city-state. Indeed, this is a fertile encounter, one that sees the development of the newly formed city-state, the soon-to-become democratic *polis*, as inextricably tied to the negotiation of public mourning and lamentation.

Laws attributed to Solon and established in the sixth century set out deliberately to curtail or reform funeral rites.[33] To quote Plutarch, the sixth-century legislation prohibited 'everything disorderly and excessive in women's festivals, processions [*exodoi*] and funeral rites' (*Solon* 21.4). The process of outlawing female mourning, which in the same gesture underlines its theatrical and public dimension, is parallel to the development of the democratic *polis* and its two crucial discursive and institutional formations: the tragedy and the funeral oration. Furthermore, as scholars have stressed, funeral legislation may have also been part of the attempt to diminish the power of the aristocracy in the newly formed democratic *polis*. Before the introduction of Solon's laws, during the archaic period, aristocratic funerals were lavish displays of wealth and power. As grand public events, they served to reinforce the civic and political power of the aristocracy. They were highly codified and ritualised events. Women's lamentation was crucial at every stage of this process: at the wake, or *prothesis*, during the procession, or *ekphora*, when the body was carried to the grave site, and finally at the grave site itself. Professional mourners, usually older women, were famous for their grief-inducing qualities. All in all, during the archaic period, as we know from Homer or vase paintings, funerals were highly staged and codified events, where the function of gender, family and social status was demarcated clearly.

The sixth century saw a shift in this civic dimension of funeral rites. The role of the state became more prominent and the loyalty expressed to the family in the practices of the funeral had to be curtailed. In general this attempt to redefine death rites forms part of the new negotiation between public and private as the power of the great aristocratic families came to be contained within the newly formed democratic *polis*. For example, the *prothesis*, according to Solon's legislation, was to be held indoors and the *ekphora* could only take place in silence and before dawn. Whereas in Homer, Hector's body was burned after a lengthy and very public lamentation on the ninth day, according to the new law such displays of both the dead body and public grief were to be banned. Interestingly enough, male lament in Homer does not carry the connotations of femininity and theatricality that are attached to it after Solon's laws are implemented.

The restrictions imposed on aristocratic families regarding funeral rites saw a parallel involvement of the state in matters of burial. Indeed, the public participation in funeral rites, according to Richard Seaford, helped create the identity of the newly formed democratic *polis*.[34] It is not so much that ritual lamentation was banned outright, in a simply direct oppressive manner. Rather the *polis* itself wanted to regulate and form the new modes of mourning, the ones that would be deemed appropriate to the new state. In controlling the power of the aristocratic families through a regulation of death ritual, the democratic *polis* also created new modes of citizenship. It tested its own limits in relation to those citizens. That this should happen over the whole realm of 'who controls death' is particularly interesting. Death rites became a discursive *topos* where the relationships between the living and the dead, between the citizen and the state, are constantly negotiated. That these debates were gendered is crucial. Indeed, gender is a constitutive aspect of this whole *topos*. It is not merely an added characteristic, an epithet that markedly inflects the discussion, but a central feature of the way this debate unfolds.

As scholars have shown, this process of the state's appropriation of funeral rites probably took centuries, and the fact that aspects of particularly female lamentation were banned does not necessarily mean that they ceased to take place. Our dependence on written sources proves inadequate in charting the genealogy of this stubbornly oral tradition. Either way, the shift in funeral rites from the family to the jurisdiction of the state can be read as a founding aspect of the development of that very city-state. In the same gesture the differentiation of gender, the role of male and female in this new (proto) democratic state, also seems central to its founding.

Tragedy is central to this process, helping in the imaginative, artistic and political renegotiation of the relationship between the family and the state, between men and women. In turn, this redefinition of death ritual and citizenship helps to 'invent' the democratic *polis*. Helen Foley writes:

> Tragedy is full of the public laceration of cheeks and the lamentation at other people's tombs supposedly forbidden by Solon. Revenge and funerary lamentation are intimately related in tragedy, and women play a public and dominant role in awakening it . . .
> Did the audience simply view these activities as justified (at least partially) because they were leading to the overthrow of the tyrants Clytemnestra and Aegisthus? Or should we consider the possibility that this *kommos* (a choral lament shared between chorus and actors) was meant to offer a display of precisely those uncontrolled lamentations by women that purportedly led in earlier Greek history to the enactment of the funerary legislation and, more speculatively, to the replacement of vendetta justice by the all male institution of trial jury?[35]

Rather than simply and directly reflecting contemporary tensions over death rites and ritual, tragedy helps to rework them. It helps create the cultural shift concerning 'who claims the dead' in the democratic *polis*. That this relationship should always involve the law is also telling. Foley touches upon one of the main tensions that is enacted through tragic form: the relationship between mourning and the law. The competing discourses over the dead are also marked by differing systems of jurisdiction. The so-called female 'vendetta' system of justice is gradually replaced by the more enlightened male system of trial jury. By the time we reach *Antigone*, however, this model is somewhat turned on its head as the female system of justice returns with a vengeance. Traditionally tragedy has been read as charting the linear development of a progression, from darkness to light, from barbarism to civilisation, from blood vengeance to democratic jurisdiction. This, however, is not a straightforward path since the emphasis on mourning tends to throw up the contradictions, the exclusions and the ambiguities involved in this process. My attempt to read mourning as constituting not only tragic themes but also tragic forms might reconfigure the ways that tragedy relates to its historical context. Instead of mirroring the shifts taking place or even providing an outlet for banned forms of mourning, tragedy actively takes part in the new negotiations taking place within the democratic *polis*. Neither a direct translation of the new law nor necessarily an expression of resistance against it, tragedy embodies both these modes. It creates a site of struggle where the tensions between mourning and law constantly are enacted but never fully resolved.

In *Mourning Becomes the Law*, Gillian Rose looks at the ways in which practices of mourning turn into legislation.[36] Although she cites Antigone as her primary example, her reading of Antigone is not one that sees her as the female outsider. Rather her proposition is a more liberal and hopeful one – where the function of Antigone is seen as primarily one of critique.[37] Rather than representing the outside of the law, the irony of society (as Hegel would have it), for her Antigone represents the possibility of change and progress within the law itself. Rather than negate the law, Antigone's mourning presents the possibility of a new and, by definition, better law. This reading is, however, one that carries more of the hope of its author than that of its subject. It is not so much that mourning becomes the law, making it a better law in the process, as that mourning becomes embodied in the law. It is a process not of transformation but rather one of masking, traversing and disguising, to the point of course where the actor and the role fuse into one. The conglomerate that results from this encounter can never be reduced to its constitutive parts. Viewed in more Foucauldian terms, the relationship between mourning and the law can be read as the law's ability to have always and already inscribed within itself its own critique and resistance.[38]

By the same token tragedy does not directly mirror contemporary debates about the law, nor does it present a subversive, critical privileging of mourning in its place. It probably does both: it helps create a new discourse of death in the new democratic culture, while also embodying a critique towards that culture. As a quintessentially democratic institution, it embodies one of the primary characteristics of the democratic state: the liberal and institutional coexistence of the law and its undoing. In truth, it could be read as one of the first institutions, historically, to embody such a negotiation. The centrality of mourning points to that historical negotiation. Reintroducing mourning to the study of tragic form places it within a historical and political context, but most importantly it might help to show how that context was formed in the first place, and what ideologies and what exclusions helped to give it form and substance.

Antigone (Again): Philosophy's Designated Mourner

Any discussion of mourning and tragic form, particularly one that bears relevance to the workings of the law and the state, will inevitably lead us back to Antigone. Between the great mournful figures of Atossa and Pentheus, who were cited at the start of this chapter, lies Antigone in all her charm and splendour Antigone appears as the liberal dream of the negotiation between mourning and the law. Between the two extremes of the barbaric, lamenting, raw and unmediated mourning of the Persian Queen and the self-referential, 'citational', almost meta-mourning of the fallen Theban King, we find Antigone. In the newly formed democratic *polis*, Antigone comes to represent both the law and its transgression. She tests the limits of the state and in the end reinforces its power. The fact that she does this through practices of mourning is very significant. The fact that she represents a woman or rather a girl (always played by a man) is equally significant. The outside of the law, the irony of society, tests the limits of that law. Whether this is the way for progress, as Rose would claim, or the inevitable recirculation of power, as Foucault would claim, is open to discussion and debate. Either way, as positive or negative critique, Antigone and her fascination with death have occupied philosophy for centuries. Perhaps her unique position, in which she embodies all the debates mentioned here, is what makes her philosophy's designated mourner. The type of mourning that she represents (highly mediated, state controlled, even in its transgression) in the end fails to challenge the discursive hegemony of philosophy. The fact that this supposed challenge is enacted by a girl, or a man dressed as a girl, also briefly critiques the gender blindness of philosophy. This critical excursion, however, is itself traversed, masked, highly theatrical; there to test momentarily the limits of the law, expanding to include its outside, but only to bounce back again reinforced. This could account for philosophy's love affair with Antigone.

The choice of the phrase 'love affair' is not coincidental in this context. The thanatoerotic dimension of Antigone is endemic to the kind of philosophy that presents itself as an antidote to excessive mourning. From

Plato to Lacan, as Staten suggests, there is a tradition of metaphysical philosophy that sees mourning as a challenge, as bad thinking, as travestied philosophy. That this tradition is also anti-theatrical is telling. Despite psychoanalysis' adoption of theatrical rhetoric (enactment, role-play, audience, etc.), or possibly because of it, both discourses seem to share a hostility towards the theatrical which parallels their hostility towards the feminine. Indeed, both the feminine and the theatrical in this sense are seen as almost interchangeable.

Lacan's famous reading of Antigone brings together these attitudes and is itself exemplary of the thanatoerotic tradition in metaphysical thinking that sees mourning, theatricality and femininity as embodying the obscene and the unknowable. His identification of 'otherness', of the 'thing', with femininity itself has been scrutinised in well-documented debates.[39] Despite his claims that the mother is merely an example of 'otherness', critics are quick to point out that this is not merely an empirical lapse but something that is fundamental to Lacanian thinking. The mother becomes more than a mere example; she is the paradigm through and on which the concept of 'otherness' is based:

> It is in the interval between these two signifiers that resides the desire offered to the mapping of the subject in the experience of the discourse of the Other, of the first Other he has to deal with, let us say, by way of illustration, the mother.[40]

This particular evocation of the mother has ignited a whole school of criticism. For the purposes of our analysis, it is crucial to point out that the tradition of psychoanalysis in which Lacan partakes mirrors the same concerns of the metaphysical, idealistic tradition in philosophy. This connection has been eloquently made by Staten, who writes:

> In this account Lacan repeats practically verbatim the main themes of the thanatoerotophobic tradition. One might wish to follow him when he does so, but at least one should know to what metaphysics one is declaring allegiance – as Lacan most certainly knows, even if many of his followers do not. Lacan consciously brews a mixture of Platonism and Augustinianism when he writes that 'every object relation' is 'infected with a fundamental uncertainty' because the empirical object is 'only ever graspable as a mirage' (2.169) and warns us that 'in effect, when we are in another's power, we are in great danger' (7.84). And we confirm once again that this danger, which is the danger of the libidinal object in general, has a peculiar relation to women: the words 'damage' and 'danger' are etymologically related to 'domination' and to 'dame in the archaic French sense, our lady' (ibid.).[41]

This accounts for Lacan's fascination with Antigone, which functions as a subtle critique of the emphasis placed by Freud on Oedipus. Indeed,

Antigone appears as the darling of the anti-Oedipal legacy in psychoanalysis and philosophy. However, as I have tried to demonstrate earlier in this book, a more materialist and historical analysis of Antigone places her within the Oedipal tradition. The fact that she is read as woman and primarily as a female mourner allows for these more liberal interpretations.

Fittingly, Lacan presents his analysis of Antigone as part of his seminars on Ethics. After a brief and schematic excursion on the concept of *katharsis* and on the function of the chorus and, after the obligatory critique of Hegel's reading of Antigone, Lacan presents us with his own view:

> We know very well that over and beyond the dialogue, over and beyond the question of family and country, over and beyond the moralizing arguments, it is Antigone herself who fascinates us, Antigone in her unbearable splendour. She has a quality that both attracts us and startles us, in the sense of intimidates us; this terrible, self-willed victim disturbs us.[42]

Antigone seems to embody all the qualities of this thanatoerotic, misogynist tradition. Indeed, she is described in words that almost echo the previous quotation. She is dangerous but alluring; her splendour is unbearable; she frightens us but we are also attracted to her; she is a victim but a self-willed one. This double-edged notion of desire fits in very well with the love–hate nexus that the original object of desire inspires. Lacan writes: 'In effect, *Antigone* reveals to us the line of sight that defines desire.'[43] Lacan finds this identification of Antigone with the 'other' or the 'thing' itself appealing. Interestingly enough, in this quotation, unlike elsewhere in his essay, the word Antigone is italicised, indicating that he refers to the whole play and not merely the character. Since this is the case and since the play presupposes performance, it is tempting to question whether Lacan would have found Antigone so full of 'unbearable splendour' had he been aware that she is really a man playing a woman. How would the cross-dressing element together with the homosociality of the event of *Antigone* inflect his assessment of 'her'?

In a long tradition of humanistic readings of Antigone, Lacan ignores the fact that she is part of a performance, one that relies on the existence of a civic institution. Like Butler, whose interpretation is markedly different from Lacan's, he sees 'her' as basically animating and embodying a philosophical debate which existed before 'her' and which she graphically displays through her actions.[44] How those actions and the gestic language they comprise may help to constitute the terms of this debate remains unexamined by Lacan and the tradition he exemplifies. Of course, this is part of the more general ambivalence of philosophy towards theatre and performance. However, in Lacan's case this difficult relationship is fuelled with a revived and particularly problematic hostility. He writes about what he dismissively calls the *mise en scène*:

> On the level of what occurs in reality, an auditor rather than a spectator is involved. And I can hardly be more pleased with myself since Aristotle agrees with me; for him the whole development of the arts of the theatre takes place at the level of what is heard, the spectacle itself being no more than something arranged on the margin. Technique is not without significance, but it is not essential; it plays the same role as elocution in rhetoric.[45]

This disregard is spectacular in itself. Even a strict, formalist structuralist would allow for more space than the term 'technique' implies. This total and almost disdainful view of the act of performance typifies the philosophical tradition to which Lacan pays homage here. It is a tradition in many ways initiated by Aristotle himself, as Lacan quite rightly points out. In privileging the auditory over the spectacular, Lacan, like Aristotle, reads the performance event as a metaphor for the act of reading. This is a familiar turn in philosophical writing about performance. Among other things, it diminishes the performance event, in all its civic and political dimensions, into a one-to-one personal communication (like that between the analyst and the patient?). Like characters in a pop-up book, the roles of the play *Antigone* animate a debate that already has been written and formulated. They are there for amusement, to add a little 'drama' to an otherwise sophisticated debate. Still, the emphasis has to be placed on the auditory rather than the spectacular in case we get carried away by the 'sensational', physical elements. Lacan continues his damning assessment of the spectacle:

> The spectacle here is a secondary medium. It is a point of view that puts in its place the modern concerns with *mise en scène* or stagecraft. The importance of *mise en scène* should not be underrated, and I always appreciate it both in the theatre and in the cinema. But we shouldn't forget that it is only important – and I hope you will forgive the expression – if our third eye doesn't get a hard-on; it is, so to speak, jerked off a little with the *mise en scène*.[46]

With puritanical zeal, Lacan defends the written word and the auditory imagination against the stage and the visual or physiognomic imagination. His use of the term 'stagecraft' is condescending, as it implies manual labour. His appreciation of the *mise en scène* he patronisingly acknowledges in a gesture that conflates live performance with the cinema. But he leaves his most important blow for the end of the paragraph, which turns into a pornographic account of the spectacular and the scenic. It is fascinating that the only way he can conceptualise the impact of the 'spectacle' is in terms of a 'hard-on'. If the third eye does not get excited with the level of philosophical debate, then it gets the lower and debased version of that interaction: 'a hard-on' it is jerked off with the *mise en scène*. The *mise en scène* provides the rhetorical elocution of an 'Oh' or rather 'Oh, no!'

We are catapulted back into the Platonic loathing of theatre as the agent that arouses the worst and lowest emotions in the audience. Lacan's use of pornographic rhetoric echoes Plato's fear and loathing of the power of the spectacle to ignite overwhelming emotions on a collective level. More often than not these feelings are related to acts of mourning. We are in familiar Platonic territory, where the stage is seen as potentially triggering an epidemic of uncontrollable grief. It interferes with the ability to think clearly and properly; it is bad, sloppy philosophy since it relies on a physical and emotional reaction rather than on one of reason, or rather it tends to blur the separation between the two.

This is more or less the tradition of anti-theatricality in wich Lacan participates. The figure of Antigone proves particularly attractive, allowing him to eroticise the debate while also maintaining its philosophical credibility. How else other than through the workings of the *mise en scène* can he experience what he calls the 'splendour of Antigone'? Only if he experiences her, as he does, not as something made, through a complicated series of modes of production, not as something that relies on a civic, interpretive community to make sense, but as something 'ideal' in the Platonic sense. All in all, it is better to read Antigone as part of philosophical tradition about ethics, rather than as part of a tradition of performance about mourning and gender.

It is difficult, however, even in Lacan's strict differentiation between the splendour and the disgust, not to conflate the two. Antigone presents the ideal candidate for such a conflation. For a moment she allows for the transgression and the disgust: she is a woman challenging the law. In the end that very law is recuperated and reinforced, allowing for the splendour to surface. She does this through the various acts of mourning, thereby epitomising the thanatoerotic tradition that has a particularly difficult relationship with the feminine.

Antigone makes a crucial appearance in Joan Copjec's recent study *Imagine There's No Woman*.[47] As part of her reassessment of Lacan, Copjec assigns to Antigone the vital function of *sexualising* a debate that in Hegel was seen only in terms of biological difference. In other words, Lacan's use of Antigone in his Ethics seminar is a way of placing ethics 'in our bodies, and nowhere else'. This way of reading Antigone as embodying Lacanian ethics is, more or less, contrary to the interpretations we have been proposing so far. Copjec writes:

> My argument, in sum, is that Lacan attacks Hegel's argument by (1) sexualizing work or, better, the act and (2) debiologizing death in an effort, in both cases, to corporealize the ethical subject.[48]

For Copjec this places Lacan firmly on the side of Antigone, rather than equally seeing Antigone and Creon as markers of singularity, as Hegel does. In an illuminating study that also revalidates the functions of the sacred and immortality, Copjec sees in Lacan's reading of Antigone a formula that redeems psychoanalysis. The 'regime of biopolitics', with the immortal and scared at one extreme and death and annihilation at the other, is set up against the discourse of Lacanian psychoanalysis. It is primarily the sexualisation of the body proposed here that challenges the natural or sacred readings put forward by biopolitics. She writes:

> The notion to which I refer is the one suggested by psychoanalysis, where the body is conceived not 'biopolitically' as the seat of *death* but, rather, as the seat of sex. Contrary to what Foucault has claimed, the sexualization of the body by psychoanalysis does not participate in the regime of biopolitics: it opposes it.[49]

This is a very insightful comment, which is probably true of psychoanalysis in general, but seems less clear when we are dealing with Antigone (and indeed Lacan's view of her). Turning Antigone's predicament into an act, a work, as this analysis demands, would have to engage with her as a performative being. Furthermore, if Antigone comes to stand in for the process of sexualising both her identity and her revolt, how are we to read her in the knowledge that she is played by a man, a knowledge that is compounded by the fact that this is not an aberration but a structural element of this story? This aspect of her performative quality inflects any reading that sees her as enacting the process of sexualising the body, a process that has direct ethical implications. Rather than viewing Antigone as the site of the sexualisation that redeems death, I would claim that reading her as a performative being might mean that she has more in common with the regimes of biopolitics than with any opposition against it. Antigone's travesty of the law also entails a travesty of sex. In a double blow, or in a double bind, she comes to enact the law and its transgression but, also, the relationships between biology and sex. If Hegel's reading is accused by Copjec of being 'free of libido', then this performative reading of Antigone sees her/him as a desiring creature, not one, however, who unproblematically stands in for the category of sex. Indeed, what this reading may point towards is the interdependency of the discourses governing the law (and its transgression) and the discourses of sexualisation. I would claim that in relation to Antigone these are based on a thanatoerotic drive that doesn't as much substitute death with sex (as the locus of the body) but rather conflates the two, with a deep ambivalence towards the feminine.

Things, Objects and Ruins: The Materiality of Mourning

The anti-theatrical legacy initiated by the metaphysics of Plato is one that I would claim continues in the Freudian and Lacanian traditions of psychoanalysis. Just as Plato appropriates and rewrites the 'dramatic dialogue' and turns it into his signature, classical psychoanalysis is also based on a rhetoric of performance. In a familiar turn that appropriates the alterity it seeks to overcome, mourning, femininity and theatricality are taken over, subsumed by the voice of metaphysical, idealist philosophy. Since the primary imagination in this instance claims to be auditory and not bodily or physiognomic, the analogy of ventriloquy might aptly apply. This long and grand tradition of the reception of tragedy from Aristotle to George Steiner places tragedy within the workings of an idealist philosophical tradition. Typically, it ignores or rather negates the impact of mourning, femininity and theatricality. The whole function of performance and the performative, so central to tragic form, is totally bypassed. When it is mentioned, like the references to the feminine, it is in terms of a debased spectacle, one that is deemed necessary but in the end needs to be overcome.[50]

A reading of tragic form as a discourse of mourning would at the same time investigate its idealist-metaphysical reception. The 'sense of tragedy' which is aligned to this philosophical ideal has been recently rehearsed by George Steiner, who writes:

> 'Tragedy' is a dramatic representation, enactment, or generation of a highly specific world-view. This world-view is summarized in the adage preserved among the elegies ascribed to Theognis, but certainly older, and present also in Middle Eastern sacred texts: 'It is best not to be born, next best to die young.' This dictum is transparent shorthand for a larger conception. It entails the view that human life *per se*, both ontologically and existentially, is an affliction . . .
>
> We are unwelcome guests, old enough at the moment of birth (as Montaigne says) to be a corpse and blessed only if this potentiality is realized as swiftly as it can be.[51]

It is primarily this reading of tragedy as quasi-existential and deeply anti-historical and apolitical that has reached mainstream reception. It prohibits critique, let alone change. It sees tragedy as a universal, metaphysical and idealist trope sprinkled with Steiner's particular brand of existentialism. Despite its pretensions, this reading belongs to a long humanist tradition. It is the double of the tradition that sees in tragedy the agency of progress and civilisation. It is the 'black hole' to the glowing light within which tragedy is usually read. Steiner elaborates on his argument:

> But the translation of the pure tragic axiom into a performative act is infrequent. It is exceedingly difficult to document. Motives invite sceptical enquiry. And the intellectual convictions or psychological states or 'moods' (Heidegger's *Stimmungen*) which would dictate self-annihilation tend, except in psychotic lesions, to be brief and intermittent. 'Black holes' are formidably difficult to locate; they yield little testimony, not only in astrophysics.[52]

Despite such difficulties, the human psyche manages to excel: therein lies its greatness and there lies the fundamental anti-historicism of this view. The reference to 'black holes' also evokes the thanatoerotic legacy this tradition fulfils. As mentioned earlier, the trope of this analysis easily dissolves into melodrama and bourgeois self-absorption.

However, there are other ways of introducing negativity into the discourse of tragedy. Mourning may do just that. It is not a matter of choosing between two extremes, either the reading that sees tragedy as a steady and linear progress into light and civilisation (the essence of the dream of democracy) or as a rhetoric that is steeped in quasi-existentialist, nihilistic terms. Either side of this binary enacts a dialectic of enlightenment, with the negative, dark side acting not as a critique but as a constitutive element of this dynamic. After all, darkness, blindness, black holes are all fundamental characteristics of this dialectic. We recall Oedipus, whose blindness marks his entry into consciousness. Hegel comments on this interdependent relationship between darkness and light: 'Here the external, physical sun rises and goes down in the west: but in its place the inner sun of self-consciousness rises with a higher light.'[53] The same gesture grants philosophy the inner sun of knowledge, albeit a knowledge that underlines the pointlessness and meaninglessness of life. The black hole is more than compensated for by the power that the awareness of its existence brings. This sublimation of the darkness into light also involves a series of complex modes of representation which repudiate the theatrical, the performative and the feminine. What is seen as a desperate loss for tragedy becomes a triumphant gain for philosophy. In this shift from tragedy's loss to philosophy's gain we have an appropriation of the negativity of tragedy in which what is rewritten is the discourse of mourning itself. It shifts from a historical and political rhetoric to one of universalising, homogenising impact. Tragic form is rewritten as forming part of the tragic nature of human character. It becomes a prop within a 'grander' philosophical discussion about the futility of existence. The only character that such a rhetoric privileges is that of the philosopher himself. The tragic poet and the actor are merely doomed to enact endlessly what the philosopher in his wisdom has known all along: that we are all going to die and that life is meaningless. It is at this point that this rhetoric easily dissolves into melodrama.

Reading tragedy as a discourse of mourning rather than of ahistorical and apolitical negativity allows for possibilities both within the genre itself and with its fraught relationship to philosophy. If Plato's anti-theatrical philosophy promises deliverance from mourning, then tragedy presents a complex and somewhat contradictory validation of mourning. It is not simply that it presents us with a straightforward celebration of mourning in confrontation with the law and Plato. Mourning comprises a discursive *topos* that examines the function of the law, the citizen, gender and the power over the dead and the past in the new democratic *polis*. It becomes the site where the subject-in-the-making is confronted with the *polis*-in-the-making. What mourning emphasises is that the two are interdependent; one cannot be read without the other. Whereas the previous reading of negativity tends to disassociate the subject from the historical process, mourning helps create the site that stages their absolute interdependency. Indeed, this reading of mourning might enable us to reconcile psychoanalysis and history.[54]

Rather than the 'anguished scream over the abyss', so beloved of Romanticism, tragedy comes to enact a language of critique. Through the discourse of mourning, it deals with catastrophe and ruins not in a metaphysical sense but in the sense of enacting historical memory. Walter Benjamin's writings on the German *Trauerspiel* might help to bridge the gap between the mourning of the ancients and that of the moderns. His emphasis on the loss and the ruins of history not merely as debris and waste but as constitutive parts of historical memory parallels the foundational role played by mourning within tragic form. Despite Benjamin's own protestations that he was chiefly concerned in differentiating between tragedy and Baroque *Trauerspiel*, his reworking of the concept of the *Trauerspiel* might point to ways of reconceptualising tragedy within modernity. Asja Lacis records Benjamin's response to her question regarding the futility of studying dead literature:

> I show the essential difference between tragedy and *Trauerspiel*. The plays of the Baroque express despair and contempt of the world – they are really sad plays,

whereas the attitude of the Greek and of the real tragedians remains unbending toward world and fate... Second, he said, his investigation was not mere academic research but had an immediate relation to very current problems of contemporary literature... Therefore, he said, I have extensively treated the artistic problems of allegory, emblems, and ritual. Until now aesthetic theory has valued allegory as a lower ranking artistic means. He wanted to prove that allegory was an artistic means of high value, even more than it was a special form of artistic perception.[55]

Just as the introduction to Benjamin's book on the German *Trauerspiel* has been read as proposing a modern theory of subjectivity, I suggest that, despite his intentions, Benjamin tries to find a place for tragedy within modernity. His stark differentiation between the 'attitude' of the Greeks and that of the Baroque, and in turn modernity, is based within a humanist tradition of the reception of tragedy, and, in many ways, it is similar to the opposition that Brecht sets up when he tries to define his epic theatre against the Greek model. Both men are trying to create a theory of theatre for modernity. For both, the 'tragedy of the Greeks' forms a benchmark against which they proceed to define their own projects. Benjamin would later discover his 'ideal' model in Brecht's epic theatre. However, had his model kept some of the elements of the 'sad plays of the Baroque', or rather had he been able to see these elements in the Greek plays themselves, then, possibly, Brecht's epic theatre might have been infused with the negativity that, according to Adorno, it so badly needed.

In his later work Brecht comes round to the idea of tragedy. Quite predictably he was attracted to Antigone and the work of Samuel Beckett.[56] However, the main thrust of his analysis remains anti-tragic. Epic theatre emerges as a scathing critique of primarily Greek tragedy, which is seen as the precursor to bourgeois naturalism. Tragedy comes to stand in for the great European tradition of the Enlightenment and within it originates the notion of the human subject that leads directly to bourgeois individuation – all categories which were anathema to Brecht and to Benjamin. In this dialogue between the ancients and the moderns, the moderns had to eradicate any trace of a 'tradition' that may have placed their project within a historical trajectory.

Reading tragedy as part of a discourse of mourning might help sketch out such a historical trajectory. This story would account for negativity within tragic form without resorting to conceptual black holes; it also would help to reconcile tragedy and modernity. Epic theatre itself would not need to be read in opposition to tragic form but could be read as part of the same aesthetic and epistemological legacy. In turn, mourning can act as a corrective to epic theatre's somewhat uncritical optimism, a characteristic that Adorno rightly criticises. Benjamin and Brecht never really saw eye-to-eye regarding the workings of epic theatre, despite the received opinion about their relationship.[57] Benjamin's insistence on ruins, melancholy and catastrophe as an integral part of history never fitted comfortably with Brecht's somewhat 'crude' vision of hope and progress. However, there is more negativity in Brecht's work than this schematic reading allows for (and more space for research than this analysis permits). Highlighting the function of mourning might help underline the parallels rather than the differences between tragic and epic form.

Notes

1. Euripides, *The Bacchae*, lines 358–69, in *The Bacchae and Other Plays*, trans. Philip Vellacot (London: Penguin Books, 1973).
2. See Nicole Loraux, *The Invention of Athens: The Funeral Oration in the Classical City*, trans. Alan Sheridan (Cambridge, MA, and London: Harvard University Press, 1986).
3. See Sigmund Freud, 'Mourning and Melancholia', in *The Ego and the Id*, *The Standard Edition of the Complete Psychological Works of Sigmund Freud*, ed. and trans. James Strachey, 24 vols (London: Hogarth, 1953–74), vol. 18. Also see John Bowlby, *Attachment and Loss* (New York: Basic Books, 1969).
4. See Judith Butler, 'Melancholy Gender/Refused Identification', in *The Psychic Life of Power: Theories in Subjection* (Stanford: Stanford University Press, 1997), pp. 132–50.
5. Stephen Halliwell, 'Plato's Repudiation of the Tragic', in M. S. Silk (ed.), *Tragedy and the Tragic: Greek Theatre and Beyond* (Oxford: Clarendon Press, 1996), pp. 332–49, p. 333.
6. Ibid. p. 334.
7. Edith Hall, 'Is there a *Polis* in Aristotle's *Poetics*?', in M. S. Silk, ed., *Tragedy and the Tragic*, p. 305. Interestingly, she quotes Aristotle's famous dictum about the relationships between art and politics: 'Correctness in the art of poetry is not the same thing as correctness in the art of politics. (Ouch e aute orthotes estin tes politikes kai tes poietikes technes)', (Aristotle, *Poetics*, 1460b 13–15), Hall's translation.
8. See Halliwell, 'Plato's Repudiation of the Tragic', p. 347.
9. Ibid.
10. Plato, *Republic*, 606 a–b. Quoted in Henry Staten, *Eros in Mourning* (London and Baltimore: The Johns Hopkins University Press, 1995), p. 4, Staten's translation.
11. Staten, *Eros in Mourning*, p. 5; see chapter entitled, 'The Argument', pp. 1–17.
12. Plato, *Symposium*, 210a-b, quoted in Staten, *Eros in Mourning*, p. 3.
13. See Staten, *Eros in Mourning*, p. 3.
14. Ibid. p. 73.
15. See Julia Kristeva, *Black Sun: Depression and Melancholia* (New York: Columbia University Press, 1989), p. 5; Montaigne quoted, p. 4.
16. For an analysis of Aristotle's view of Melancholia not as an illness but as a trait of the philosopher, see Kristeva, *Black Sun*, pp. 6–9.
17. See Kristeva, *Black Sun*, p. 27.

18. Ibid. pp. 27–8.
19. Ibid. p. 23.
20. Ibid. pp. 28–9.
21. This is true of the Japanese Noh and Kabuki theatres and of the Peking Opera. It is interesting to note that the term 'impersonator' is used rather than 'actor', as if to imply that real acting deals with character whereas representing the feminine requires a series of performative acts.
22. See Kristeva, *Black Sun*, p. 102.
23. See Butler, *The Psychic Life of Power*, p. 137.
24. Ibid.
25. This formulation reaches its thematic and rhetorical peak when Butler exclaims that 'the "truest" lesbian melancholic is the strictly straight woman, and the "truest" gay male melancholic is the strictly straight man', see *The Psychic Life of Power*, pp. 146–7. Jonathan Dollimore presents a critique of Butler's views in 'Bisexuality, Heterosexuality and Wishful Theory', in *Textual Practice* 10 (3), (1996): pp. 523–39. He writes of the above formulation that it is 'such a theoretically exquisite irony that it seems churlish to wonder whether it is true, or whether Butler is not herself partaking of that hyperbole she has just discerned in that "mundane heterosexual masculinity and femininity,"' p. 537.
26. This is part of her overall project. Also see *Bodies that Matter: On the Discursive Limits of Sex* (London and New York: Routledge, 1993). In the above article Dollimore continues his critique of Butler, 'in Butler's account gay desire usually figures *in an intense relationship to* heterosexuality – so much so that it might be said to have an antagonistic desire *for* it; reading Butler one occasionally gets the impression that gay desire is not complete unless somehow it is installed inside heterosexuality . . . something generally missed by those who have mis/appropriated her work for the facile politics of subversion', p. 535. I would claim that this interdependency, which runs throughout her work, derives from her strong 'attachment' to Hegel.
27. Adam Phillips, 'Keeping it Moving: Commentary on Judith Butler's "Melancholy Gender/Refused Identification"', in Butler, *The Psychic Life of Power*, pp. 151–9, p. 151.
28. See Mikkel Borch-Jacobsen, *Psychoanalysis, Mimesis and Affect*, trans. Douglas Brick et al. (Stanford: Stanford University Press, 1992).
29. Staten, *Eros in Mourning*, p. 7.
30. Butler, *The Psychic Life of Power*, p. 146.
31. Ibid.
32. For studies in this area, see Gail Holst-Warhaft, *Dangerous Voices: Women's Laments and Greek Literature* (London and New York: Routledge, 1992); Katherine Derderian, *Leaving Words to Remember: Greek Mourning and the Advent of Literacy* (Lieden and Boston: Brill, Mnemosyne, Bibliotheca Classica Batava, 2001).
33. For an excellent account of Greek funerary legislation and funeral rites, see Helen P. Foley, 'The Politics of Tragic Lamentation', in *Female Acts in Greek Tragedy* (Princeton and Oxford: Princeton University Press, 2001), pp. 19–55.
34. See Richard Seaford, *Reciprocity and Ritual: Homer and Tragedy in the Developing City-State* (Oxford: Clarendon Press, 1994).
35. See Foley, *Female Acts in Greek Tragedy*, p. 27.

36. Gillian Rose, *Mourning Becomes the Law* (Cambridge: Cambridge University Press, 1996).
37. For a critical reading of this theory see Chapter 1.
38. Foucault writes: 'There is no binary division between the dominators and the dominated, or the master and the mastered ... there are no relations of power without resistances, and these resistances are formed precisely where power is being exercised,' quoted in Philip Barker, *Michael Foucault: Subversions of the Subject* (London and New York: Harvester Wheatsheaf, 1993), p. 78.
39. See Elizabeth Grosz, *Jacques Lacan: A Feminist Introduction* (London: Routledge, 1990); Mikkel Borch-Jacobsen, *Lacan: The Absolute Master*, trans. Douglas Brick (Stanford: Stanford University Press, 1991); Soshana Felman, *Jacques Lacan and the Adventure of Insight: Psychoanalysis in Contemporary Culture* (Cambridge, MA: Harvard University Press, 1987); for a critique, see François Roustang, *The Lacanian Delusion: Why Did We Follow Him for so Long?*, trans. Greg Simms (Oxford: Oxford University Press, 1990).
40. Jacques Lacan, *The Seminars of Jacques Lacan: Book II, The Ego in Freud's Theory and in the Technique of Psychoanalysis*, trans. Sylvia Tomaselli (New York: Norton, 1998), p. 218.
41. Staten, *Eros in Mourning*, p. 182.
42. Jacques Lacan, 'The Splendour of Antigone', in John Drakakis and Naomi Liebler (eds), *Tragedy* (London and New York: Longman, 1998), p. 189. Reprinted from Jacques-Alain Miller (ed.), *The Ethics of Psychoanalysis 1959–1960*, Book VII, trans. with notes by Dennis Porter (London: Routledge, 1992).
43. Ibid. p. 188.
44. Indeed Butler's reading of Antigone attempts to trace an alternative line of kinship. It also has been read as a critique of Lacan. She writes: 'I remember hearing stories about how radical socialists who refused monogamy and family structure at the beginning of the seventies ended that decade by filing into offices and throwing themselves in pain on the analytic coach. And it seemed to me that the turn to psychoanalysis and, in particular, to Lacanian theory was prompted in part by the realization by some of those socialists that there were some constraints on sexual practice that were necessary for psychic survival and that the utopian effort to nullify prohibitions often culminated in excruciating scenes of psychic pain ... That this constraint is understood to be beyond social alteration, indeed, to constitute the conditon and limit of all social alterations, indicates something of the theological status it has assumed.' Judith Butler, *Antigone's Claim* (New York: Colombia University Press, 2000), p. 75.
45. Jacques Lacan, 'The Splendour of Antigone,' p. 194.
46. Ibid. p. 194.
47. Joan Copjec, *Imagine There's No Woman: Ethics and Sublimation* (Cambridge, MA: MIT Press, 2002). See chapter entitled, 'The Tomb of Perseverance: On Antigone', pp. 12–47.
48. Ibid. p. 19.
49. Ibid. p. 29.
50. Staten comments interestingly on this relationship between mourning, femininity and theatricality. Even Nietzsche, the great anti-metaphysical philosopher, is drawn into the argument. Staten writes: 'Lacan, who rarely mentions Nietzsche, is actually very close to him in some ways, at least to the Nietzsche who defends

to the last the boundary of his absolute particularity, who fears most of all *to be torn* by sexual desire, by a woman, by the universality of the species, and who, at least in his earliest phase, developed the pathos of *sparagmos*, like Lacan, into an interpretation of tragedy and a "tragic sense of life" (7.313). "It is in the nature of desire to be radically torn," says Lacan, because the subject is "irremediably separated" from the object, an object that by "essence destroys him" (2.166). "The perfect woman always tears to pieces when she loves," Nietzsche wrote in *Ecce Homo*, in what Lacan might have recognized as a profound insight into the nature of *das Ding*.' See Staten, *Eros in Mourning*, p. 176.

51. George Steiner, 'Tragedy Pure and Simple', in Silk (ed.), *Tragedy and the Tragic*, pp. 534–46, p. 536.
52. Ibid. p. 537.
53. G. W. F. Hegel, *Werke in zwanzig Banden, Vol.12, Vorlesungen über die Philosophie der Geschichte* (Frankfurt am Main: Suhrkamp, 1970), p. 134; quoted in Rainer Nägele, *Theatre, Theory, Speculation: Walter Benjamin and the Scenes of Modernity* (Baltimore and London: The Johns Hopkins University Press, 1991), p. 8.
54. For other ways of reconciling these two discourses, see the work of Cornelius Castoriadis, particularly, *The Imaginary Institution of Society: Creativity and Autonomy in the Social-Historical World* (Cambridge: Polity Press, 1987); *The Castoriadis Reader*, ed. David Curtis (Oxford: Blackwell, 1997).
55. Quoted in Rainer Nägele, *Theatre, Theory, Speculation*, p. 78.
56. The debate about the incompatibility of tragedy and epic theatre is yet another inflection on the debate about engagement and autonomy. Schematically this has been read as Brecht/Benjamin versus Adorno (and Lukacs for different reasons). Benjamin's championing of Brecht is read against Adorno's endorsement of Beckett. Brecht and Beckett emerge on opposing ends of the engagement/autonomy debate. For a concise summary, see Elizabeth Wright, 'Placing the Theory: Brecht and Modernity', in *Postmodern Brecht* (Cambridge: Cambridge University Press, 1989), pp. 68–89. Also see Theodor Adorno, *Notes to Literature*, trans. Rolf Tiedemann (New York: Columbia University Press, 1991).
57. For an analysis, see Peter Wolin, 'Benjamin and Brecht', in *Walter Benjamin: An Aesthetic of Redemption* (Berkeley, CA: University of California Press, 1994), pp. 139–54.

CHAPTER 7

Brecht – Beckett – Müller: Modern Tragedy and Engagement

In *Brecht and Method*, Fredric Jameson examines the ways in which the Brechtian project comes out of the experiments of modernism and proposes epic theatre as an aesthetic equivalent of dialectic materialism.[1] While acknowledging Brecht's impact on contemporary thinking about performativity and embodiment, he proceeds to underline a difference between Brecht's 'method' and that of 'other philosophical methods or world-views':

> It would have to be a defence profoundly related to Hegel's own case for what he called the 'speculative': namely, the way in which the very idea of a concept carries in question, at the same time as it passes judgement on worlds that have not yet raised themselves to that level. Change in Brecht would then qualify as a speculative concept of precisely that kind: a purely formal notion that implies and projects its own content by virtue of its unique form.[2]

What constitutes a 'method' rather than a philosophy for Jameson would have to be the very theatrical quality of the Brechtian work. The emphasis on the speculative will invariably lead, as we have seen elsewhere in this book, to the spectacular. Indeed, we may say that the 'form' that Brecht proposes strives to reconcile the speculative with the spectacular, in a gesture (or *gestus*) that embodies both critique and enactment. Hölderlin applies the same phrase when talking about Greek tragedy. His reading of tragedy as 'a metaphor of an intellectual intuition' proposes tragedy as a speculative theory, a *theoria*. We could go so far as to claim that Hölderlin's 'metaphor of an intellectual intuition' could equally apply as a definition of epic theatre. In turn, we can trace a genealogy of the term from Hölderlin, through Hegel and Benjamin to Brecht, acknowledging Brecht's debt to German Idealism.

Is it, however, the same historical and political debt from which Brecht wants to vehemently disassociate himself in rewriting the term epic, which Hölderlin reserves as 'a metaphor of great aspirations'.[3] I would like to suggest that when Brecht rewrites the term epic he infuses it with tragedy's 'intellectual intuition'. As a result, his epic theatre strives to combine the somewhat utopian aspirations of traditional epic with the speculative and spectacular modes of tragedy. This 'method' of reading epic back into tragic form could also be seen as an example of Brecht's famous strategy of 'crude' thinking.

The parallels drawn between epic and tragic forms through the function of the speculative/spectacular allow for a reading of both forms through the discourse of mourning. The constitutive relationships between tragedy and mourning have been charted throughout this book. It proves a little harder to read epic as a discourse of mourning. However, through the legacy of German Idealism and through the infusion of the 'intellectual intuition', the purely utopian exaltations of epic are constantly questioned, critiqued, counterbalanced. This adds a quality of negativity to epic; it brings with it melancholy and speculation, while also accounting for the possibility of change. As Brecht succinctly put it: 'Although the purely biological death of the individual is uninteresting to society, dying ought none the less to be taught.'[4] Epic theatre here contests the power of philosophy as the sole instructor of death. Epic theatre as a speculative *theoria* offers lessons in death, but, crucially, does so through the possibility of change. Birth–death–resurrection, so often linked structurally to the genesis of theatre, here are removed from their usual cyclical and metaphysical patterns and through the function of the dialectic are infused with the possibility of change. This change, however, is not simply and mechanistically, as epic theatre is so often read, a march to all-increasing progress but is informed by death and mourning.

Brecht's repudiation of tragedy is matched by a supposed championing of the form by his great counterpart in twentieth-century theatre, Samuel Beckett. The Brecht–Beckett opposition becomes more pronounced as the two projects are seen as paradigms of differing schools of Marxist criticism. Predictably, Brecht's epic theatre comes to stand as a Benjaminian model of engaged art, whereas the work of Beckett is put forward by Adorno as explicating the political possibilities of autonomous art. This debate between engagement and autonomy is inflected by differing attitudes towards the tragic. Schematically drawn, epic is said to be devoid of negativity and Beckett's tragic theatre is said to disallow the possibility of change. Darko Suvin writes of the unease felt within a Marxist tradition when faced with the work of Beckett. Interestingly, a similar awkwardness characterises the encounter with tragedy:

A critic of modern dramaturgy with a bent for Brecht and Chekhov, for the Berliner Ensemble . . . for Marx and Bloch – one in other words, who enjoys the dramaturgy and theatre fully when they participate, by means of their specific exemplary sensual presentness, in the great liberating effort of our century – has one outstanding difficulty to come to terms with, if he or she is to be sincere to his trade and even to her or his (*ex hypothesi*) encompassing horizons: Samuel Beckett.[5]

Like tragedy, Beckett's work is concerned with the large questions of death, loss and suffering, and thereby causes a slight embarrassment to the critic who looks for issues of labour, productivity and historical change within the same project. However, this reading of Beckett, parallel in many ways to the mechanistic reading of Brecht, is itself part of the same metaphysical trajectory that consigns tragedy to the inevitable, the mythical and the apolitical. In many ways it can be read as part of a cold war rhetoric, one that identifies Beckett with the individual and Brecht with the collective. In turn this argument sees Beckett's work as expressing the power of individual freedom, while Brecht's theatre expresses the confining restrictions of a collective, mechanistic aesthetic that is no more than propaganda. This thesis is further punctuated by the fact that Beckett is seen to be able to 'do' tragedy, while Brecht obviously cannot accommodate the form.

This oppositional way of reading Beckett against Brecht results primarily from two schools of Beckettian criticism. Jennifer Birkett and Kate Ince very usefully summarise these as the 'existentialist humanist' school,[6] prompted by Martin Esslin's reading of Beckett as part of the so-called 'Theatre of the Absurd' and seen as a direct enactment of Parisian existentialism, and the 'mimetic nihilist' school, which sees Beckett as 'a darkly destructive pessimist whose form represents his dark vision of social and human potential for transformation'.[7] However, as Birkett and Ince acknowledge, both these approaches 'belong to the same epistemology'. This epistemology also positions tragedy within the same trajectory. This view sees no possibility of transformation and critique within the work of Beckett. If tragedy is seen to occupy the metaphysical, the inevitable, the unaccountable, which is translated into the 'human', then Beckett is seen as its main representative for the twentieth century. The convergence formulated by this humanist/existential/nihilist approach manages in the same stroke to revive the metaphysical/idealist school of tragedy, and to remove the possibility of critique, transformation and change from the work of Beckett.

It is only in the Lukácsian analysis that Brecht and Beckett are not read in opposition to each other as both are seen as occupying the same decadent, formalist position, and Lukács uses both as examples in his attack on modernism and the avant-garde. This is the analysis that has been discredited by humanists and Marxists alike. Ignoring for a moment the actual content of Lukács' criticisms, we may note that these projects can indeed be read in tandem and not solely in opposition. Like Plato, whose actual attack on enactment, mimesis and theatre might contain a grain of truth (as contagion, distortion and so on), Lukács' position on realism might reflect back on Brecht and Beckett in interesting ways. Lukács' essentially Platonic mode of reading Brecht and Beckett might inadvertently bring out some of the parallels in their work.

Adorno's criticisms of Lukács for applying 'socialist realist' criteria to avant-garde texts quite predictably acts as a rehabilitation of Beckett but not of Brecht. Adorno champions Beckett as part of his attack of 'engaged art'. He writes in his essay 'Commitment' (1962):

> Kafka's prose and Beckett's plays and his genuinely colossal novel *The Unnamable* have an effect in comparison to which official works of committed art look like children's games – they arouse the anxiety that existentialism only talks about. In dismantling illusion they explode art from the inside, whereas proclaimed commitment only subjugates art from the outside, hence only illusorily. Their implacability compels the change in attitude that committed works only demand.[8]

In this way, Adorno proceeds to 'rescue' Beckett from humanist and mechanistic Marxist criticism. Beckett is seen to be more existential than existentialism itself and more political than self-proclaimed political art. Particularly through his analysis of *Endgame*, Adorno proposes a Marxist reading of Beckett that allows for critique, and not simply 'nihilist mimesis'. This is a crucial essay both for Beckett studies and for Marxist aesthetics.[9] According to Adorno, Beckett's work, far from mirroring existentialism and/or nihilism, places the individual firmly within the workings of capitalism. He writes:

> The catastrophes that inspire *Endgame* have shattered the individual whose substantiality and absoluteness was the common thread in Kierkegaard, Jaspers, and Sartre's version of existentialism . . .
> The individual himself is revealed to be a historical category, both the outcome of the capitalist process of alienation and a defiant protest against it, something transient himself.[10]

By the same token, the exposure undergone by the subject exposes the workings of capital together with its processes of representation. Through the emphasis on the notion of 'dismantling illusion', Beckett's theatre moves, or rather bridges, the aesthetic and the philosophical. Adorno writes:

> In order to underbid history and thereby perhaps survive it, *Endgame* takes up a position at the nadir of what the construction of the subject-object laid claim to at the zenith of philosophy; pure identity becomes the identity of what has been annihilated, the identity of subject and object in a state of complete alienation.[11]

It is this original split of subject and object – the individual and the collective, the aesthetic and the political – that tragedy was supposed to heal. In a supposedly organic unity, the two halves were rendered whole through the humanist function of tragedy within the democratic *polis*. Beckett's theatre announces the total concretisation of that split – a complete state of alienation. It also hints at the fact that it may never have existed.

It has been announced often in contemporary criticism that philosophy has never had a body. Theatre and tragedy have always had bodies, but they remain notoriously difficult to render beyond humanism. In making an ontological theatre, in ways similar to Brecht, Beckett's theatre had to encounter the problem of the body in representation. Brecht works out a sophisticated system of acting but Beckett takes another direction. His bodies, rather than enacting a dialectical relationship with the process of representation itself, as is the case in Brecht, become bodies that need to be contained. They appear in other things, subjects/objects, half-buried, completely disembodied and so on. This inability to contain the body on stage at the same time enacts all the ways in which European theatre has thought of representing the body on stage. The Beckettian theatre can be read as a philosophy with a body which acknowledges that the status of that body within the philosophical tradition he is reworking is non-existent, or rather is a corpse. Reviving it and placing it on to the stage again proves an almost impossible task. On the one hand, there are no models for an embodied philosophy within the philosophical tradition. On the other, tragic form is unable to provide the required medium as:

> Exposition, complication, plot, peripetia and catastrophe return in decomposed form as participants in an examination of the dramaturgical corpse. Representing the catastrophe, for instance, is the announcement that there are no more painkillers.[12]

In one of Beckett's late plays, characteristically entitled *Catastrophe* (1982), the protagonist on stage is positioned like a statue that awaits instructions in order to be moulded. This image, commenting on the tense relationships between playwright and director, is seen as the site of the catastrophe of representation itself.

From Beckett's early plays to the later one-act plays, the notion of catastrophe, as Adorno noted earlier on, informs and helps shape his theatre.

However, this is not an apocalyptic, metaphysical catastrophe; it is catastrophe as a mode of analysis, as an aesthetic and as a form of critique. Some critics are led to see this as a negation of the dialectic:

> To put an end to the terrorism of rationality that permeates our culture, 'the only strategy is a *catastrophical* one, and not at all dialectical. Things must be pushed to their limit, where quite naturally they reverse themselves and collapse' [*Exchange*, p. 11]. The poetic mode must be enhanced at the expense of rationality, ambiguity must replace the tyranny of sense, of things that 'make sense', reversibility must take the place of linearity and accumulation.[13]

Read in this poststructuralist manner, the strategy of catastrophe leads to ambiguity, ambivalence, the end of 'the tyranny of sense' and so on. However, as its critics proclaim, this approach can lead to a kind of transcendental relativism. On the other hand, if the notion of catastrophe is read as an aspect of negative dialectics, in the way Adorno uses the term, then a different set of possibilities arises. The rubble, the fragmentation, the waste and detritus that occupy the Beckettian stage, including the human body, are not merely seen as a bleak meditation on the human condition. They are constitutive elements of that condition and of the historical process itself. Catastrophe read as negativity allows for this detritus of history to be read as a form of critique rather than as a solipsistic, nihilist meditation on the cyclical nature of history and the pointlessness of human agency.

Adorno's infusion of Beckett with negative dialectics also allows for his notion of tragedy to be read historically and politically. And, of course, the way catastrophe is primarily remembered is through mourning. Mourning in Beckett's theatre becomes mourning for the impossibility of tragedy itself. Adorno writes:

> As in utopia, it is its last day that decides on the species. But mourning over this must reflect – in the spirit – the fact that mourning itself is no longer possible. No weeping melts the armour; the only face left is the one whose tears have dried up.[14]

It is always a cited mourning that is reiterated in a meta-theatrical way. In a sense, 'the death of tragedy', as long as it occupies a transcendental realm, will always be part of the essential discourse of tragedy itself. As is the case with the 'oral tradition', read in a pre-Derridean way, its immanent death comes to define its life. As long as tragedy is seen as a pre-discursive (or non-discursive) part of the human condition, and as long as that human condition occupies the position of a 'fall' (from God, from organic community, from the democratic *polis*, from language), its death will haunt its presence. For the discourse of the death of tragedy has probably existed as long as tragedy itself. Once the 'fall' has occurred, the organic relationship between tragedy and the *polis* severed, its death will always inform its life. In this way, mourning in the theatre of Beckett will always be the mourning of theatre itself. In the same gesture, this acts as a critique of the transcendental discourse that has created this ghost of tragedy in the first place. This tragic view of human existence, which interprets human suffering as inevitable and metaphysical, is seen as part of the capitalist process of commodification and alienation.

As an enactment of historical catastrophes, mourning presents the rubble of history not as part of the inevitable, pointless condition of being human, but as part of the rise of capitalism, which is linked with the specific development of the democratic state. Far from working against the notion of the dialectic and creating a poststructuralist funfair, catastrophe underlines the negativity that is structural to that dialectic in the first place. In his defence of Beckett against Lukács, Adorno writes:

> [Beckett] makes thematic something that Horkheimer and I, in the *Dialectic of Enlightenment*, called the convergence between a society totally in the grips of the culture industry and the reactions of an amphibian. The substantive content of a work of art can consist in the accurate and tacitly polemical representation of emerging meaninglessness . . .[15]

Tragedy has always been read as one of the defining moments of the dialectic of the Enlightenment. It is the mode of theatre to which the Beckettian stage refers and cites in a meta-theatrical manner. By dragging the catastrophes on to the stage, his theatre constantly enacts 'the impossibility of tragedy', an impossibility, however, that defines tragic form itself. This 'polemical representation' of the impossibility casts its reflection both on this fictional death, but also on the fictional birth of tragedy, as resulting from that forever lost, never-to-be regained organic oneness both within ourselves and in our relationships with each other and the state.

Reading catastrophe in this way in the work of Beckett leads us back to Benjamin and Brecht. However, I do not want to conflate Brecht with Beckett. Rather, I want to underline the fact that their work responds to the same question: the question of tragedy. Both projects seek to create a theory and performance (a praxis) for tragedy within modernity. Significantly, both are defined against the transcendental and idealist school of tragedy. Brecht in his commitment to 'engagement' created a manifesto-type proclamation. Beckett in his commitment to 'autonomy' remained hermetically silent about his work throughout his life. Both appear as paradigmatic cases of the Benjamin–Adorno debate, and both projects revitalise the political efficacy of tragedy within the context of modernity.

Towards the end of his life Brecht contemplated directing *Endgame*. It is significant that he chose this particular play, the one also chosen by Adorno in his analysis of Beckett. This hypothetical performance would have been Brecht's answer to both Lukács and Adorno. In his characteristic way, that of using praxis, he would have shown the possibilities in uniting these otherwise incongruous projects. As this analysis hopes to have shown, the projects themselves might not be as contrasting as we are led to believe. However, they are not identical and cannot be reduced to each other. Clearly there are striking differences between the two. The infusion of Brecht with negativity and the political reading of Beckett put forward by Adorno might create areas of overlap. In this way Brecht does not simply stand for the ultimate engaged theatre, which dissolves into propaganda, while Beckett presents autonomy, which has been read as existentialist humanism. The sharpness and severity of these positions is somewhat curved, mellowed, injected with both historical awareness and melancholy. At the same time, both projects strike graphic poses towards tragic form. In denying the possibility of tragedy within modernity, each from a different perspective, what they challenge is the idealist/metaphysical trajectory that tragedy has occupied since ancient Athens. In its place they posit a performative praxis that tries to reinvent the form.

The analysis of Brecht and Beckett undertaken here does not attempt to alleviate the stark differences in their work and does not identify one with the other. What it suggests is that they are responding to the same set of problems through, more or less, the same medium. The encounter with tragedy is unavoidable, as it is in the work of Heiner Müller, who quite consciously tries to reconcile epic and tragic form while also resuscitating the debate about commitment. In an interview with Horst Laube in 1990, Heiner Müller said:

> Sooner or later one should perhaps admit that one takes pleasure in destruction and that things fall apart. 1945, for instance, was an important experience for me. This wonderful 'swinging country' feeling after a very confined childhood and youth. Everything had been destroyed, nothing worked. It was the most wonderful time . . . In front of us was a void and the past no longer existed, so that an incredible free space was created in which it was easy to move. These depressive, negative interpretations always come from the past or the future, and are made by people who are fixated so far in the past that they can only conceive of living in the future. The true pleasure of writing consists, after all, in the enjoyment of catastrophe.[16]

Heiner Müller employs this aesthetic of catastrophe in his modern tragedies. We might even claim that his work is all about reclaiming tragedy for the purposes of modernity. This, however, might prove to be a difficult task, especially since his inheritance is Brechtian. Müller was one of Brecht's successors at the Berliner Ensemble and, throughout his life, showed an equal fascination with the works of Brecht and the great tragedies of the European canon. Most of his 'plays' consist of radical rewritings of the tragic canon. He is particularly interested in Euripides and Shakespeare. Instead of rewriting parables, in a classically Brechtian gesture he chooses to rewrite classic tragedies, almost using them as parables for the project of the Enlightenment. He writes in his *Hamletmachine*:

> SOMETHING IS ROTTEN IN THIS AGE OF HOPE
> LET'S DELVE IN EARTH AND BLOW HER AT THE MOON[17]

Müller brings a Brechtian sensibility to his critique. However, his relationship with Brecht is not straightforward. In his own words, 'to use Brecht without criticising him is betrayal'.[18] His aesthetic of destruction tears up and spits out classical European tragedies and can be applied to his relationship with Brecht. His Brecht, however, is read through the work of Benjamin. In many ways, the crude thinking of Brecht and the apocalyptic thinking of Benjamin come together to create his own particular strand of aesthetic catastrophe, his own version of tragedy. Müller writes:

> The formula for theatre is just birth and death. The effect of theatre, its impact, is the fear of change because the last change is death. There are two ways of dealing with this fear: as comedy, by deflating the fear of death; and as tragedy, by elevating it.[19]

In the creation of this theatre of death Müller also adds his Artaudian influences, bridging another of the great divides in modernist performance. The two high priests of performance theory in the twentieth century, one presenting the political, the other the mythical and archetypal, are brought together and, in many ways, allowed to 'fight it out' in Müller's plays until there is nothing left but total destruction. This destruction, however, has in the process imbibed both traditions and through the rubble has created something new. Müller writes of Artaud:

> Thought at the end of the enlightenment, which began with the death of God; the enlightenment is the coffin in which he is buried, rotting with the corpse ... The lightning that split Artaud's consciousness was Nietzsche's experience, it could be the last. The emergency is Artaud. He tore literature away from the police, theatre

away from medicine. Under the sun of torture, which shines equally on all continents of this planet, his texts blossom. Read on the ruins of Europe, they will be classics.[20]

In a style of writing that is reminiscent of Benjamin, Artaud is heralded as the last flicker of the Enlightenment. The classics that he has created, however, rely on ruins. Later in his life, Müller would write himself into this scheme by claiming to be the last German playwright. In the meantime, this mirroring of Brecht through Artaud and vice versa helps bridge one of the great divides of modernist performance. Artaud appears to be politicised and Brecht is injected with a melancholic, catastrophic aesthetic. Müller remoulds both these legacies into his version of the tragic, a sense of the tragic that is built on the detritus of these great traditions. On this rubble he creates texts that are fragmentary, highly dense in reference and citation. Discursive machines, they not only refer directly to a specific text but also to the impact that text may have had on the canon in general. Hence, his reworking of the Medea myth is a homage to Euripides but also is scattered with the intertextual history of the myth, while at the same time making contemporary allusions:

> On the way we heard the screen ripping
> And saw the pictures crash
> The forests burned down in EASTMAN COLOUR
> But the journey was without arrival NO PARKING
> At the crossroads with one eye
> Polyphemus guided the traffic
> Our harbour was a dead cinema
> On the screen the stars were in a race
> To see who can decompose the fastest
> In the box office Fritz Lang was throttling Boris Karloff
> The wind in from the south played with old posters
> OR THE UNHAPPY LANDING[21]

In this version of Medea, where she is explicitly read as a postcolonial subject, Müller rereads the east–west relationship (and the barbarism/civilisation narrative) in post-Second World War terms. The play is littered with images of Americana, as emblems both of post-war modernity and imperial oppression. The opening of *Waterfront Wasteland* contains the words 'FREUD'S DUREX MARLBORO (BUDWEISER)', as slogans almost of the occupying army at Colchis, together with 'The torn-up tampons The blood – Of the women of Colchis'.[22] The legacy of Euripides, and the contradictions embedded within the democratic *polis* he exposes, are reinterpreted in terms of the new dynamics of empire created after 'the great catastrophe' of the Second World War. The aesthetic that he employs to do this transpires as a fusion of Brecht and Artaud, with a nod towards the experiments of high modernism. He writes in his preface to *Medea Material*:

> The material, apart from being extracted from my life with women, came from Euripides, Hans Henny Jahnn and above all, Seneca. I could not have written the third part, *Landscape with Argonauts*, without T. S. Eliot's *The Waste Land*, and also not without Ezra Pound.[23]

It is rare that a Brechtian tradition is quite consciously fused with the traditional modernist high-art legacy. Müller seeks to explore possibilities beyond the great divisions within modernism. His work also signals the dominance of anglophone modernism within the critical canon. In turn, through the extensive use of the English language, his work underlines the hegemony of that language and anglophone culture for the post-war period. Of course, the fascination with the United States and 'Americana' in general is present in the work of Brecht, but is turned into a more visceral critique by Müller, going far beyond the somewhat caricatured images of 'American capitalists' that Adorno accused Brecht of portraying. The fascination with the English language in his work also acts as a comment on the fate of the European avant-garde once it was appropriated by the culture industry in the United States. The references to Fritz Lang and Boris Karloff quoted above are also subtle reminders of the complex encounters between the refugees from the European avant-garde and their host language/country. Indeed, the fascination with the English language as a site of both emancipation and appropriation was something that Adorno recounts as part of his on-going discussions with Brecht. He writes:

> Brecht once provoked me in conversation by asserting that the literature of the future should be composed in pidgin English. At this point in the discussion Benjamin refused to follow him and went over to my side. The barbaric futurism of such proclamations – which Brecht himself probably did not intend very seriously, by the way – is an alarming confirmation in the domain of language of the positivist enlightenment's tendency to regress when left to its own devices. Truth . . . shrivels up like pidgin or basic English and then becomes truly fit for giving commands . . .
> The universal system of communication, which on the face of it brings human beings together and which allegedly exists for their sake, is forced upon them.[24]

Even Adorno, however, allows for the critical possibility in the use of foreign words. This anticipates a current postcolonial reading of the use of English in the writing of literature. He continues in 'Words from Abroad':

> Like Greeks in Imperial Rome, foreign words, used correctly and responsibly, should lend support to the lost cause of a flexibility . . . In this way foreign words could preserve something of the utopia of language . . . Hopelessly, like death's heads, foreign words await their resurrection in a better order of things.[25]

For those of us who come to English as outsders (if this is still possible), this formulation touches a nerve. This may account for Müller's on-going exploration of the use of English. We might recall here the old argument that the use of Greek in Imperial Rome was a way of undermining the power of the Roman Empire. The same line of thinking claims that the Romans, crude and vulgar, had no civilisation to speak of and, although they invaded the Greeks, the Greeks conquered the Romans through their language and culture. In Adorno's admittedly Eurocentric way of reading this, he posits the great European traditions of the past as an antidote to the overwhelming impact of the US Empire. However, the use of pidgin English, to which Brecht schematically referred, points to the very utopian possibilities that Adorno mentions. Their positions do not appear to be as incompatible as Adorno might think, even if their manner and style are somewhat different. The use of pidgin English, scattered throughout Müller's work, acts as both an exploration of the language for 'giving commands' and as a messenger for the 'resurrection in a better order of things'. This fascination with images of 'Americana' and the English language is something that Müller inherits from Brecht, even as he injects it with a tragic sensibility.

Such an interaction would also have to encounter the problem of representing gender. The classical legacy inherited from both the Athenian and the Renaissance model displays a certain difficulty in the presentation of the female on the stage. Müller's work tackles this problem by reiddressing the whole issue of gender and representation and making it both thematically and formally central to his work. In the same gesture, he also 'corrects' Brecht's somewhat problematic position regarding the role of gender in the overall politics of epic theatre. Although there have been more recent feminist appropriations of Brechtian epic techniques, his reading of gender exhibits a traditional 'blind spot' within Marxist theory.[26] His strong female characters – in particular the 'epic' mothers – in some cases are reminiscent of the 'woman as/of revolution' image so prevalent within socialist realism.

Whereas Brecht looks towards the so-called 'theatres of the orient' in search of a language of performance, Müller addresses the traditions he is himself rewriting. His texts are almost void of stage directions (in stark contrast to Beckett) and, in most cases, are only plays because he has named them as such. The theatrical conventions he problematises are all rewritten within the text itself. They become thematic rather than conventional. They could even be seen as dramatic poems, if not for the fact that they are meant to be performed. This is not a mere meta-theatrical gesture; his work negotiates a new relationship between tragedy and philosophy. Diametrically opposed to Beckett's work, which does this through very strict explication of performance, Müller's tragedies are almost bare of stage directions. In an exalted Brechtian manner, these directions become part of the 'character' of the performer. The following quotation from *The Hamletmachine*, spoken by the HAMLETPERFORMER is paradigmatic of this approach:

> The set is a monument. It shows a man a hundred times larger than life who made history. The petrification of hope. His name is interchangeable. The hope was not fulfilled. The monument lies on the ground, razed three years after the state funeral of the hated and honoured one by his successor to power. The stone is inhabited. In the spacious nostrils and ear cavities, in the wrinkles on the skin the creases in the uniform of the shattered statue the poorer people of the capital have found accommodation. After the fall of the monument the revolt will follow on in due course. My drama, if it were to take place, would happen at the time of the uprising.[27]

Similarly the conventions for representing women on stage are seen as constituent of tragic form itself. This is how Müller comments on the tense relationship between tragic form and the reproducing female body:

> Here comes the ghost that begot me, the axe still in his skull. You can keep your hat on, I know you've got one hole too many. I wish my mother had had one less when you were still dressed in flesh; it would have spared me myself. Women should be stitched up, a world without mothers. We could get on butchering each other in peace and quiet, and with some chance of success, when life gets to be too long, or our throats too tight for screaming.[28]

The fantasy of a 'world without mothers', as we have seen, forms one of the great themes of Athenian tragedy and also helps create its performance conventions. It is a far cry from Brecht's epic mothers. Müller's theatre exhibits a genuine anxiety in the representation of women on the stage. In some plays, like in *Quartet*, his version of Laclos', *Les Liaisons Dangereuses*, he employs cross-gender casting, but on the whole he does not chose direct inversion to tackle the issue. The difficulty of representing the female is constantly enacted, both thematically and formally on the stage. His *Hamletmachine* ends with Ophelia in a wheelchair being wrapped up in muslin while she says:

> Here speaks Electra. In the heart of darkness. Under the sun of torture. To the metropolis of the world. In the name of the victims. I discharge all the sperm I ever received. I transform the milk from my breasts into deadly poison. I take back the world I gave birth to. Between my thighs I strangle the world I gave birth to. I bury it in my crotch. Down with the happiness of surrender. Long live hatred, contempt, uprising, death. When it walks through your bedrooms with butchers' knives you will know the truth.[29]

The conflation of Electra with Ophelia is interesting, as it is usually Hamlet who is read as an Orestes-like character. In blending these two traditions, the text comments on the conventions that both tragedies use. This examination of tragic convention in relation to gender is never undertaken by Brecht. The technique of estrangement is never applied to the function of gender.

Form, as Müller's theatre is glaringly aware, carries within it a type of historical memory and is itself implicated in the historical process. If we sketch out a brief genealogy of Brecht's famous *Verfremdungseffekt*, we can question whether it might be 'inherently' critical and progressive and we can perhaps ascertain why it proves lacking when dealing with the representation of gender. Its legacy carries all the passion of revolution inherited from the Russian and Soviet avant-garde. Brecht's interactions with the Soviet constructivists, either directly or through the intervention of Benjamin, have been well documented.[30] There is, however, another historical source for Brecht's V-effect and that is his encounter with Chinese acting.

At one of the famous Writers' Conferences organised by Stalin in the late 1930s, Brecht encountered the Chinese actor Mei Lan-fang, who, with his troupe, performed for the guests; among them were Brecht, Eisenstein, Tretiakov and Meyerhold. He performed a female character through the use of stylisation and fixed gesture. Those present were stunned with the effect that such stylisation and distantiation could produce. Here was a man playing a woman without resorting to any notion of inner character or naturalistic representation. The event was hailed as a triumphant success and had a huge impact on everyone present.[31] This kind of non-mimetic, stylised acting fuelled Brecht's notion of the *Verfremdungseffekt*.

Mei Lan-fang belonged to a theatrical tradition that had no female performers, although it did have an equally long tradition of female impersonators. The fact that Brecht's V-effect could be implicated in its genealogy with a system of representation that denies female visibility puts a somewhat negative slant on the interpretation of alienation and distancing as radical and critical formal conventions. Indeed, it problematises the relationship between formal experiment and critique. This interaction between Brecht and the 'theatres of the orient' needs to be read critically within a postcolonial context. In his quest for radical formal conventions, Brecht was borrowing forms without necessarily taking on board their history. Interestingly enough, one of the reasons that Mei Lan-fang was in Moscow in the 1930s was because he was fascinated by the naturalism of Stanislavsky. In China at the time the stylisation and abstraction of the classical Chinese theatre were considered old-fashioned and even bourgeois (after all, this was the eve of the Chinese revolution). Naturalism, and its emphasis on the inner life of character and individuation, was considered to be the emblem of modernity and change.

A complex network of relationships surfaces when we try to discuss the role of these conventions for theatrical representation . Like the Athenian model, the Chinese theatre and the Japanese Noh and Kabuki all have the men-playing-women convention as central to their language of performance. The alterity that sometimes has to occur in order for mimesis to take place is in each instance provided by the female. This distance is supposed to provide us with critical awareness and insight. In this historical trajectory that sees parallels in the conventions of the Athenian, Chinese and Japanese theatres, the primary object of distancing is the female. If this model of distancing has at its centre an otherness that relies on the repudiation of the female, then this somewhat diminishes the radical potential of such a convention.

It is almost a pity that Brecht had to turn his weary European eyes towards the so-called theatres of the orient for inspiration. The theatres of China and Japan are seen as immune from the workings of class, empire and capital, and their emphasis on stylisation, abstraction and distance is seen as inherently radical. Similar conventions in tragic form are seen as implicated in the failures of the European project of the Enlightenment.

It is in this respect that the theatres of Beckett and Müller act as both correctives and supplements to Brecht. In trying to restore the political efficacy of tragedy for modernity, they engage, albeit critically and destructively, the long and fraught history of tragic form. They present ways in which tragedy and philosophy might be reconciled, investigating the possibility of a philosophical theatre. Through an aesthetic of catastrophe they propose ways of relating to the past and creating historical memory. In the words of Walter Benjamin: 'Some hand things down by making them inviolable and conserving them; others pass on situations by making them handy and liquidating them.'[32]

The disassociation of tragedy from the long and complex metaphysical trajectory it has occupied from Plato onwards forms a crucial step in talking about tragic form in terms that are historical, and at the same time critically useful for the present. A material and materialist reading of mourning might help create a critical language for tragedy that differentiates it from idealist readings and opens up possibilities for critique. If philosophy can be read as a deliverance from mourning, then tragedy might present us with ways to embrace mourning, grief and loss as part of our historical, aesthetic and political experience.

Notes

1. Fredric Jameson, *Brecht and Method* (London and New York: Verso, 1998).
2. Ibid. pp. 168–9.
3. Friedrich Hölderlin, *Essays and Letters on Theory*, ed. Thomas Pfau (Albany: SUNY Press, 1988), p. 83.
4. Quoted in *Brecht and Method*, p. 171. Original: *Grosse Kommentierte Berliner und Frankfurter Ausgabe* (Aufbau/Suhrkamp, 1989–98), ed. Werner Hecht, Jan Kopf, Werner Mittenzwei and Klaus-Detlef Muller, XXI, p. 402.
5. Darko Suvin, *To Brecht and Beyond: Soundings in Modern Dramaturgy* (Brighton: Harvester Press; Totowa, NJ: Barnes and Noble Books, 1984), p. 209.
6. Jennifer Birkett and Kate Ince, *Samuel Beckett: Longman Critical Readers* (London and New York, 2000), pp. 2–3.
7. Ibid. p. 2.
8. Theodor Adorno, 'Commitment', in *Notes to Literature*, vol. 2, trans. Shierry Weber Nicholson (New York: Columbia University Press, 1992). First given as a talk on radio Bremen, 28 March 1962; published in *Die Neue Rundschau*, 73, 1 (1962): p. 90.
9. See Birkett and Ince, *Samuel Beckett: Longman Critical Readers*, for an assessment, pp. 10–12.
10. Theodor Adorno, 'Trying to Understand *Endgame*', in *Notes to Literature*, vol. 1, trans. Shierry Weber Nicholson, ed. Rolf Tiedmann (New York: Columbia University Press, 1991), p. 249. First published in *Der Monat*, 11 November 1958.
11. Ibid. p. 249.
12. Ibid. p. 260. The tragedy that Adorno compares *Endgame* to is *Oedipus Rex*.
13. Karlis Racevskis, 'The Theoretical Violence of a Catastrophic Strategy', in *Diacritics* 9 (September 1979): 35. Quoted in Birkett and Ince, *Samuel Beckett: Longman Critical Readers*, p. 16.
14. Adorno, 'Trying to Understand *Endgame*', p. 261.
15. Adorno, 'Extorted Reconciliation: On Georg Lukács' *Realism in Our Time*', in *Notes to Literature*, vol. 1, p. 226. He continues, 'Lukács' conflation of Beckett with the cult of Being in particular ... demonstrates his blindness to the phenomenon under consideration. It derives from the fact that he stubbornly refuses to accord literary technique its rightful central place.'
16. See Heiner Müller, *Germania*, trans. Bernard and Caroline Schütze, ed. Sylvère Lotringer (New York: Semiotext(e), 1990), p. 190.

17. Heiner Müller, *Theatremachine*, trans. and ed. Marc von Henning (London and Boston: Faber and Faber, 1995), p. 87.
18. See Müller, *Germania*, p. 133.
19. Ibid. p. 56.
20. Ibid. p. 175.
21. Müller, *Theatremachine*, p. 56.
22. Ibid. p. 47.
23. *Medea Material* in Ibid. p. 46.
24. See Adorno, 'Words from Abroad', in *Notes to Literature*, vol. 1, p. 191.
25. Ibid. p. 192.
26. The role of gender in the Brechtian project, both in the plays and in the theory has generated much interest lately. For an apolitical, neo-conservative reading, see John Fuegi, *The Lives and Lies of Bertolt Brecht* (London and New York: Harper Collins, 1994); for a critical review of this, see, Olga Taxidou, 'Crude Thinking: Recent Brecht Criticism', *New Theatre Quarterly* vol. II, no. 44 (Autumn 1995): 381–4; also see Elin Diamond, 'Brechtian Theory/Feminist Theory: Toward a Gestic Feminist Criticism', in *The Drama Review*, vol. 32, no. 1 (1988): 82–91; Elizabeth Wright, 'The Good Person of Szechwan: Discourse of a Masquerade', in Peter Thomson and Glendyr Sacks (eds), *The Cambridge Companion to Brecht* (Cambridge: Cambridge University Press, 1994), pp. 117–28; Iris Smith, 'Brecht and the Mothers of Epic Theatre', *Theatre Journal*, vol. 43, no. 4 (Dec. 1991): 491–505; Sara Lennox, 'Women in Brecht's Work', *New German Critique*, 14 (Spring 1978): 83–96.
27. Müller, *Theatremachine*, p. 91.
28. Ibid. p. 88.
29. Ibid. p. 94.
30. See Lars Kleberg, *Theatre as Action* (London: Macmillan, 1993); see also Walter Benjamin, *The Moscow Diaries* (Cambridge, MA; London: Harvard University Press, 1986).
31. For an analysis of this event, see Kleberg, *Theatre as Action*, p. 90.
32. Quoted in Irving Wohlfarth, 'No-Man's Land: On Walter Benjamin's "Destructive Character"', in Andrew Benjamin and Peter Osbourne (eds), *Walter Benjamin's Philosophy: Destruction and Experience* (London and New York: Routledge, 1994), p. 172, Wohlfarth's translation.

Index

Adorno, Theodor, 15, 21, 49, 73, 188, 194, 196–200, 203–4
Aeschylus, 14, 74, 82, 100, 106, 112; *see also Oresteia, The, Persians, The, Seven against Thebes*
AIDS crisis, 20, 21
Alcestis (Euripides), 123
allegory, 14, 20, 37, 72–3, 74, 77, 81–8, 91, 92, 95, 98–9, 103, 174, 188
anthropocentrism, 27, 45–6, 47, 61, 84, 122
anthropology, 8, 30, 42, 44, 47, 50, 51, 77, 88, 89, 91, 95
Antigone, 18–41, 177–85
  anti-humanism of, 78, 84, 108, 109, 116
  anti-Oedipal philosophy, 11, 22, 43, 55, 58, 61, 62, 141, 168, 181
  death of, 54, 63, 28–9
  and Oedipus, 11–12, 63, 79, 126–8, 180–1
  and *philia*, 24–5, 30, 119, 127
  and the right to mourn, 11, 30–3, 37, 66–7, 125–8, 177–82
anti-theatricalism, 6, 7, 11, 29, 35, 103, 111, 161, 162, 163, 166, 172, 180, 183, 185, 187
Aquinas, Thomas, 34–5
Archelaos, King of Macedon, 13, 99, 134
Aristophanes, 100, 147, 151, 155
Aristotle, 12–14, 106–25, 160–3
  and Boal, 15
  and Brecht, 14–15
  and Iphigenia, 117–18, 128, 147

  and mimesis, 12, 110–12
  and mothers, 56
  and Oedipus, 42, 54
  and performance, 7, 182
  and Plato, 111, 112, 160–3
  and the relationship between tragedy and philosophy, 5–7
  and Sophocles, 107–8, 113
  and tragedy as transcendental, 5–7
Aristotelianism, 13–14
  and Benjamin, 73, 93
  and Brecht, 73, 88, 91, 112–13, 128
  and mimesis, 110–11
  and Oedipus, 13, 42
  and spectacular philosophy, 109
Artaud, Antonin, 20, 46, 113, 201, 202, 203
Asklypios, 57
Athenian tragedy
  and Chinese and Japanese theatre, 207
  and cross-dressing, 36–7, 174
  and death, 28
  and the feminine, 9–10, 26, 54, 57, 98, 142, 174, 175
  and German Idealism, 1, 4
  and the homosocial, 9–10, 19, 23, 26, 30, 91
  and hysteria, 142–3
  and mourning, 30, 36, 98, 159
  and *philia*, 121–2, 124–5
Athens
  as a democracy, 2, 3, 8, 12, 13, 30, 115, 126, 129, 155

Euripides' criticisms of, 94, 100–3, 106, 117, 134, 155
and Hercules, 141, 144, 145, 146
and homosexuality, 171, 173
mirrored by Thebes, 45, 63, 67, 68, 100, 127, 128, 133, 160
and mourning, 30–1, 89, 175
and Oedipus, 45, 46, 63–9, 126–8
and the Persians, 15–16, 97–9, 159
the *polis* inventing itself through tragedy, 121, 159
treatment of women, 91, 152, 174, 175
avant-garde, 14, 74, 196, 203, 206

Baader–Meinhof group, 18
Bacchae, The (Euripides), 82–3, 90, 99, 101–3, 108, 116, 140, 143, 159
barbarism
in the democratic *polis*, 2, 8
and the female, 9, 10, 11, 96, 98, 159, 175, 179
and mourning, 11, 30, 98, 159, 175, 179
towards civilisation, 53, 178, 202
in war, 9, 16, 52
Beckett, Samuel, 15, 188, 193–200, 205, 207
Belfiore, Elizabeth, 110, 119
Benjamin, Walter, 72–94
and allegory, 72, 84, 87, 98, 99
and Brecht, 73–5, 188–9
criticism of Nietzsche, 5, 76, 129
and mourning, 160
Origin of German Tragic Drama, 14, 36, 72–4
politicising the aesthetic, 20
reconciling ancients and moderns, 82, 187
reconciling tragedy and modernity, 72–3, 160
and spectacular tragedy, 7
and *Trauerspiel*, 72, 74, 77, 78, 80–1, 187–9
Boal, Augusto, 15
Boethius, 34

Brecht, Bertolt, 193–7, 200–7
and allegory, 83, 113
and Beckett, 194, 195–6, 200
and Benjamin, 73–5, 188–9, 199
and the death of tragedy, 14, 15
and dialectical actors, 85, 193, 197
and epic theatre, 14, 15, 82, 93, 115, 188, 193–4, 204
and German Idealism, 14, 74, 81, 163, 193
and *gestus*, 36, 80, 91, 113, 129
opposed to Aristotle, 14, 15, 91, 112, 128
and Plato, 115, 160, 163
politicising the aesthetic, 20, 114–15, 160
brother/sister relationships, 18, 21–2, 24, 25, 30, 31, 37, 60–1, 118–20, 127, 134
Butler, Judith, 10–11, 21–6, 33, 36–8, 62, 90–1, 170–5, 181

'Cambridge ritualists', 51
Chinese theatre, 206, 207
Chow, Rey, 93
Christianity, 3, 4, 34, 35, 41–2, 50, 114, 115, 173
citizenship *see* democracy
city-states, 8, 12, 13, 31, 48, 77, 97, 103, 160, 164, 175, 177
classicism, 7, 8, 10, 42, 89
Copjec, Joan, 10–11, 183–5
Creon, King of Thebes, 20–4, 27, 28, 33, 37, 134–5, 184
critical thinking, 5, 11, 14, 15, 19, 87, 88, 92, 93
cross-dressing, 36–7, 85, 87, 90, 92, 102, 174, 181

death
of Antigone, 20, 23–5, 28–32
feminisation of, 9, 10, 28, 30–1, 53–4, 65, 137
and funeral rites, 175–9
of the Sphinx, 50–4, 65
of tragedy, 4, 5, 14, 15, 81, 198–9
see also funeral orations, mourning

democracy
  in Athens, 2, 3, 8, 12, 13, 30, 115, 126, 129, 155
  and barbarism, 7–8
  challenged by Antigone, 30, 31–2, 37, 179
  Euripides' opposition to, 14–15, 100, 106–7
  and mourning, 8, 100, 127, 175–7, 186, 187, 199
  and Oedipus, 45, 126
  and *philia*, 120–2, 127, 133, 145–6
  and tragedy, 2, 6, 7, 115, 178, 198
Derrida, Jacques, 10, 11, 13, 119–27
dialectical materialism, 74, 193
Dionysus, 4, 49–51, 76, 84, 100, 101, 108, 109, 117, 140, 159
drag, 37, 91, 102, 174; *see also* cross-dressing

Eagleton, Terry, 2–3, 98
Electra (Euripides), 24, 25, 100, 206
Enlightenment, the, 2, 14, 42, 43, 74, 77, 120, 188, 199, 201, 202, 207
epic theatre, 14, 15, 73, 80, 82, 83, 93, 112, 115, 128, 188–9, 193–4, 200, 204, 205
ethics, 1, 3, 4, 10, 20, 32, 90, 120, 122, 162, 181, 183–4
Euripides, 106–18, 123–30
  and Aeschylus, 100
  and allegory, 82
  and Aristophanes, 100, 147, 151, 155
  critical of the polis, 12–13, 101, 103, 117, 202
  death of, 13, 99, 151
  and mourning, 96, 100, 123
  and Müller, 200–3
  and myth, 14, 82, 136
  opposition to Peloponnesian War, 12, 117, 119, 155, 159
  and *philia*, 120, 133, 136, 146
  and slaves, 13, 106, 117, 151
  and representation of women, 26, 28, 96, 117, 118, 137, 143, 151
  see also Alcestis, Bacchae, The, Electra, Helen, Iphigenia in Tauris, Madness of Hercules, The

fathers
  and Antigone, 24–6, 125–8
  and Hercules, 139, 145
  and Iphigenia, 118
  and Oedipus, 42, 43, 45, 47, 52–5, 57, 59–61, 64, 66, 67, 127
  as 'prehistoric', 169
females
  absent from the Athenian stage, 9–10, 91, 204, 206–7
  Antigone as, 20, 26, 28, 30, 34, 54, 177–8, 181
  love/hate relationship with tragedy, 9–10, 26, 37, 91
  and melancholia, 168–70
  and *philia*, 10, 136
  and reproduction, 87, 91, 95, 141–2, 173, 174, 205
  and romantic love, 27–8
  and systems of justice, 177–8
  see also brother/sister relationships, 'monstrous females', mothers
feminisation
  and aesthetic politics, 94
  and allegory, 103
  of death, 9, 145–6
  of hysteria, 58–9, 68–9, 142–4
  of the law, 38
  and mourning, 11, 30, 90, 96, 124, 137, 164, 175
  of Oedipus, 6, 12, 41–2, 55, 58, 65, 68–9
  and *philia*, 124, 125, 126
  and Plato's anti-theatricalism, 7, 11, 164
feminism, 3, 10, 11, 21, 23, 30, 42, 75, 86, 90, 122, 152, 204
Foley, Helen, 177
formalism, 7, 93, 161–2, 182, 195
Frankfurt School, 15
Freud, Sigmund, 1, 43, 49, 55, 58–62, 67, 90, 167–9, 172, 180
funeral orations, 8–9, 31, 89, 125, 137, 144, 153, 175, 176
Furies, the, 64–6, 68, 127, 138, 145

German Idealism, 1, 4, 11, 14, 18–20, 73–4, 76, 81, 193, 194

Germany in Autumn (film), 18
Goethe, 83, 103
'golden era', 3, 5, 12, 31
Gordon Craig, Edward, 75
Graves, Robert, 48–9, 55, 56
'Greek miracle', 5, 7, 15, 45, 77, 106

Hall, Edith, 161
Hegel, G. W. F., 11, 21, 22–3, 28, 35, 38, 42, 44, 64, 80, 83–7, 103, 183–4, 186
Heidegger, Martin, 19–20, 46, 120, 186
Helen (Euripides), 107–8, 123, 147–56, 177
Hercules, 44, 107–8, 123, 127, 133–47, 156, 176
heroes/heroines, 2, 7, 13–14, 108, 117
    Antigone as a heroine, 18, 23, 24, 26, 30
    and feminine monsters, 44, 47, 139
    and feminism, 3, 23, 30
    Hercules as a hero, 134, 135, 137, 139, 140, 145, 146
    immortality of, 9
    Oedipus as a hero, 44, 46, 47, 48–9
heterosexuality, 23, 26–30, 37, 58, 90, 118, 120–1, 168–71, 173
holy rape, 41–2, 135, 136
Homer, 123, 124, 164, 176
homosexuality, 11, 24–6, 86, 90–1, 95, 121, 170–1, 173–4
homosocial friendship
    and the absence of women in theatres, 23, 121
    and Antigone, 19, 26, 30, 181
    and Euripides, 107
    and feminisation, 86
    and kinship, 26
    and the negation of the female, 9
    and *philia*, 24–5, 66, 119, 120–2, 124
    and reproduction, 26, 87, 173
    and war, 143–4
humanism, 2, 10, 12, 13–14, 20, 27–9, 33, 34, 47, 73, 77, 84, 90, 115, 122, 162, 181, 196
hysteria, 12, 55, 58–60, 63, 65–9, 141–4

Ibsen, Henrik, 14, 74, 112
idealism, 1, 4, 11, 14, 18–20, 73–4, 76, 81, 193, 194
Iphigenia in Tauris (Euripides), 117

Jameson, Fredric, 193
Japanese theatre, 207

Kant, Emmanuel, 19, 35, 120
katharis, 108, 112–17, 163, 181
kings
    blasphemed by wearing rags, 99, 151, 154
    and the concept of power, 5, 7, 13–14, 23
    and female reproduction, 87
    Oedipus as a king, 43, 48
    see also Archelaos, Creon, Pentheus, Theoclymenus
kinship, 11, 18, 22, 24–6, 65, 87, 119, 173; *see also* brother/sister relationships, fathers, mothers
Klytemnestra, 23, 24, 124, 141
Kosman, Aryeh, 111–12, 114
Kristeva, Julia, 36–7, 167, 168–70

Lacan, Jacques, 21, 58, 61, 180–5
Lacis, Asja, 187–8
law, the
    challenged by Antigone, 11, 18, 20–4, 30, 31–3, 36–8, 125, 127, 178–9, 183–5
    dialogue between tragedy and the city-state, 8, 24, 160, 176, 178, 179, 187
    and mourning, 8, 9, 31, 89, 123–4, 127, 175–8
    and *philoxenia*, 154
Lear, Jonathan, 114
Loraux, Nicole, 28, 31, 89, 96–7, 121, 159
love, 26–9, 170–1, 173

Madness of Hercules (Euripides), 44, 107–8, 123, 127, 133–47, 156, 176
Marxism, 3, 15, 34, 73, 83, 93, 194–5, 196, 204

materialism, 3–4, 9, 74, 75, 77, 82, 83, 181, 193, 208
matricide, 44, 47, 52, 67, 168–9
Medea, 21, 23, 87, 118, 119, 137, 141, 202, 203
melancholia, 20, 36–8, 72, 88, 90–2, 95, 167–70, 174–5
men-playing-women, 9, 28, 38, 84, 85, 87, 95, 175, 207; see also cross-dressing
metaphysics, 1–5, 7–8, 14, 15, 35, 75, 97, 160–3, 166, 168, 180, 185–6, 195, 200, 208
mimesis, 6, 43, 59, 61–2, 67–9, 87–8, 110–12, 115, 129, 164–5, 172, 175, 196, 207
'monstrous females', 44, 48, 50, 52, 55, 64, 65, 94, 126, 135
Montaigne, Michel de, 36, 120, 167, 174, 185
mothers, 43, 55, 56, 57, 205; see also females: and reproduction
mourning
  and Antigone, 20–1, 24, 31–2, 36
  centrality in tragedy, 8, 10, 13, 36, 100, 128, 208
  and epic theatre, 15, 194, 198, 199
  and the feminisation of death, 9, 11, 143
  and the laws of democracy, 8, 9, 21, 32–3
  and melancholia, 88–9
  and Oedipus, 62–3, 66–7, 126–8
  and *The Persians*, 15–16, 96–8, 100–3
  and *philia*, 124–9, 137, 146
Müller, Heiner, 200–6
Myson, 50

Nägele, Rainer, 78–80, 83, 86, 88, 103
naturalism, 14, 74, 84, 91, 112, 129, 188, 206, 207
Nietzsche, Friedrich, 4, 8, 57, 74, 85, 90, 101, 108, 129, 202
  Beyond Good and Evil, 47
  Birth of Tragedy, 5, 76
nihilism, 4, 76, 186, 195, 196, 198

Nussbaum, Martha C., 108, 115, 116–17

Oedipus, 11–13, 16, 22, 24, 41–71, 75, 79, 114, 125–8, 133–4, 141
Oedipus at Colonus (Sophocles), 22, 43, 46, 60, 63, 68, 125, 133–4
Oedipus complex, 22, 42, 49, 57–63, 67, 170
Oresteia, The (Aeschylus), 24, 26, 64, 65–6, 100, 127

parricide, 44, 49, 52, 67, 168
Peloponnesian War, 8, 12, 31, 117, 155, 159
Pentheus, King of Thebes, 84, 96, 99–103, 124, 159–60, 179
Pericles, 8–9, 12, 31, 89, 106
Persians, The (Aeschylus), 15–16, 97, 98
Philia, 118–29
  Antigone and Polyneices, 24–5, 127–8
  in brother/sister relationships, 24–5, 118–20, 125–8
  and democracy, 120–2, 136, 145–6
  and Euripides, 13
  Helen and Menelaos, 123
  Iphigenia and Orestes, 118–19
  and the negation of the female, 10, 25, 30, 124–5, 145, 173
  Theseus and Hercules, 144–6
  Theseus and Oedipus, 66, 126
Phillips, Adam, 172
philoxenia, 13, 124–8, 130
polis
  and Aristotle, 113, 161–3
  and barbarism, 8
  developed through tragedy, 2, 5, 6, 8, 106, 176–8, 187, 198–9
  and Euripides, 100, 103, 107, 134, 136, 202
  as an extension of the male psyche, 48, 127–8
  and homosocial friendship, 25, 26, 30
  and mourning, 8, 24, 33, 66–7, 100, 127, 175–8, 187

and *philia*, 127–8, 133, 136, 145–6
  see also Athens, city-states, democracy
Phrynichus, 96–7
Plato, 1, 3, 97, 110–12, 117, 160–6, 172, 180
  antitheatricality of, 11, 29, 35, 103, 113, 162, 183, 185, 187
  Phaedo, 116
  Republic, The, 6, 7, 110, 115, 164
Plutarch, 49, 123–4, 155, 175
postmodernism, 3, 5
poststructuralism, 7, 91, 198, 199
Poussin, Nicolas, *Gathering the Ashes of Phocion* (painting), 32
psychoanalysis, 10–12, 24, 29, 42–5, 56, 58–60, 69, 90, 95, 141–2, 160, 166–8, 171–3, 180–1, 184–5
Pynchon, Thomas *The Crying of Lot 49*, 41–2

queer readings, 21, 26, 30, 94–5

Rich, Adrienne, 91
Romanticism, 4, 11, 18–19, 30, 187
Rose, Gillian, 9, 21, 31–4, 178, 179

Seaford, Richard, 31, 176
secularism, 4–5, 8, 14–15, 50
Seven against Thebes (Aeschylus), 56, 60
sisters *see* brother/sister relationships
slaves, 13, 106, 117, 151
Segal, Charles, 123–4, 151–2
Solon, 8, 123, 175–7
Sophocles, 5, 12, 13, 18–20, 28, 30, 31; see also *Electra*, *Oedipus at Colonus*
Sphinx, the, 43–57, 61, 64–6, 68–9, 141
Staten, Henry, 164–6, 174, 180
Steiner, George, 4, 20, 24, 29–30, 77, 185–6
structuralism, 30, 113, 182
subject/object divide, 44–5, 80, 81, 197
subjectivity, 2, 4, 10, 12, 22, 42–4, 46–7, 52, 55, 57–65, 73, 75, 84–93, 141, 143–4, 188

suicide, 18, 28–30, 43, 46–7, 52, 141, 144, 151

Thebes, 21, 23, 47–8, 49, 52, 56, 96
  as the mirror of Athens, 45, 63, 67, 68, 100, 127, 128, 133, 160
Theoclymenus, King of Egypt, 149, 151, 154
theology, 3, 4, 5, 170; *see also* Christianity
theoria, 34–5, 49, 78, 79, 94–5, 151, 160, 173, 193, 194
Theseus, 63, 64, 66–7, 126–7, 133–5, 141, 144–6
Thucydides, 89
Tiresias, 47, 100, 159–60
tragedy
  Aristotle's view of, 4, 6–7, 12, 15, 109–13, 117, 124, 147, 161–3, 185
  centrality of mourning to, 8, 10, 13, 36, 100, 128, 208
  death of, 4, 5, 14, 15, 81, 198–9
  and development of the democratic *polis*, 2, 5, 6, 8, 106, 176–8, 187, 198–9
  and *philia*, 119, 124, 136, 146
  and the subject/object divide, 197
transcendentalism, 2–8, 15, 97, 165, 166, 172, 198, 200
Trauerspiel, 14, 72–103, 187–8

universalism, 2, 120, 161
US Defense Department, 1, 6, 16
utopia, 2, 18, 33, 38, 75, 119, 194, 198, 204

Wagner, Richard, 75, 76
women *see* brother-sister relationships, females, feminisation, feminism, 'monstrous females'

Yeats, W. B., 75

Zeitlin, Froma, 25, 122
Zeus, 45, 100, 135–6, 139, 149